# PARTICIPATORY APPROACHES IN CHILD AND FAMILY SOCIAL WORK
## Creating Meaningful Relationships and Empowering Families

Edited by
Clive Diaz, Sammi Fitz-Symonds and Tim Fisher

First published in Great Britain in 2026 by

Policy Press, an imprint of
Bristol University Press
University of Bristol
1–9 Old Park Hill
Bristol
BS2 8BB
UK
t: +44 (0)117 374 6645
e: bup-info@bristol.ac.uk

Details of international sales and distribution partners are available from policy.bristoluniversitypress.co.uk

© Bristol University Press 2026

DOI: 10.51952/9781447373407

British Library Cataloguing in Publication Data
A catalogue record for this book is available from the British Library:

ISBN 978-1-4473-7337-7 hardcover
ISBN 978-1-4473-7338-4 paperback
ISBN 978-1-4473-7339-1 ePub
ISBN 978-1-4473-7340-7 ePdf

The right of Clive Diaz, Sammi Fitz-Symonds and Tim Fisher to be identified as editors of this work has been asserted by them in accordance with the Copyright, Designs and Patents Act 1988.

All rights reserved: no part of this publication may be reproduced, stored in a retrieval system, or transmitted in any form or by any means, electronic, mechanical, photocopying, recording, or otherwise without the prior permission of Bristol University Press.

Every reasonable effort has been made to obtain permission to reproduce copyrighted material. If, however, anyone knows of an oversight, please contact the publisher.

The statements and opinions contained within this publication are solely those of the editors and contributors and not of the University of Bristol or Bristol University Press. The University of Bristol and Bristol University Press disclaim responsibility for any injury to persons or property resulting from any material published in this publication.

Bristol University Press and Policy Press work to counter discrimination on grounds of gender, race, disability, age and sexuality.

Cover design: Liam Roberts
Front cover image: iStock/Miragest

# Contents

List of figures and boxes — iv
List of abbreviations — v
Notes on contributors — vii
Acknowledgements — xi
Foreword by Richard Devine — xii

| PART I | Foundations and contemporary challenges | |
|---|---|---|
| 1 | Introduction<br>*Hayley Pert, Clive Diaz, Sammi Fitz-Symonds and Shane Powell* | 3 |
| 2 | Increasing and varying rates of children in out-of-home care: insights from Ecological Systems Theory<br>*Sophie Wood* | 13 |
| 3 | Contemporary challenges in social work service delivery to children and families<br>*Liz Frost* | 33 |
| 4 | Participation and decision-making<br>*Hayley Pert* | 50 |

| PART II | Advocacy and family participation | |
|---|---|---|
| 5 | Family Drug and Alcohol Courts<br>*David Westlake and Melissa Meindl* | 73 |
| 6 | Strengthening families through Family Group Conferencing<br>*Lorna Stabler, Tim Fisher and Kar Man Au* | 87 |
| 7 | Parent activism in child welfare in high-income countries<br>*David Tobis and Fae Rowley* | 111 |
| 8 | Models of parental advocacy in child and family social work<br>*Shane Powell, Clive Diaz, Tim Fisher, Kar Man Au and Jourdelle Bennett* | 139 |
| 9 | Advocacy for children in care<br>*Sammi Fitz-Symonds and Lorna Stabler* | 167 |

| PART III | Rights and innovation | |
|---|---|---|
| 10 | Children in Care Councils<br>*Clive Diaz, Sammi Fitz-Symonds and Elen Newton* | 191 |
| 11 | Digital participation and technology in social work<br>*Sammi Fitz-Symonds and Shane Powell* | 206 |
| 12 | Concluding reflections<br>*Clive Diaz and Tim Fisher* | 223 |

Index — 235

# List of figures and boxes

## Figures
| | | |
|---|---|---|
| 2.1 | Bronfenbrenner's Ecological Systems Theory adapted to reflect factors influencing rates of children in care | 20 |
| 6.1 | Painting by Family Group Conferencing researcher and artist Alankrita S reflecting on the special environment of a Family Group Conference | 91 |

## Boxes
| | | |
|---|---|---|
| 6.1 | Tim's reflections on Family Group Conferences | 88 |
| 6.2 | Kar Man's reflections on Family Group Conferences | 92 |
| 6.3 | A Family Group Conference as a tool for relationship repair | 94 |
| 6.4 | The importance of community connections | 95 |
| 6.5 | Kar Man's reflections on private family time | 97 |
| 6.6 | Challenges for research focusing on Family Group Conferencing | 99 |
| 6.7 | Lorna's reflections on evidence | 103 |
| 6.8 | Reflections on the role of practitioners | 104 |

# List of abbreviations

| | |
|---|---|
| AbSec | NSW Child, Family and Community Peak Aboriginal Corporation |
| ACS | Administration for Children's Services |
| AFST | Allegheny Family Screening Tool |
| AI | Artificial Intelligence |
| BASW | British Association of Social Workers |
| BPNN | Birth Parents National Network |
| CAMHS | Child and Adolescent Mental Health Services |
| CASCADE | Children's Social Care Research and Development Centre |
| CIC | Children in Care |
| CiCC | Children in Care Councils |
| CWOP | Child Welfare Organizing Project |
| DCSF | Department for Children, Schools and Families |
| DfE | Department for Education |
| EEC | Ecological Systems Theory |
| FAB | Family Advisory Board |
| FDAC | Family Drug and Alcohol Court |
| FGC | Family Group Conference/ing |
| FIN | Family Inclusion Network |
| FINseq | Family Inclusion Network, South-East Queensland |
| FISH | Family Inclusion Strategies in the Hunter |
| FPC | Family Proceedings Court |
| IPAN | International Parent Advocacy Network |
| IRO | Independent Reviewing Officer |
| LA | Local authority |
| LAC | Looked after children |
| MCWIC | Midwest Child Welfare Implementation Center |
| MFP | Movement for Family Power |
| NGO | Non-Governmental Organisation |
| NIHR | National Institute for Health and Care Research |
| NLR | Non-lawyer review |
| NSW | New South Wales |
| Ofsted | Office for Standards in Education, Children's Services and Skills |
| OCN | Open College Network |
| ORID | Objective, Reflective, Interpretive, Decisional |
| PAN | Parent Advocacy Network |
| PAPCP | Poverty-Aware Paradigm for Child Protection |
| PFAN | Parent, Family and Allies Network |

| | |
|---|---|
| PPA | Peer Parental Advocacy/Advocate |
| RCT | Randomised Control Trial |
| SEND | Special Educational Needs and Disabilities |
| UNCRC | United Nations Convention on the Rights of the Child |

# Notes on contributors

**Kar Man Au** is a lived experience research assistant, educator, accredited Family Group Conference (FGC) co-ordinator and parent advocate. With a background that includes co-authoring work on strengths-based practice, she promotes relationship-centered and rights-based participation across research, teaching and practice. She works with universities, local authorities and communities, and supports relational approaches and efforts towards constructive change. By bringing her experiences to the forefront, she challenges power imbalances and contributes to reshaping systems and more meaningful involvement in social care and research.

**Jourdelle Bennett** is a professional with an LLB (Hons) dedicated to challenging stereotypes and reshaping narratives, particularly around fatherhood, family and systemic bias. Since 2017, he has dedicated his work to empowering fathers, advocating for child-focused outcomes and breaking down barriers that hinder equitable involvement in family life. Drawing from both professional expertise and lived experience as a service user, he delivers impactful training that promotes inclusivity and highlights the vital role fathers play within the family unit. As a consultant to the Chief of Police, he works in the intersection of law, equity and community.

**Clive Diaz** has over 17 years' experience as a social worker, child protection conference chair, Safeguarding and Quality Assurance Manager and Principal Social Worker. More recently, Clive has held a number of academic roles including at Bath University, the Open University and Oxford Brooks University. Since 2018, Clive has worked as a Researcher for Cardiff University's Children's Social Care Research and Development Centre (CASCADE) and in 2025 he took up the role of Professor of Social Work at Swansea University. He has authored over 20 publications on the topic of children's social care, and he published his first book on decision-making in child and family social work with Policy Press in 2020.

**Tim Fisher** is one of the UK's leading experts in facilitation and participatory methods. A social worker for 18 years, he held roles in local authority management, including Principal Social Worker, for more than a decade Throughout his career, he has collaborated with a range of organisations to develop inclusive approaches such as Family Group Conferencing, peer advocacy and other methods that centre the voices of people. He is the founder of Relational Activism and the current National Practice Lead for the organisation Kinship. His writing on social work and community-based practice has been published in *Community Care*, *The Ecologist*, and the *Stanford Social Innovation Review*.

**Sammi Fitz-Symonds** is Research Associate at the Children's Social Care Research and Development Centre (CASCADE) and a doctoral candidate at Cardiff University School of Law and Politics. Her research explores children's social care law and policy, with a particular focus on advocacy and participation. Sammi has led a study on children's advocacy and is co-investigator on research into personal advisors in Wales. She has also been involved in several studies exploring parental advocacy programmes across the UK. She has taught family law and brings a strong socio-legal perspective grounded in both law and social science. Her work is informed by her lived and first-hand experience of the care system, offering unique insight into its challenges and complexities.

**Liz Frost** is Associate Professor of Social Work and Visiting Research Fellow at the University of the West of England, Bristol. She is a member of the Executive Committee of the European Social Work Research Association, and co-editor of *The Journal of Psychosocial Studies*. Her over-riding interest is in psychosocial well-being. Undertaking small projects on the impact of shame and recognition on social workers, and looking (with Italy and Sweden) at how child protection social workers stay in these jobs, led her to undertake a series of commissioned projects (2017–23) considering the factors that resulted in workers thriving.

**Melissa Meindl** is an experienced mixed-methods researcher with extensive knowledge of Family Drug and Alcohol Courts (FDACs) and related models, having led and contributed to research in this area since 2018. Melissa's research on FDACs has been presented at multiple international conferences and to the Children and Young People Committee of the Welsh Parliament, and it has provided evidence-based insights to support FDAC practice and policy development in the UK.

**Elen Newton** is a social worker and has experience working with young people and adults across both local authority and the NHS. Alongside this role, she has been involved in several research and evaluation studies focused on parental advocacy and the impact of befriending and mentoring programmes for care-experienced young people.

**Hayley Pert** is a qualified social worker having worked with children, young people and their families across a number of local authorities in the south-west. She is currently Senior Lecturer in Social Work at the University of the West of England (Bristol). Her research interests primarily focus upon the experiences of children and young people specifically within statutory childcare social work.

**Shane Powell** is a doctoral researcher in Cardiff University's School of Social Sciences, examining transitions between Child/Adolescent and Adult Mental Health Services for 18–25-year-olds in Wales. His realist-informed mixed-methods research will identify structural, organisational and experiential barriers to inform context-sensitive service improvements. His background includes research positions at the University of South Wales Centre for Criminology and Cardiff University's Children's Social Care Research and Development Centre (CASCADE), alongside current archival and policy work. Previously, he worked as an Assistant Psychologist in a secure forensic mental health setting and lectured in Biological Psychology.

**Fae Rowley** worked as a social activist in the United States, building power in the asylum-seeking community through AsylumWorks in Washington D.C. and in the Philippines strengthening communities. She has held various positions supporting families in child welfare. She was a graduate student in public health at Columbia University in New York City when she worked on this chapter.

**Lorna Stabler** is Research Fellow at CASCADE, Cardiff University, Senior Kinship Fellow at Foundations, and Specialty Lead for Social Care at Health and Social Care Research Wales. Her research focuses on what is needed to strengthen the relationships and networks of families and children who are involved with social services for any reason, and to improve their experiences and outcomes. She is passionate about ensuring that those with lived and living experience of social care systems are at the forefront of creating meaningful change to improve family lives – including through involvement in social care research, service design and evaluation.

**David Tobis** is a world leader of parent advocacy and activism in child welfare. He was executive director of the Child Welfare Fund, which helped launch parent activism in child welfare. His book, *From Pariahs to Partners*, documents the dramatic changes parents and their allies helped bring about in New York's child welfare system. He consulted with UNICEF, the World Bank, governments, NGOs and foundations in over 30 countries. He is Ambassador-At-Large for the International Parent Advocacy Network (IPAN) that builds a parent-led movement to reform child welfare systems globally.

**David Westlake** is Principal Research Fellow in Children's Social Care at Cardiff University. He has done a wide range of research in this and related areas, including the evaluation of the Family Drug and Alcohol Court pilot in Wales, which is the basis for the chapter he contributed to this collection. David led the world's largest randomised controlled trial in social work and is jointly leading the evaluation of the groundbreaking Basic Income for Care Leavers in Wales pilot. He is a Health and Care Research Wales 'Advancing Researcher' and provides advice to UK government on evaluation design.

**Sophie Wood** is Postdoctoral Fellow in the School of Public Health at the University of Alberta. She is also Honorary Research Fellow at Cardiff University. Her PhD research concerns the rising and varied rates of children in out-of-home care in the UK and internationally. Sophie is a mixed-methods researcher with a strong background in evaluation, administrative data linkage and advanced quantitative analysis. Her work spans a wide range of social policy areas, including children's social care, mental health services, secure children's homes, Family Group Conferencing, and parental alcohol use.

# Acknowledgements

We would like to thank all the contributors to this book for sharing their expertise and insights, and for their commitment to documenting and reflecting on the practice and policy landscapes explored across the chapters.

Our deepest thanks go to the many participants, families and professionals who took part in the research projects and studies on which this book draws. In particular, we are grateful to the parents and young people who contributed through advisory groups, whose perspectives and experiences have been central to shaping the work presented here.

We gratefully acknowledge the support of the funders who made these projects possible, including What Works for Children's Social Care (now Foundations), Health and Care Research Wales (HCRW), the Nuffield Foundation and the National Institute for Health and Care Research (NIHR).

We are also thankful to the various reviewers for their thoughtful feedback on the manuscript, and to the editorial and production teams at Bristol University Press for their guidance throughout the publishing process.

# Foreword

*Richard Devine*

The title of this book doesn't do it justice. I know that's an unusual way to start a foreword, but hear me out.

Technically, the title is accurate: this book explores 'Participatory Approaches in Child and Family Social Work'.

But I would contend that it's so much more than that.

This book is for the tenacious optimists – the determined idealists – the compassionate crusaders – and, most importantly, the doers of social work.

It is for those who work within, on the periphery of, or outside the system, and who believe deeply that there's a better way to do this work.

Those who believe in connection, collaboration and creating contexts that facilitate change.

Before diving in, it's worth noting: this book is the product of deep collaboration. It benefits from the rich intersection of lived experience, practitioner wisdom and academic rigour. More impressively, no one perspective is privileged. These authors act in accordance with the values they advocate – and that alone makes them worth listening to.

The first section presents an unflinching account of the challenges faced by contemporary social workers – those working in a system that, despite its rhetoric, often fails to live up to the ideals it aspires to: a system that hinders social workers from acting in alignment with their values and their hearts.

It speaks plainly about the mounting pressures – rising demand, more children entering care, unmanageable caseloads and systems that hinder meaningful connection with children. Crucially, it avoids the trap of blaming social workers for the many dissatisfactions experienced by those receiving social work services. Instead, it brings to light the real tensions in ways that open up new – hopeful and disruptive – possibilities.

This leads into the second section, which explores, in a systematic, rigorous, yet accessible way, several approaches that fundamentally reorient how social work is done. Approaches like the Family Drug and Alcohol Courts (FDACs), Family Group Conferences (FGCs), and Parental Advocacy are unpacked – all grounded in both evidence and ethical integrity. This section is likely to leave you inspired – and, better yet, equipped with practical tools to transform your practice.

I use the word 'transform' carefully. Like many terms in our field, it risks being co-opted to maintain appearances rather than dismantle barriers. But transformation is possible – for practitioners, managers and policy shapers – and, more critically, for children and their parents.

The final section offers reflections on rights and innovation. Rights-based social work is a moral, ethical and legal imperative – but rights alone are not enough. We also need systems and infrastructure that make those rights real. The ideas in this section move us closer to that goal. As the final chapter reminds us, "the future of child and family social work must be fundamentally participatory – centred on the rights, experiences and contributions of children, families and communities."

'Future' is the key word here. This book is an invaluable guide for practitioners who want to help shape a new future – one grounded in dialogue, community and participation – a future where the lives of children and families are improved in ways that also nourish and transform the lives of practitioners.

Ultimately, this book will equip you to support children and parents in imagining – and building – their own futures.

# PART I

# Foundations and contemporary challenges

# 1

# Introduction

*Hayley Pert, Clive Diaz, Sammi Fitz-Symonds and Shane Powell*

## Context

Child and family social work is complex, multifaceted and hugely consequential. Decisions made by social workers have long-term impacts on families, and the relationships formed in these interactions can prove fundamental to an individual or family's experience of social work as a profession. Effective interventions have the potential to help vulnerable families make changes that can dramatically improve their lives and long-term outcomes.

The current context presents practitioners with a range of new challenges and opportunities, particularly in terms of meaningfully involving children and families in decision-making. For example, the role of Artificial Intelligence (AI) in social work offers both significant promise and risks. On one hand, AI can enhance efficiency by automating administrative tasks, allowing social workers to focus more on direct client interactions. Indeed, pilot projects in some English local authorities have rolled out AI systems that record conversations, draft letters, and even propose action points that humans might otherwise miss (Camden Council, 2024). The company behind one such software estimates that it could save up to £2 billion per year in social worker time alone (*The Guardian*, 2024).

However, on the other hand, major challenges include ensuring data privacy and security when using AI because sensitive client information must be protected. There is also the risk of bias being encoded into AI algorithms, which can perpetuate existing inequalities if not carefully managed. Furthermore, the human elements of empathy and understanding, which are so crucial in social work, cannot be fully replicated by AI systems. These developments necessitate a careful and balanced integration of technology and the human touch. They also raise important questions about participation, defined in this book as the meaningful and ongoing involvement of children, young people and families in decisions that affect their lives. As digital tools become increasingly embedded in practice, we must ensure that they enhance, rather than diminish, opportunities for inclusive and ethical engagement.

These considerations are especially relevant when examining the role that structural disadvantage plays in determining outcomes for children, young people and families. The war in Ukraine has seen energy prices soar in the past two years, which, taken alongside the widening disadvantage following the COVID-19 pandemic, is particularly troubling.

Since the onset of COVID-19, inequalities and poverty in the UK have been exacerbated in several ways. The pandemic disproportionately affected lower-income households, with many facing job losses and reduced working hours, leading to financial instability. School closures had a significant impact on the education of children from poorer backgrounds, thereby widening the attainment gap. Health inequalities also deepened, as those from disadvantaged communities – in particular, those from minoritised backgrounds – experienced higher rates of infection and mortality. Despite government support measures, the overall rate of absolute poverty rose slightly, highlighting the persistent challenges in addressing economic disparities (Ofsted, 2022).

COVID-19 also had a major impact on children and family social work practice in the UK. During lockdowns, social workers faced difficulties in maintaining regular contact with vulnerable children and families because in-person visits were restricted. This led to concerns about unreported cases of abuse and neglect because children were less visible to professionals. The pandemic also exacerbated mental health issues among children and young people, increasing the demand for social services (Ofsted, 2022).

Social workers had to adapt quickly to remote working, which, while necessary, reduced opportunities for peer support and professional development. Despite these challenges, the sector demonstrated resilience with many social workers finding innovative ways to support families, such as virtual check-ins and online resources, thereby widening the possibilities for including, involving and engaging with service users and other professionals.

The impact of the pandemic and the ongoing financial pressures exacerbated by the cost-of-living crisis have also intensified the retention crisis within children's social care. The government's own assessment rates this issue as 'critical' (Department for Education [DfE], 2024a). In 2023, the DfE reported that one in five children's social work positions were vacant – the highest rate since 2017, before the COVID-19 pandemic and financial crisis (DfE, 2024b). The reasons for this crisis are multifaceted and contested, with factors like organisational culture and job demands regularly positioned as key drivers. Regardless of the causes, the reality is stark.

The current challenges faced by social workers, only a few of which have been touched upon here, are in some ways unique, shaped by events like the COVID-19 pandemic and the war in Ukraine. However, their impact is not new – social workers and the communities they serve are under more pressure than ever before.

These complexities require practitioners to have a deep understanding of the issues facing children and families, the skills and knowledge to support families in very difficult circumstances, and the ability to navigate complex systems and policies. However, despite the importance of this work, there are still significant challenges and gaps in the field, particularly in terms of addressing the needs of the families that social workers work with and ensuring that they have a meaningful voice in decision-making.

One of the key motivations behind writing this book is to help address these challenges and gaps. It provides a resource that draws together emerging research, critical reflections and practice innovations in order to support more participatory and equitable models of practice. In doing so, the book explores interventions such as parental advocacy, peer support and Family Group Conferencing (FGC), all of which show promise in supporting families and strengthening their engagement with services. It also highlights alternative forms of family and child-led change, such as activism and grassroots organising.

In this book, we define 'advocacy' as organised actions that support or amplify the voices of children and families in navigating services or asserting their rights. 'Activism' refers to organised efforts by individuals or groups, including parents and young people themselves, to challenge systemic inequalities or drive reform in policy and practice. These concepts sit alongside participation as complementary forms of engagement and influence, each shaped by different power dynamics and forms of agency. At times, these concepts overlap or blur, especially in broader international contexts as illustrated in Chapter 7, underscoring the complex and context-dependent nature of parent-led efforts to influence child and family social work.

By capturing the perspectives of young people, parents, professionals and researchers, this book aims to contribute to the ongoing development of child and family social work, promoting best practice and outlining areas where further change is needed. It is our hope that the book will serve as a practical and reflective tool for students, practitioners and academics alike.

New research, policies and practice approaches are constantly emerging, and it can be challenging for social work managers, practitioners and academics to stay up to date with the latest developments. In this ever-evolving landscape, practitioners are required to adapt and innovate in order to meet the complex needs of children, young people and families.

There is a growing recognition that families and children should be more meaningfully involved in decision-making processes. However, what we know is that improvement in doing so has been painfully slow, despite the efforts of practitioners, academics and social work leaders to remedy this. This book will draw on a range of empirical research studies to shed light on the current challenges faced in child and family social work, while highlighting innovative and alternative models that offer solutions to these challenges.

## Book overview

This book provides a comprehensive examination of contemporary child and family social work, organised into three interconnected sections that explore foundations, developing practices and innovation. These sections reflect a deliberate editorial structure that moves from conceptual framing and systemic analysis through examples of participatory practices, and – finally – toward emerging innovations that have the potential to reshape how children and families engage with support services. This progression mirrors the logic of reflective practice – understanding the context, acting within it and imagining better futures.

Thematically, the book begins by grounding the reader in the current challenges facing child and family social work. This includes systemic pressures, legal frameworks and shifting patterns in care. It then moves to examine practice-based responses that amplify the voices of families and children through advocacy and relational approaches. Finally, it explores new and under-examined frontiers in participation, particularly digital and youth-led innovations, recognising their growing significance in a rapidly changing world. Each chapter contributes to a broader narrative: that meaningful participation is not a one-size-fits-all model but rather a diverse, evolving set of practices shaped by context, power and the lived experiences of children, families and practitioners.

### *Part I: Foundations and contemporary challenges*

Chapter 2 considers the complex patterns in out-of-home care rates through Ecological Systems Theory. By examining international trends, it explores why some regions see increasing numbers while others achieve reductions, and it provides evidence-based strategies for safely supporting more children to remain with their families.

Chapter 3 delves into the human experience of social work delivery through comprehensive research spanning 11 English local authorities. Through the voices of practitioners, it illuminates how emotional strain, discrimination and overwhelming caseloads affect both workforce retention and practice quality, while offering pathways toward sustainable change.

Chapter 4 focuses on the importance of social workers involving children and families meaningfully in decision-making. It provides an overview of the current legal and policy frameworks for participation, discusses the benefits and challenges (for social workers) of meaningful participation for families, and presents practical strategies for practitioners to involve children and families in the decision-making processes more effectively.

## *Part II: Advocacy and family participation*

Chapter 5 showcases innovation through the Family Drug and Alcohol Court model. Drawing on evaluative research, it demonstrates how this therapeutic, problem-solving approach and collaborative intervention transforms outcomes for families affected by substance misuse.

Chapter 6 examines how FGC empowers extended family networks in collective decision-making by analysing both implementation challenges and evidence of positive impact on strengthening families.

Chapter 7 offers a deliberately broad international perspective on parent activism and advocacy across eight high-income countries, providing a wide-ranging account of how parents have organised to challenge and influence child welfare systems. This panoramic overview sets the scene for the more focused and analytically grounded case studies within the remainder of the book.

Chapter 8 explores peer parental support and the diverse models represented within this form of advocacy. Through empirical research carried out in the UK, the chapter outlines how different approaches can amplify parents' voices and improve family outcomes.

Chapter 9 centres on advocacy for children in care, analysing legal frameworks and empirical evidence of its effectiveness in promoting children's rights and participation. It thoughtfully considers ethical challenges while providing practical guidance for implementation.

## *Part III: Rights and innovation*

Chapter 10 explores the role of Children in Care Councils (CiCCs) and their contribution to participatory practices. It draws on empirical research carried out during the COVID-19 pandemic and discusses how CiCCs were then trying to provide care to experienced young people with an opportunity to play a role in decision-making at a strategic level.

Chapter 11 examines digital participation in child and family social work, and how digital transformation enables, constrains or shifts the nature of participation. In addition, it weighs benefits against risks around privacy, security and digital exclusion while considering ethical implications for future practice.

This comprehensive work offers insights for practitioners, researchers and policy makers committed to reforming child welfare systems. By emphasising meaningful engagement with children and families while acknowledging systemic challenges, it charts a path toward more participatory, family-centred approaches that honour both rights and relationships.

## Key theories of participation

Fundamental to all the chapters in this book is an appreciation of the theoretical underpinnings of children's and families' participation in social work practice. These are rooted in several influential models that have shaped our understanding of how children can be meaningfully involved in decisions affecting their lives. While these models provide valuable insights into the nature and implementation of participatory practices, it's important to consider their practical applications and limitations within the complex realities of child and family social work. This serves as a backdrop for discussion of key issues affecting children and young people, and helps lay the context for understanding forums that support parental involvement and engagement between social care and families in order to reduce risk and meet need.

In selecting the theoretical frameworks to be discussed, we have prioritised models that are both foundational in the field and actively referenced in practice across different national contexts. These models – Hart's Ladder of Participation, Shier's Pathways to Participation and Lundy's Model of Participation – have been chosen because they each offer distinct but complementary perspectives on how participation can be conceptualised, supported and critiqued. Together, they provide a theoretical scaffold for the chapters that follow, offering tools for reflection, principles for design and benchmarks for evaluating participatory practice.

What follows is a brief overview of some of the key theoretical frameworks that have influenced child and family social work in the past few decades and continue to shape the field today:

- Roger Hart's (1992) Ladder of Participation has been particularly influential in conceptualising children's participation. This model presents eight rungs, representing different levels of involvement ranging from non-participation (manipulation, decoration and tokenism) to genuine participation. The upper five rungs of Hart's Ladder depict increasing degrees of participation, with the highest levels involving child-initiated actions and shared decision-making with adults. This model serves as a useful tool for practitioners to critically examine their approaches and to strive for more authentic involvement of children and young people in decision-making processes.
- Building on Hart's work, Harry Shier's (2001) Pathways to Participation model shifts the focus to organisational commitment to participatory processes. Shier's framework consists of five levels, progressing from simply listening to children to sharing power and responsibility

for decision-making. Each level is associated with three stages of commitment: openings, opportunities and obligations. This model provides a practical road map for organisations to assess and enhance their participatory practices, emphasising the systemic changes required to support genuine participation.
- Laura Lundy's (2007) Model of Participation offers a rights-based perspective. Her framework emphasises four key elements necessary for meaningful participation: Space, Voice, Audience and Influence. This model underscores the importance of not only providing opportunities for children to express their views but also ensuring that these views are genuinely heard and acted upon.

Each of these models contributes something essential to the themes explored throughout this book. Hart's Ladder provides an intuitive framework for recognising and challenging tokenism, and this is echoed in Chapters 4 and 10, which explore how children's involvement can range from passive consultation to active influence in decision-making. Shier's model supports the organisational and systemic focus in Chapters 6 and 9, offering insight into how structures can enable or restrict participation in processes like FGC and formal advocacy. Lundy's rights-based emphasis is especially relevant in Chapters 7, 9 and 11 which discuss where children and parents seek space and influence in systems that have often excluded them. Across the book as a whole, these frameworks help clarify what is meant by participation and what it looks like in practice.

These theoretical frameworks have profound implications for child and family social work practice, informing approaches, empowering service users and challenging traditional power dynamics. In terms of informing practice, social workers can use Hart's Ladder to critically reflect on their own practice, ensuring that they move beyond tokenistic involvement towards more collaborative approaches. For instance, in child protection conferences, practitioners might strive to actively involve children in decision-making processes rather than merely informing them of outcomes. Similarly, Shier's Pathways to Participation model can guide organisations in developing policies and procedures that systematically support meaningful participation, such as in care planning for looked-after children.

Lundy's model is particularly relevant in ensuring that participation is not just a box-ticking exercise but a genuine attempt to incorporate children's views into decision-making processes. In the context of looked-after children's reviews, for example, social workers must create safe spaces for children to express their opinions, actively listen to these views and demonstrably consider them in subsequent actions and decisions.

These theories also emphasise the importance of empowering children and families, moving beyond mere consultation to active involvement and shared decision-making. In family support services, this might involve collaborating with families in the design and delivery of services, rather than simply asking about their needs. Moreover, these models highlight the need for capacity-building among service users, prompting social workers to identify areas where additional support might be necessary to enable meaningful participation, such as providing advocacy services or adapting communication methods for children with special needs.

Importantly, all three models implicitly address power dynamics between professionals and service users. By striving for higher levels of participation, social workers are challenged to share power and decision-making authority with children and families. This aligns with anti-oppressive practice principles in social work (Dominelli, 2002), encouraging a more equitable relationship between practitioners and those whom they serve.

While these theoretical frameworks offer valuable insights, it is crucial to consider their limitations in real-world applications. For instance, they may not fully account for the complex realities of child protection work, where safeguarding concerns might necessarily limit the extent of children's participation (Healy and Darlington, 2009). Social workers must navigate the delicate balance between promoting participation and ensuring child safety, a nuance not explicitly addressed in these theoretical frameworks. Moreover, these models provide only limited guidance on navigating participation with very young children or those with significant developmental delays. While they acknowledge that children's capacity for participation increases with age and maturity, practical strategies for meaningful engagement with these groups are less clearly defined.

Resource implications pose a further challenge. Achieving higher levels of participation often requires significant time and resources, which may be difficult to secure in the context of stretched social services (Vis et al, 2011). This reality can create tension between the ideal of full participation and the practical constraints of day-to-day social work practice. Finally, there is a risk that these models could be used in a superficial, tick-box manner, leading to tokenistic rather than meaningful participation (Gallagher et al, 2012). It is crucial that practitioners and organisations engage with these frameworks thoughtfully and critically, rather than viewing them as simple checklists to be completed.

Despite these limitations, these theoretical models provide invaluable frameworks for understanding and implementing participatory practices in child and family social work. They offer clear structures for assessing and improving participation, aligning with rights-based approaches and challenging traditional power dynamics. By thoughtfully applying these theories while remaining mindful of their limitations, practitioners can work towards more effective, ethical and empowering participatory practices in child and family social work.

## Final thoughts

The aim of this book is to serve as a comprehensive guide for both students and practitioners, offering insights into intentional and reflective practice. It delves into the heart of contemporary practice, exploring the critical themes that shape childcare social work today and have been outlined here.

No doubt the sector, and the families that social workers support, are experiencing unprecedented challenges. This book seeks to offer new perspectives on both long-standing and emerging issues, bridging theory, practice and policy with grounded, real-world insights. In doing so, it addresses a significant gap in the literature: while much has been written about participation in principle, less attention has been given to how it is experienced and enacted by children, parents and practitioners across diverse systems and settings. The book responds to that gap by offering a collection that is both critically reflective and practically grounded.

We have deliberately integrated practice, research, policy and the voices of those with lived experience to provide a multilayered overview of participation, advocacy and innovation. The contributions span a range of disciplines, including social work, law, psychology and education, and draw on empirical studies from across the UK and internationally. We have prioritised the inclusion of authors with diverse positionalities and experiences – those who have worked in front line practice, who conduct participatory research and who bring insight from advocacy, activism and care experience. This diversity enriches the text and reflects our commitment to ensuring that multiple perspectives shape how we understand and improve practice.

At its core, this book is motivated by a desire to improve the experiences of children, young people and their families, and to support the dedicated professionals who work tirelessly in challenging circumstances. Readers will find practical tools, critical frameworks and real life case studies to inform and inspire their work. We hope that the book will help foster a more participatory, equitable, and values-led approach to social work: one that confronts inequality and holds space for complexity, while staying grounded in relational practice and respect.

By sharing knowledge and best practices, we aim to empower practitioners to make a meaningful difference to the lives of children and families. We call for a return to core social work values and a renewed focus on humane, collaborative and inclusive practice.

## References

Camden Council (2024) *Impact assessment: magic notes AI pilot*. Available from: https://opendatastore.camden.gov.uk/data-charter/DPIA-PRE/DPIA-PRE_25_214.pdf

Department for Education (2024a) *Consolidated annual report and accounts.* Available from: https://www.govwire.co.uk/news/department-for-educat ion/corporate-report-department-for-education-consolidated-annual-rep ort-and-accounts-2023-to-2024-96874#:~:text=This%20report%20s ets%20out%20the%20expenditure%20and%20performance,annual%20 report%20and%2

Department for Education (2024b) *Children's social work workforce.* Available from: https://explore-education-statistics.service.gov.uk/find-statistics/ children-s-social-work-workforce/2023

Dominelli, L. (2002) *Anti-Oppressive Social Work Theory and Practice,* Palgrave Macmillan.

Gallagher, M., Smith, M., Hardy, M. and Wilkinson, H. (2012) 'Children and families' involvement in social work decision making', *Children & Society,* 26(1): 74–85. Available from: https://doi.org/10.1111/ j.1099-0860.2011.00409.x

Hart, R.A. (1992) *Children's Participation: From Tokenism to Citizenship,* UNICEF International Child Development Centre.

Healy, K. and Darlington, Y. (2009) 'Service user participation in diverse child protection contexts: principles for practice', *Child & Family Social Work,* 14(4): 420–30. Available from: https://onlinelibrary.wiley.com/doi/ abs/10.1111/j.1365-2206.2009.00613.x

Lundy, L. (2007) ' "Voice" is not enough: conceptualising Article 12 of the United Nations Convention on the Rights of the Child', *British Educational Research Journal,* 33(6): 927–42. Available from: https://bera-journals.online library.wiley.com/doi/10.1080/01411920701657033

Ofsted (2022) *Children's Social Care 2022: Recovering From the COVID-19 Pandemic.* Available from: https://www.gov.uk/government/publications/ childrens-social-care-2022-recovering-from-the-covid-19-pandemic/ childrens-social-care-2022-recovering-from-the-covid-19-pandemic

Shier, H. (2001) 'Pathways to participation: openings, opportunities and obligations', *Children & Society,* 15(2): 107–17. Available from: https:// doi.org/10.1002/chi.617

*The Guardian* (2024) *Social workers in England begin using AI system to assist their work.* Available from: https://www.pslhub.org/blogs/entry/7483-soc ial-workers-in-england-begin-using-ai-system-to-assist-their-work

Vis, S.A., Holtan, A. and Thomas, N. (2011) 'Obstacles for child participation in care and protection cases – why Norwegian social workers find it difficult', *Child Abuse Review,* 21(1): 7–23. Available from: https:// onlinelibrary.wiley.com/doi/10.1002/car.1155

# 2

# Increasing and varying rates of children in out-of-home care: insights from Ecological Systems Theory

*Sophie Wood*

## Context

This chapter delves into the notable variation in the rates of children in care across different local authorities in the UK, and the consequential impact on the child and family social work sector. It highlights the breadth of the issue, supported by research that reveals significant disparities in care rates between local authorities. These variations raise concerns, especially considering the well-documented negative impacts of care on children's outcomes. The chapter further examines the literature to explore potential causes, including demographic differences, social and economic factors, and local authority policy and practice variations. It applies an ecological systems framework to consider the interconnected and diverse factors influencing rates of children in care. It then discusses potential solutions, emphasising early intervention, a stronger focus on reunification, changes to social care practices and policy reform.

## The extent of variation in rates of children in care

The high rates of children in care in the UK and other developed nations are prominent on the political agenda (Dickens et al, 2007); McGhee et al, 2018; Bennett et al, 2020; Bywaters et al, 2020; Goldacre and Hood, 2022; Welsh Government, 2023; Department for Education, 2023) and several studies (for example, Hodges and Scourfield, 2023; have explored why care rates are rising and vary between local authorities. Bringing these studies together highlighted the fragmented nature of existing approaches to understanding rising and variable care rates, and suggested the value of applying an ecological systems framework. This considers the complex interplay between individual, familial, community, societal and political factors, providing a more holistic understanding of the issue.

The care system has witnessed a substantial rise in the number of children under its supervision in the past decade (Stabler et al, 2021; Wood and

Forrester, 2023), rising by 23 per cent in England and 25 per cent in Wales between 2013 and 2023 (UK Government, 2023; StatsWales, 2024). A similar pattern exists in Northern Ireland (an increase of 35 per cent between 2013 and 2023; Northern Ireland Department of Health 2017; 2023) and other nations, including Australia (Australian Government, 2023), Canada (Hélie et al, 2022) and Belgium (Van Holen et al, 2023). However, in Scotland, the number of children in care actually *decreased* by 24 per cent between 2013 and 2023 (Scottish Government, 2024). There exists no consensus regarding the reasons behind these fluctuations (Bywaters et al, 2020).

Although overall out-of-home care is usually considered harmful, certain outcomes for children may improve upon entering care (Forrester et al, 2009). Sebba et al (2015) found that children in longer-term care in England performed better educationally than those who were 'in need' but not in care, and better than those in short-term care, suggesting a protective effect. However, each additional care placement change after age 11 was linked to a decrease of one-third of a grade at GCSE. Also, children in residential or other forms of care at age 16 scored over six grades lower than those in kinship or foster care. Other studies indicate that children not in care, but in need or on child protection plans, may face challenges in educational attainment (Berridge et al, 2021; Green et al, 2021). The suitability of care differs for each child, considering their unique care experiences and home situation. Determining the optimal level of care is akin to a 'Goldilocks' measure – not too high or too low – yet establishing the precise balance is challenging (Cordis Bright, 2013).

Children within the care system frequently encounter adverse outcomes, including heightened rates of psychological disorders and reduced educational achievement (Ford et al, 2007; Trout et al, 2008). Concerns are mounting regarding the potential harms of care for children and families, as well as its limited ability to reverse the impact of past harms. There is evidence of enduring harm to parents after their children are removed (Broadhurst and Mason, 2020; Russell et al, 2022). Furthermore, a high proportion of care experienced mothers (17 per cent) have their own children placed in care, indicating intergenerational trauma and a system stacked against individuals with past encounters with it (Doebler et al, 2024). Most children maintain contact with their birth families into adulthood, with a substantial proportion (11 per cent) returning home when they leave care at age 18 (UK Government, 2023). This underscores the significance of these enduring relationships and the role they play in a child's identity (Dallas-Childs, 2022), as well as the challenges the state faces in replicating lifelong support. Moreover, care is costly, prompting legitimate concerns about its cost-effectiveness. The high rate of care raises crucial questions related to social justice, social policy and practices within children's social services, such as whether decision-making processes are equitable and transparent. Consequently, preventing children from entering state care is a primary objective in numerous countries, including England (Trowler, 2018), Wales (Ministerial Advisory Group on Improving Outcomes for Children, 2019), New Zealand (Katz et al, 2015) and Norway (Skivenes, 2011).

There is a consensus, therefore, on the necessity of averting risk factors leading to entry into care (Department for Education, 2016; Family Rights Group, 2018). This aligns with the principles of the United Nations Convention on the Rights of the Child (1989) and the Children Act UK (1989), emphasising the significance of children being cared for by their parents whenever feasible, while acknowledging that state care may be the safest option in some cases. However, the issue is complex, with rising rates in many countries, though not all, influenced by a variety of factors including the challenge of responding appropriately to diverse children's needs and potentially shifting norms and practices within child welfare organisations, such as evolving responses to risk (Thomas, 2018).

## Why are care rates so high?

Multiple factors contribute to high care rates, but the evidence is fragmented, making it difficult to grasp the overall picture because we cannot see how these factors interact. Some operate on a UK-wide or country level, such as national policy frameworks and economic conditions, while others are more locally driven, including specific community dynamics, local authority practices and the availability of support services. Policy divergence across the UK can further contribute to regional variations, often reflecting differing legal and operational practices rather than higher levels of need for public care (McGhee et al, 2018). Despite the differences in devolution settlements, there is a noticeable convergence in policy direction across the UK towards early intervention, the extensive use of kinship care, and adoption as an exit route from public care. This convergence is particularly evident in the increased entry of very young children into public care in Scotland, Northern Ireland and Wales (McGhee et al, 2018). Another example was the surge in rates of out-of-home care in Wales in the early 2000s, influenced by increased risk aversion by social workers in response to high-profile cases like Peter Connolly's death, although the impact was felt most acutely in the poorest neighbourhoods (Elliott, 2020). Applying Ecological Systems Theory could help to integrate these various layers – national, regional and local – into a comprehensive framework, enabling a deeper understanding of their complex interactions and their collective influence on care rates.

Deprivation is strongly associated with high care rates and local authorities in more deprived areas have more children in care (Bywaters et al, 2020). Goldacre and Hood's (2022) study in England identified a social gradient in children's social care, highlighting how lower socio-economic status influences a higher likelihood of child welfare intervention. They identified stronger social gradients for younger, white children and children assessed with neglect or on protection plans for neglect. However, there is no substantial evidence of significant changes in deprivation over time to explain the increase in rates (Forrester et al, 2021a).

The societal recognition of new risks to children, such as parental substance use or domestic abuse, could be contributing to the increased number of children in care. Also, evolving forms of harm, like child sexual or criminal exploitation, have been identified over recent decades (Thomas, 2018).

Government cuts in benefits and services associated with austerity are suggested to contribute to the recent increases in care rates as more families come under pressure and spending fails to meet rising needs (Thomas, 2018). However, care rates were already rising considerably before austerity, indicating that this does not fully explain the increase. The COVID-19 pandemic (Forrester et al, 2021b) and the cost-of-living crisis could be further exacerbating the issue. Furthermore, ways of working within children's social care may play a role, with 'risk-averse' practices potentially contributing to the rise (Thomas, 2018).

While care rates have increased overall in England and Wales, there are significant variations between local authorities (Wood and Forrester, 2023) and some areas have experienced a decline in rates. The specific reasons for these differences remain unknown.

## Why do care rates vary?

Variations in care rates among local authorities in Wales are significant (Wijedasa et al, 2018; UK Government, 2023). For instance, a child in Torfaen is five times more likely to be in care than one in Carmarthenshire. For context, Torfaen is in South East Wales and encompasses urban and rural areas with high levels of deprivation. In contrast, Carmarthenshire, situated in the south-west, is predominantly rural and not considered a deprived area overall, although there are pockets of relatively high deprivation. Hodges (2020a) found that in Wales approximately half the differences in care rates among local authorities could be explained by deprivation rates. Therefore, while the role of deprivation is understood, it does not adequately explain variation alone (Hodges, 2020a).

Hodges (2020a) found differences in collaboration between children's social care and related agencies likely account for around 25 per cent of the variation between local authorities in Wales. Fitzsimons et al (2022) found that local authority characteristics, possibly reflecting local practice, explain an additional 7 per cent of the variation in the likelihood of children entering residential or foster care, beyond the 20 per cent attributed to the characteristics of children, families and neighbourhoods. These local authority characteristics could include differences in how they managed social care thresholds, the practices they followed and, potentially, other organisational or policy factors that were not directly measured in the analysis.

Bunting et al (2018) examined child welfare trends across the UK and observed a general shift toward increased child protection. However, variations in case processing may have an impact on overall care rates. For example, in Northern Ireland, high referral levels to children's social care result in only one in ten referrals leading to a child protection investigation, compared with one in five in England. In Wales, although referrals have decreased, a higher proportion have proceeded to assessment. Meanwhile, Scotland's alternative legal route complicates direct comparisons. The study suggests that variations in child protection practices across the UK nations could be due to differences in the integration of health and social care systems (in Northern Ireland), mandatory reporting practices, socio-economic factors (such as deprivation and child poverty) and varying professional orientations toward family support.

The changes in care rates have also exhibited diversity across local authorities. Since 2015, there has been an overall 29 per cent increase in care rates in Wales, but the rates of change vary significantly (StatsWales, 2024). Notably, four local authorities have experienced increases of 40 per cent or more, while two have seen decreases exceeding 20 per cent (Wood and Forrester, 2023). These disparities do not align with changes in underlying factors such as deprivation levels (Forrester et al, 2021a). Moreover, national influences, which we might expect to drive local variation ranging from media coverage to family policy, fail to fully account for such variations (Forrester et al, 2021a). Importantly, if certain local authorities are successfully reducing the need for children to be in care, there may be valuable lessons for others to learn.

Workers' views, values and social work practices vary significantly by local authority. Wood and Forrester (2023) found that workers in local authorities with decreasing care rates exhibited stronger pro-family values, were less risk-averse when responding to case study vignettes (based on genuine social work cases where respondents were asked how they would respond to a situation), had greater confidence in the decisions made within their local authority, and were more positive about the support available for their practice. Other studies have explored variations in social worker decision-making, such as Strolin-Goltzman and Holbrook (2023) who found that, regardless of years of job experience, workers were more likely to make decisions in favour of family preservation if they had experienced secondary traumatic stress or reported collaboration with other child-serving community professionals. Furthermore, Keddell (2023) discusses the problem of decision variability in child protection in New Zealand and highlights the ethical challenges social workers face. The author argues that decision variability represents a justice issue because children in similar circumstances should receive consistent protection across different locations. They found that variability is influenced by individual decision-makers and the broader decision-making ecology, despite the use of assessment tools aimed at reducing inconsistency.

Wijedasa et al (2018) investigated how macro-level factors, such as the percentage of low-income families, and social work system variables, including expenditure on children in need, social work turnover, innovation funding and Ofsted ratings (Ofsted inspects and regulates services for children), were associated with changes in the rate of children in care in England. They found areas that experienced a reduction in the rate of children in care were linked to a decrease in the number of low-income families, participation in the Department for Education's Innovation Programme and better Ofsted ratings. A better Ofsted rating could suggest a correlation between the quality of service and the ability to manage and reduce the need for state intervention in family life.

To summarise, while we know that rates are rising and vary significantly, the underlying reasons remain only partially understood. Although some contributing factors, such as deprivation, have been identified, they cannot fully explain the variations because these rates often fluctuate in ways that defy singular explanations. While existing evidence suggests the presence of interconnected factors, our understanding is hampered by a fragmented and siloed evidence base. Applying Ecological Systems Theory could offer a more comprehensive framework, bridging these gaps and integrating the complex, context-dependent factors involved.

## Why Ecological Systems Theory?

The factors influencing rates (and their variation) of children in care are complex and diverse. Ecological Systems Theory is effective for unpacking complex issues because it helps to understand the relationships between different elements of a problem and it has been applied to other aspects of social work (for example, Barber, 2002; Gordon et al, 2012; Piel et al, 2017). It emphasises the importance of considering not just the individual but also their relationships, community, and broader societal influences. Piel et al (2017) applied an ecological systems approach to understanding social support in foster family resilience and their interactions with child welfare agencies, healthcare providers and educational institutions. It emphasised the importance of support networks, reciprocal relationships, systemic challenges and adapting to life transitions, ultimately aiding in the development of resilient and stable foster families through targeted interventions.

Ecological Systems Theory offers a comprehensive framework to advance our understanding of changing and varied rates of out-of-home care. By considering the multiple levels of influence from the microsystem to the macrosystem, Ecological Systems Theory helps to identify how broader structural socio-economic conditions have an impact on individual and family dynamics, thereby influencing the rates of children in care. This theory is particularly helpful in understanding the variability of problems and issues across different local contexts because it integrates the influence of local practices, policies and resources within the overarching structural environment, providing a nuanced perspective on regional disparities in out-of-home care.

## Ecological Systems Theory explained

Ecological Systems Theory emerged from the amalgamation of systems theory, ecological theory and bioecological systems theory (Teater, 2021). These frameworks analyse the reciprocal influence between individuals and the various physical, interpersonal, social, political and cultural systems that shape their lives (Langer and Lietz, 2015). Bronfenbrenner (1977) applied Ecological Systems Theory to child development (explained later). This chapter applies it to understanding the complex, multi-level factors influencing the rates of children in out-of-home care. Figure 2.1 visualises the factors influencing rates of children in care identified in this chapter and splits them into the five layers of the ecological system.

The microsystem is closest to the individual, encompassing their immediate relationships and interactions. These include direct engagements with parents, siblings, teachers and peers. It is where most direct social interactions occur, shaping much of an individual's early experiences and influencing their development (Bronfenbrenner, 1977). Understanding the microsystem is key to grasping how immediate personal relationships and environments have an impact on a child's well-being and possible need for out-of-home care. For example, a child who experiences consistent parental support and positive school interactions is likely to develop resilience and a strong sense of security, reducing the risk of entering out-of-home care. Conversely, a child exposed to parental neglect or conflict within the home may be more vulnerable to adverse outcomes, necessitating protective interventions such as foster care.

The mesosystem connects different systems within the microsystem involving relationships and/or bidirectional influences. An example is the relationship between parents and social workers or other support systems such as school. If families have good relationships with these services/systems, then they are more likely to engage with them and receive support when needed. It is vital to assess the quality of relationships among these microsystems because they can facilitate or obstruct a child's development (Bronfenbrenner, 1977). For instance, in cases where a school regularly communicates with a child's social worker and the parents are actively involved in school meetings, issues can be identified and addressed early, preventing escalation to the point

**Figure 2.1**: Bronfenbrenner's Ecological Systems Theory adapted to reflect factors influencing rates of children in care

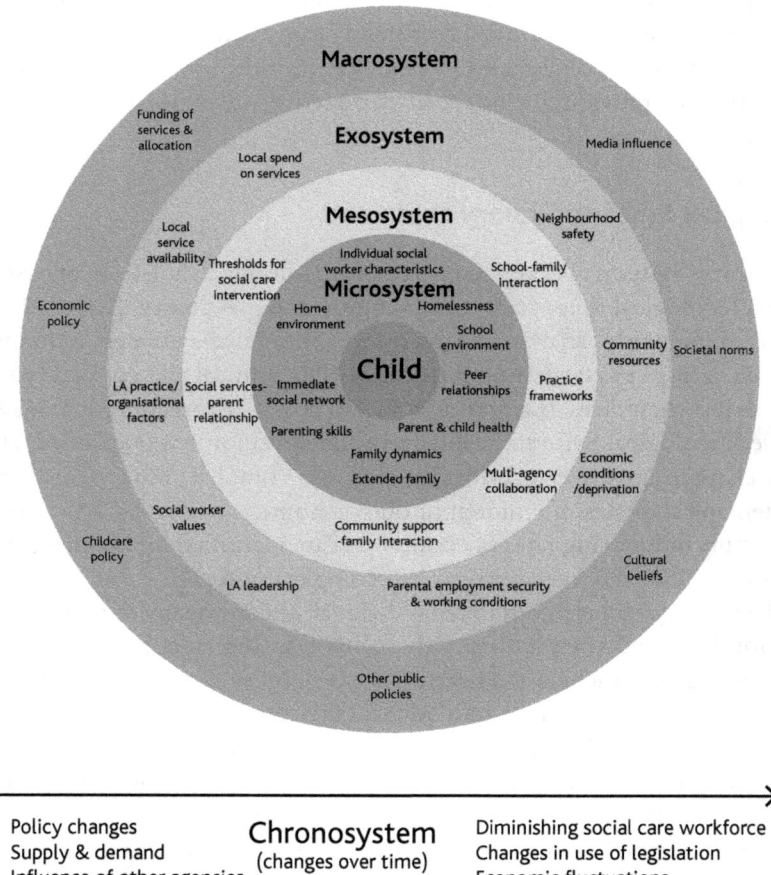

where out-of-home care is considered. However, if there is a breakdown in communication between these systems, crucial support might not be provided, leading to the child being placed into care.

The exosystem consists of interactions between two or more systems indirectly influencing another system. Unlike the mesosystem, it involves external environmental settings that have an impact on child well-being and development, such as a parent's workplace affecting a child indirectly (for example, due to stress). Or the introduction of a new practice framework in a local authority could alter how social workers engage with families. If the framework promotes a strength-based approach, it could encourage families to be more receptive to support and more willing to make behavioural changes, which could in turn influence whether or not their children enter care.

The macrosystem comprises larger systems influencing an individual's life, including policies, cultural values and resources. It infiltrates all layers of the ecological model, thereby having a profound impact on individuals (Bronfenbrenner, 1977). For instance, societal views on mental health care accessibility can affect whether a parent seeks treatment and, in turn, a parent's ability to meet their child's needs. It represents the broader socio-cultural context in which individuals develop. Furthermore, macro-economic policies, such as cuts to welfare benefits or austerity measures, can significantly increase financial stress on families, leading to a higher likelihood of children entering care due to the compounded effects of poverty.

The chronosystem incorporates the dimension of time, considering how life transitions and historical changes influence child well-being and development (Bronfenbrenner, 1977). This layer emphasises that development is dynamic, influenced by societal and environmental changes. For example, the influence of high-profile child deaths has a temporal influence on rates of children in care by prompting practitioners to adopt a more risk-averse approach due to heightened awareness of risk factors and the fear of becoming the focus of the next media story.

Stabler et al's (2021) scoping review of interventions influencing rates of children in care found that evaluations focused mainly on individualised approaches within the microsystem. This assumes that parental problems are the main cause of children entering care and thereby overlooking the wider ecological system. Featherstone et al (2018) supports this, arguing that the child protection system often neglects economic, environmental and cultural barriers, thereby obscuring the social determinants of harm. One challenge is that evaluating small-scale interventions with parents is often simpler than assessing broader system-level interventions which, although potentially more impactful, are complex and costly to study because of the many mechanisms involved. There is also a shortage of economic evaluations (El-Banna et al, 2021; Suh and Holmes, 2022) in children's social care, thereby posing challenges for evidence-based decision-making for policy makers.

## The possible solutions to increasing rates of out-of-home care

This section considers possible solutions to increasing rates of care through an ecological systems lens, covering themes such as early intervention, a stronger focus on reunification, social care practices and policy reform.

### Early intervention

It is clear that early intervention is key to reducing the need for out-of-home care. By adopting comprehensive strategies that integrate services across family, community, organisational and policy domains (Stabler et al,

2021), social workers can address root causes and intervene proactively to prevent care placements and their escalation (Williams et al, 2022; Wood et al, 2024b).

Hood (2015) explains that the UK care system is structured into tiers of primary, secondary and tertiary services. It is designed around a series of thresholds where the levels of need and risk are assessed at each point to determine the necessary resources. Decisions in one tier affect those in others: for instance, placing a child in residential care when they could be in foster care has an impact on the entire system.

One key issue is the system's focus on protective interventions rather than preventive measures. Hood et al's (2016) analysis of national datasets found that more children are placed on child protection plans than on child in need plans. Allocating more resources to meet needs before protection is required might reduce the number of children entering care.

Also, the likelihood of children exiting the care system through reunification or adoption decreases as problematic behaviour becomes more entrenched. National figures from England (UK Government, 2023) show a 3 per cent decrease in the proportion of children under 18 leaving care (excluding those aging out) from 2019 to 2023. Hodges' (2020b) analysis found that fewer children were leaving care over time, thereby contributing to the rising overall rates of children in care.

Another related concept is 'failure demand' (Hood et al, 2016), which occurs when service users do not receive necessary support and therefore re-enter the system. It also raises a broader question about the effectiveness of a tiered system in children's social care. Currently, expertise is concentrated in Tier 3 services, which handle the most acute cases. However, reserving the 'best' services for these cases can inadvertently create failure demand elsewhere in the system because issues are not adequately addressed when they first arise (Hood, 2015). If expertise in higher tiers were more readily available in Tier 1 and Tier 2, social workers might receive better clinical consultation, thereby improving assessment and planning, especially in cases that reach court (Family Justice Review Panel, 2011). Also, services designed around multiple isolated tiers of triage and assessment can de-contextualise children from their social circumstances (Hood et al, 2020). Greater fluidity between tiers, with a focus on child development and shifting from placement type to placement purpose, could better support children and their families (Holmes et al, 2018).

However, it is important to recognise that some factors influencing child welfare are driven by higher-level aspects of the ecological system and beyond social workers' control. Therefore, changes are needed at multiple levels. An early intervention approach informed by Ecological Systems Theory would address issues across the entire ecosystem. These might include family therapy or substance use treatment to address family dynamics; social workers using a strengths-based approach to improve relationships; strong multi-agency collaboration; a social care workforce prioritising family unity; and economic policy changes to provide families with more resources to care for their children. Each family will have unique considerations.

## Reunification

We know that fewer children are leaving care (Hodges, 2020b). Therefore, addressing rising care rates requires a stronger focus on reunification. This includes advocating for better multi-agency collaboration and parental skill-building (Stabler et al, 2021), addressing root causes while strengthening support mechanisms for families (Williams et al, 2022; Wood et al, 2024b), and promoting Family Group Conferences (FGCs) for family involvement and kinship care (Wood et al, 2024a).

FGCs involve extended family members in planning and decision-making for children at risk or in need, aiming to keep children with their birth families when safe and to support social workers in their work with families (mesosystem). They empower families by allowing them to lead decision-making and planning, thereby fostering a sense of ownership and responsibility (microsystem). They also help identify broader family networks (microsystem) to support the child, thereby reducing reliance on external interventions. By involving families in decision-making, FGCs seek to limit removals to cases of absolute necessity. They also aid in reunification by involving families in plans to address issues leading to removal.

However, evidence of FGCs' impact on reducing the number of children in care is mixed (Scourfield et al, 2024). Wood et al (2024a) shows that FGCs are correlated with higher rates of children entering care. However, this could be because FGCs are also associated with increased kinship foster care, indicating a successful alignment with the goal of keeping children within their familial networks. Additionally, higher FGC rates by local authority are linked to more children leaving care, suggesting their effectiveness in facilitating reunifications or other resolutions.

## Social care working practices

It is evident from the literature that divergent social work practice influences variations in rates of care. Key messages for social care practices include fostering family-oriented cultures within services to support children at home when safe to do so (Wood and Forrester, 2023) and adopting a poverty-aware approach that provides direct material support to families (Wood et al, 2022a).

Wood et al (2022b) investigated how interventions which change a family's income affects rates of children in care. Most of these interventions stem from macro-level policy changes. However, the study highlights how material hardship (as a result of these interventions) impacts the microsystem. It identifies three main pathways: mothers seeking employment due to decreased income; changes in the home environment leading to increased parental stress, mental health issues, and substance misuse, which can impair caregiving and potentially result in neglect or abuse; and the heightened risk of homelessness due to income reductions, increasing child harm. Conditions in other layers of the ecosystem may also buffer how changes in the macro system (for example, benefit policy change) impact on the microsystem. The study found that welfare payment changes have a greater impact on families in poor economic conditions (exosystem) and that a family's support network (microsystem) influences how they cope with income reductions and unsuitable employment (exosystem).

Notably, the employment-related studies in the pathway focused exclusively on mothers. Historically, social work with children and families has heavily centred on mothers, often placing the primary responsibility for child protection on women, regardless of a male partner's presence. This focus can reinforce biases linking father absence with mother-blaming (Strega et al, 2008).

Conversely, improvements in family circumstances and material assistance can prevent maltreatment and reduce the need for out-of-home care. These values can be instilled through training and leadership (Wood and Forrester, 2023) but are also influenced by broader welfare system factors like funding and societal norms about poverty. Nørup and Jacobsen (2022) highlight how poverty's structural causes are often overlooked in social work practice, arguing that a focus on individual responsibility can neglect essential support needs. While Webb (2022) found that funding for children's services often fails to align with actual needs, particularly for preventative services.

Finally, social workers must adopt data-informed decision-making to address needs more effectively across the ecosystem. For instance, Wood et al's (2024c) review of publicly available multi-agency data relevant to children's social care in Wales revealed that data is accessible at every level of the ecosystem. At the microsystem level, direct environments like family and school are detailed through data on domestic abuse and children's social care. The mesosystem, showing interactions between environments, is represented by data on individuals engaged in education, training, or employment, along with education data on school absences, exclusions, and attainment. External factors at the exosystem level are illustrated by data on deprivation, local authority spending, employment, housing stock, and local crime statistics. The macrosystem, reflecting societal norms and policies, is shown through data on welfare payments, and social housing lettings. The study also addresses the chronosystem by discussing data timeliness and historical context, including changes in children's social care data collection since the Social Services and Well-being (Wales) Act 2014.

Key barriers to not using this data to inform decision making include inadequate training, capacity issues, overwhelming data volume, and inconsistent documentation. Enhancing data accessibility and clarity is crucial; establishing a central hub for social workers to easily access essential information would be highly beneficial. Integrating socio-economic data into interpretations is also vital (Hood et al, 2020). Rapid developments in artificial intelligence could further streamline this process, providing social workers with better insights to inform their decisions (Department for Education, 2024).

*Policy reform*

The changes mentioned earlier need to occur in tandem with changes at the macro level, specifically the vital role of policy reforms in driving systemic change within social care, considering the interplay between systems. Advocating for holistic, evidence-based reforms is key to reducing reliance on out-of-home care (Stabler et al, 2021). Creating a family-oriented culture in social services requires supportive policies (Wood and Forrester, 2023), while addressing economic factors through tax benefits or free childcare is crucial for lowering care rates (Wood et al, 2022b). Policy Reforms should also promote a poverty-aware approach in social work (Nørup and Jacobsen, 2022). Supportive policy frameworks and funding for FGCs is essential, with only 30 per cent of UK local authorities currently mandatorily offering FGCs before care placement (Wood et al, 2022a).

There also needs to be systemic reform in caring for vulnerable children, emphasising a shift towards preventive and community-based support and improved funding models. Franklin et al (2023) criticised increased spending on high-cost late interventions for not addressing the root causes of entry into care. Investing in data infrastructure and improving data quality and accessibility are also crucial for better service delivery and reducing reliance on out-of-home care (Wood et al, 2024c).

*Summary*

Making changes at one level of the system is challenging without addressing factors at other levels, as efforts in one area are often influenced by and dependent on conditions at other levels. Interventions aimed at improving a child's immediate environment may be limited if broader systemic issues, such as policy constraints or community resources, are not also addressed. Key recommendations from this section include the following:

- Strengthening family and community support systems.
- Addressing economic factors affecting families.

- Adapting the child welfare system to focus on placement purposes and meeting children's needs with appropriate expertise from initial contact.
- Using data to identify at-risk children earlier and implement targeted preventive measures, with a focus on accessibility of data and integrating socio-economic factors.
- Promoting reunification through Family Group Conferencing and multi-agency efforts focused on skill-building and addressing root causes.
- Advocating for family-oriented policies, poverty-aware approaches, and adequate funding for family support services.

## Conclusion

This chapter addresses variations in out-of-home care rates over time, providing a comprehensive analysis informed by Ecological Systems Theory. The findings reveal significant fluctuations in care rates across regions and periods, influenced by a myriad of interconnected factors within a larger system.

At the microsystem level, a child's immediate environments, like family and school, are crucial. Supportive family dynamics and stable homes reduce the risk of entering care, while adverse conditions increase it. The mesosystem involves interactions between environments, such as parent-social worker relationships, where effective communication can improve outcomes. The exosystem includes external factors like parental workplace conditions that indirectly affect child welfare, as stress from these systems can impact a parent's ability to provide care. At the macrosystem level, societal factors, including cultural values and social policies, significantly influence child welfare, with policies supporting economic stability helping to reduce care rates. The chronosystem considers the impact of time and societal shifts, where changes to social policies or local authority leadership can influence care trends. Overlaps exist between these systems and conditions in one can amplify or mitigate the effects of another, such as macro-level economic policy changes disproportionately affecting families in poverty.

This chapter highlights key areas for future research, including economic evaluations of social care interventions, more evaluations of interventions targeting the exo, macro, and chronosystems using a complex systems approach, and exploring technological innovations like artificial intelligence in social work to improve data-informed decision-making.

Using Ecological Systems Theory, this chapter highlights the need to address issues at multiple levels and recognise their interconnectedness. Early intervention should focus on family support, economic stability, and policy changes to tackle root causes and prevent care placements. The findings emphasise promoting a family-oriented culture in social services, adopting a strengths-based approach, and training social workers to effectively use data. Success requires systemic policy reforms to support these initiatives. Changes at one level must align with others to achieve the desired outcomes.

**References**

Australian Government (2023) *Aboriginal and Torres Strait Islander children are not overrepresented in the child protection system.* Available from: https://www.pc.gov.au/closing-the-gap-data/dashboard/se/outcome-area12/out-of-home-care

Barber, J.G. (2002) *Social Work with Addictions*, Palgrave.

Bennett, D.L., Mason, K.E., Schlüter, D.K., Wickham, S., Lai, E.T., Alexiou, A. et al (2020) 'Trends in inequalities in children looked after in England between 2004 and 2019: a local area ecological analysis', *BMJ Open*, 10(11): e041774.

Berridge, D., Sebba, J., Cartwright, M. and Staples, E. (2021) 'School experiences of children in need: learning and support', *British Educational Research Journal*, 47(6): 1700–16. Available from: https://doi.org/10.1002/berj.3750

Broadhurst, K. and Mason, C. (2020) 'Child removal as the gateway to further adversity: birth mother accounts of the immediate and enduring collateral consequences of child removal', *Qualitative Social Work*, 19(1): 15–37.

Bronfenbrenner, U. (1977) 'Toward an experimental ecology of human development', *American Psychologist*, 32(7): 513.

Bunting, L., McCartan, C., McGhee, J., Bywaters, P., Daniel, B., Featherstone, B. et al (2018) 'Trends in child protection across the UK: a comparative analysis', *The British Journal of Social Work*, 48(5): 1154–75. Available from: https://doi.org/10.1093/bjsw/bcx102

Bywaters, P., Scourfield, J., Jones, C., Sparks, T., Elliott, M., Hooper, J. et al (2020) 'Child welfare inequalities in the four nations of the UK', *Journal of Social Work*, 20(2): 193–215. Available from: https://doi.org/10.1177/1468017318793479

Cordis Bright (2013) *Research on differences in the looked after children population.* Available from: https://www.cordisbright.co.uk/admin/resources/all-wales-heads-of-childrens-services-research-on-differences-in-lac.pdf

Dallas-Childs, R. (2022) *'"It was a thing about belonging and identity. I just felt, this is who I am"· Residential care experienced children and young people actively (re)creating identity, family and community'* (PhD thesis). The University of Edinburgh.

Department for Education (2016) *Putting children first: Delivering our vision for excellent children's social care.* Available from: https://assets.publishing.service.gov.uk/government/uploads/system/uploads/attachment_data/file/554573/Putting_children_first_delivering_vision_excellent_childrens_social_care.pdf

Department for Education (2023) *Stable homes, built on love: Implementation strategy and consultation: Children's social care reform 2023*. Available from: https://assets.publishing.service.gov.uk/government/uploads/system/uploads/attachment_data/file/1147317/Children_s_social_care_stable_homes_consultation_February_2023.pdf

Department for Education (2024) *Introduction to data analytics and the development process*. Available from: https://assets.publishing.service.gov.uk/media/66214a5abe5f81890e757d42/Introduction_to_data_analytics_and_the_development_process.pdf

Dickens, J., Howell, D., Thoburn, J. and Schofield, G. (2007) 'Children starting to be looked after by local authorities in England: an analysis of inter-authority variation and case-centred decision making', *The British Journal of Social Work*, 37(4): 597–617. Available from: https://doi.org/10.1093/bjsw/bch276

Doebler, S., Bailey, G., Broadhurst, K., Robers, L., Wood, S., Cowley, L. et al (2024) Care Experienced Mothers and their Children in Care in Wales. *Centre for Child and Family Justice Research*.

El-Banna, A., Petrou, S., Yiu, H.H.E., Daher, S., Forrester, D., Scourfield, J. et al (2021) 'Systematic review of economic evaluations of children's social care interventions', *Children and Youth Services Review*, 121: 105864. Available from: https://doi.org/10.1016/j.childyouth.2020.105864

Elliott, M. (2020) 'Child welfare inequalities in a time of rising numbers of children entering out-of-home care', *British Journal of Social Work*, 50(2): 581–97.

Family Justice Review Panel (2011) *Family Justice Review: Final Report*. Ministry of Justice, Department for Education and the Welsh Government.

Family Rights Group (2018) *The Care Crisis Review: Options for Change*. Available from: https://frg.org.uk/involving-families/reforming-law-and-practice/care-crisis-review

Featherstone, B., Gupta, A., Morris, K., and Warner, J. (2018) 'Let's stop feeding the risk monster: towards a social model of "child protection"', *Families, Relationships and Societies*, 7(1), 7–22.

Fitzsimons, P., James, D., Shaw, S. and Newcombe, B. (2022) *Drivers of Activity in Children's Social Care*. Department for Education. Available from: https://assets.publishing.service.gov.uk/media/62961ec9d3bf7f036ddfe7ce/Drivers_of_Activity_in_Children_s_Social_Care.pdf

Ford, T., Vostanis, P., Meltzer, H. and Goodman, R. (2007) 'Psychiatric disorder among British children looked after by local authorities: comparison with children living in private households', *The British Journal of Psychiatry*, 190: 319–25.

Forrester, D., Goodman, K., Cocker, C., Binnie, C. and Jensch, G. (2009) 'What is the impact of public care on children's welfare? A review of research findings from England and Wales and their policy implications', *Journal of Social Policy*, 38(3): 439–56. Available from: https://doi.org/10.1017/S0047279409003110

Forrester, D., Wood, S., Waits, C., Jones, R., Bristow, D. and Taylor-Collins, E. (2021a) '*The Coronavirus pandemic and children's social care practice: Policy briefing*', Wales Centre for Public Policy.

Forrester, D., Wood, S., Waits, C., Jones, R., Bristow, D. and Taylor-Collins, E. (2021b) *Children's social services and care rates in Wales: A survey of the sector*, Wales Centre for Public Policy.

Franklin, J., Larkham, J. and Mansoor, M. (2023) *The well-worn path: Children's services spending 2010-11 to 2021-22*. Available from: https://www.barnardos.org.uk/research/well-worn-path-childrens-services-spending-2010-11-2021-22

Goldacre, A. and Hood, R. (2022) 'Factors affecting the social gradient in children's social care', *The British Journal of Social Work*, 52(6): 3599–617. Available from: https://doi.org/10.1093/bjsw/bcab255

Gordon, D.M., Oliveros, A., Hawes, S.W., Iwamoto, D.K. and Rayford, B.S. (2012) 'Engaging fathers in child protection services: a review of factors and strategies across Ecological systems', *Children and Youth Services Review*, 34(8): 1399–417.

Green, M.J., Hindmarsh, G., Harris, F., Laurens, K.L., Tzoumakis, S., Whitten, T. et al (2021) *Child protection status and developmental outcomes in early and middle childhood: A data summary from the NSW Child Development Study*. Available from: https://eprints.qut.edu.au/209780/1/green21_DCJ_Report.pdf

Hélie, S., Trocmé, S., Collin-Vézina, D., Esposito, T., Morin, S. and Saint-Girons, M. (2022) First Nations Component of the Quebec incidence study on the situations investigated by child protective services in 2019. QIS-FN report.

Hodges, H. (2020a) *Children looked after in Wales: Factors contributing to variation in local authority rates*, Wales Centre for Public Policy.

Hodges, H. (2020b) *Children looked after in Wales: Flows into and out of care*, Wales Centre for Public Policy.

Hodges, H.R. and Scourfield, J. (2023) Why are there higher rates of children looked after in Wales?', *Journal of Children's Services*, 18(3/4): 165–79. Available from: https://doi.org/10.1108/JCS-02-2022-0007

Holmes, L., Connolly, C., Mortimer, E. and Hevesi, R. (2018) 'Residential group care as a last resort: challenging the rhetoric', *Residential Treatment For Children & Youth*, 35(3): 209–24. Available from: https://doi.org/10.1080/0886571X.2018.1455562

Hood, R. (2015) 'A socio-technical critique of tiered services: implications for interprofessional care', *Journal of Interprofessional Care*, 29(1): 8–12. Available from: https://doi.org/10.3109/13561820.2014.937482

Hood, R., Goldacre, A., Grant, R. and Jones, R. (2016) 'Exploring demand and provision in English child protection services', *The British Journal of Social Work*, 46(4): 923–41. Available from: https://doi.org/10.1093/bjsw/bcw044

Hood, R., Goldacre, A., Gorin, S., Bywaters, P. and Webb, C. (2020) *Identifying and understanding the link between system conditions and welfare inequalities in children's social care services*. Nuffield Foundation. Available from: https://eprints.kingston.ac.uk/id/eprint/45716/1/Hood-R-45716-VoR.pdf

Katz, I., Cortis, N., Shlonsky, A. and Mildon, R. (2015) *Modernising child protection in New Zealand: Learning from system reforms in other jurisdictions*. Sydney: Social Policy Research Centre.

Keddell, E. (2023) 'On decision variability in child protection: respect, interactive universalism and ethics of care', *Ethics and Social Welfare*, 17(1): 4–19. Available from: https://doi.org/10.1080/17496535.2022.2073381

Langer, C.L. and Lietz, C.A. (2015) *Applying Theory to Generalist Social Work Practice: A Case Study Approach*, Wiley.

McGhee, J., Bunting, L., McCartan, C., Elliott, M., Bywaters, P. and Featherstone, B. (2018) 'Looking after children in the UK – convergence or divergence?', *British Journal of Social Work*, 48: 1176–98.

Ministerial Advisory Group on Improving Outcomes for Children (2019) *Area for action 1: Safely reducing the numbers of children in need of care*. Welsh Government. Available from: https://gov.wales/sites/default/files/publications/2019-08/reducing-the-number-of-children-in-need-of-care.pdf

Northern Ireland Department of Health (2017) *Children's social care statistics for Northern Ireland 2011/12 to 2016/17*. Available from: https://www.health-ni.gov.uk/publications/childrens-social-care-statistics-northern-ireland-201112-201617

Northern Ireland Department of Health (2023) *Children's social care statistics for Northern Ireland 2022/2023*. Available from: https://www.health-ni.gov.uk/publications/childrens-social-care-statistics-northern-ireland-202223

Nørup, I. and Jacobsen, B. (2022) 'Not seeing the elephant in the room: how policy discourses shape frontline work with child poverty', *Social Policy & Administration*, 56(4): 580–94. Available from: https://doi.org/10.1111/spol.12784

Piel, M.H., Geiger, J.M., Julien-Chinn, F.J. and Lietz, C.A. (2017) 'An ecological systems approach to understanding social support in foster family resilience', *Child & Family Social Work*, 22: 1034–43.

Russell, L., Gajwani, R., Turner, F. and Minnis, H. (2022) 'Gender, addiction, and removal of children into care', *Front Psychiatry*, 13: 887660.

Scottish Government (2024) *Children's Social Work Statistics 2022–23 – Looked After Children*. Available from: https://www.gov.scot/publications/childrens-social-work-statistics-2022-23-looked-after-children

Scourfield, J., Wood, S. and Meindl, M. (forthcoming) 'The international evidence about family group conferences', in D. Westlake, M. Sanders and V. Hirneis (eds) *RCTs in Children's Social Care*, Edward Elgar Publishing.

Sebba, J., Berridge, D., Luke, N., Fletcher, J., Bell, K., Strand, S. et al (2015) *The educational progress of looked after children in England: Linking care and educational data*. University of Oxford Department of Education/University of Bristol.

Skivenes, M. (2011) 'Norway: Toward a child-centric perspective', in N. Gilbert, N. Parton, and M. Skivenes (eds) *Child Protection Systems: International Trends and Orientations*, Oxford University Press, pp 154–80.

Stabler, L., Evans, R., Scourfield, J., Morgan, F., Weightman, A., Willis, S. et al (2021) 'A scoping review of system-level mechanisms to prevent children being in out-of-home care', *British Journal of Social Work*, 52(5): 2515–36.

StatsWales (2024) *Children looked after at 31 March by local authority, gender and age*. Available from https://statswales.gov.wales/Catalogue/Health-and-Social-Care/Social-Services/Childrens-Services/Children-Looked-After/childrenlookedafterat31march-by-localauthority-gender-age

Strega, S., Fleet, C., Brown, L., Dominelli, L., Callahan, M. and Walmsley, C. (2008) 'Connecting father absence and mother blame in child welfare policies and practice', *Children and Youth Services Review*, 30(7): 705–16. Available from: https://doi.org/10.1016/j.childyouth.2007.11.012

Strolin-Goltzman, J. and Holbrook, H. (2023) 'The influence of decision-making ecology on placement into foster care', *Children and Youth Services Review*, 148, 106882. https://doi.org/10.1016/j.childyouth.2023.106882

Suh, E. and Holmes, L. (2022) 'A critical review of cost-effectiveness research in children's social care: what have we learnt so far?', *Social Policy & Administration*, 56(5): 742–56. Available from: https://doi.org/10.1111/spol.12795

Teater, B. (2021) 'Ecological Systems Theory', in K. Bolton, C.J. Hall and P. Lehmann, P. (eds) *Theoretical Perspectives for Direct Social Work Practice*, Springer Publishing Company. Available from: https://doi.org/10.1891/9780826165565.0003

Thomas, C. (2018) *The Care Crisis Review: Factors Contributing to National Increases in Numbers of Looked after Children and Applications for Care Orders*. Family Rights Group.

Trout, A.L., Hagaman, J., Casey, K., Reid, R. and Epstein, M.H. (2008) 'The academic status of children and youth in out-of-home care: a review of the literature', *Children and Youth Services Review*, 30(9): 979–94.

Trowler, I. (2018) *Care proceedings in England: the case for clear blue water* University of Sheffield. Available from: Sheffield_Solutions_Clear_Blue_Water_Full_Report.pdf

UK Government (2023) *Reporting year 2023: children looked after in England including adoptions*. Available from: https://explore-education-statistics.service.gov.uk/find-statistics/children-looked-after-in-england-including-adoptions

Van Holen, F., Verberckmoes, L., Trogh, L., West, D. and Vanderfaeillie, J. (2023) 'Placement breakdown in Flemish family foster care for unaccompanied refugee minors: experiences of non-kinship foster parents', *Children and Youth Services Review*, 155: 107206. Available from: https://doi.org/10.1016/j.childyouth.2023.107206

Webb, C.J.R. (2022) 'More money, more problems? Addressing the funding conditions required for rights-based child welfare services in England', *Societies*, 12(1): 9. Available from: https://doi.org/10.3390/soc12010009

Welsh Government (2023) *Children and young people lead radical reform of care services in Wales*. Available from: https://www.gov.wales/children-and-young-people-lead-radical-reform-of-care-services-in-wales

Wijedasa, D., Warner, N. and Scourfield, J. (2018) *Exploratory analyses of the rates of children looked after in English local authorities (2012–2017)*. What Works Centre for Children's Social Care.

Williams, A., Cummings, A., Forrester, D., Hodges, H., Warner, N. and Wood, S. (2022) 'Even secure children's homes won't take me. Children placed in alternative accommodation', *Residential Treatment for Children and Youth*, 39(4): 370–86.

Wood, S. and Forrester, D. (2023) 'Comparing local authority rates of children in care: a survey of the children's social care workforce in Wales', *The British Journal of Social Work*, 53(6): 3089–109.

Wood, S., Roberts, L. and Trotman, C. (2024c) *Data analysis to support multi-agency working: Data discovery*, Wales Centre of Public Policy.

Wood, S., Scourfield, J., Au, K., Evans, R., Jones-Williams, D., Lugg-Widger et al (2022a) *A UK-wide survey of family group conference provision*, Cardiff, Children's Social Care Research and Development Centre.

Wood, S., Scourfield, J., Stabler, L., Addis, S., Wilkins, D., Forrester, D. et al (2022b) 'How might changes to family income affect the likelihood of children being in out-of-home care? Evidence from a realist and qualitative rapid evidence assessment of interventions', *Children and Youth Services Review*, 143: 106685.

Wood, S., Scourfield, J., Meindl, M., Au, K., Evans, R., Jones-Willams, D. et al (2024a) 'Family group conference provision in UK local authorities and associations with children looked after rates', *The British Journal of Social Work*, 54(5), 2045–66.

Wood, S., Williams, A., Warner, N., Hodges, H., Cummings, A. and Forrester, D. (2024b) 'Outcomes for high-risk young people referred to secure children's homes for welfare reasons: a population record linkage study in England', *Journal of Children's Services*, 19(2): 105–22.

# 3

# Contemporary challenges in social work service delivery to children and families

*Liz Frost*

## Introduction

The retention and well-being rates in child and family social work in the UK have been a source of concern for several years. Between 2017 and 2023, with a noticeable additional rise immediately after COVID-19, the numbers of workers leaving the profession have been increasing year on year. While 2023–2024 seems to be the first exception to this rule, it remains to be seen whether this is a blip or a new trend emerging. The importance of this to service users, practitioners, organisations responsible for delivering services and profession as a whole has been well-documented (Collins, 2016; Lonne et al, 2020; Mc Laughlin et al, 2023). Just to reinforce this important point: service users' needs are badly met by stressed and distressed staff, their absences and turnover.

A range of English local authorities have sought help in relation to the exodus of social workers in their specific context. Between 2018 and 2022, myself and *Community Care* (usually considered in England as the social work 'trade journal' and also the provider of a variety of resources for employers and workers) were commissioned to undertake research on the retention and well-being of social workers in child and family social work departments. Throughout this time period, 11 surveys were conducted with seven different councils (three councils having repeat surveys). The geographical locations varied: we worked with two Inner London boroughs, one Outer London, three counties on the fringes of major cities and two rural boroughs. We undertook surveys and interviews within these statutory organisations through which managers sought evidence to understand the factors that support staff well-being and retention, both to improve staff support and service delivery.

The surveys were conducted from April 2018 to February 2022. Using qualitative and quantitative methods, we collected data from 1,943 respondents. Of this number, 10 per cent were team managers, 6 per cent practice supervisors, 13 per cent senior or advanced social workers and 5 per cent newly qualified social workers, while the main body, 36 per cent, were currently social workers in direct practice – not in the previous categories. Additionally, 86 per cent were female.

The research used mixed methods: a questionnaire sent to all social work staff, from which there were between 100 and 200 responses in each survey. Qualitative interviews (semi-structured) with 10–15 self-selecting interviewees for each local authority were also undertaken by phone by myself or a research assistant. These were then subject to thematic analysis. The interview questions were formulated from a broad sweep review of the literature of social work stress, burn-out, emotional distress, physical threat, organisational climate, resilience, vicarious trauma, moral injury and retention. Five categories emerged from this informal review of the literature to inform the research: the questions in the survey and interviews related to safety, support, organisations, staff development and satisfaction at work.

The methodology of the research draws on a contemporary psychosocial paradigm in which contextual/social structural and relational/affective factors are interwoven, allowing a multi-faceted approach to understanding social phenomena, including individual experience and the context, as well as the context of power relations in which the individual is located and by which they are impacted. Social work conceptually occupies a uniquely psychosocial space in which the macro issues of national politics and policy – via the expectations and principles within the frequently conflicting organisational structures of both local governments and the professional body – are embedded and embodied in the roles and multi-layered identities of an individual worker. This is a worker who is simultaneously, and often unconsciously, driven by forces from within all these dimensions as they enter into an affective, dynamic relationship with a service user (Ruch, 2007; Hingley-Jones and Ruch, 2016). The work undertaken, the problems encountered, the change possible and the satisfactions arrived at are the product of socio-political contexts, organisational arrangements (and defences) and the unconscious and conscious personhood of the face-to-face participants (Trevithick, 2011; Cooper, 2018). Each of these three aspects constructs what it is to be a social worker, and the social work 'self' realised in the act of working alongside experts by experience. We asked these social workers to tell us about their feelings and responses contextualised within their specific local authority, framed by the contemporary socio-political era.

The chapter primarily focuses on aspects of the findings of the research and, specifically, findings in relation to the survey's theme of 'safety'. It also draws on responses from the sections on 'support' and 'satisfaction at work'. The informal literature review that underpins this work discovered a broad range of psychosocial issues that can be considered important for the fundamental sense of an individual's safety. Emotional distress, discrimination, being 'blamed and shamed' and unmanageable workloads are all issues that can render workers insecure and anxious at work, and certainly unhappy.

Physical safety was also considered. However, as the chapter goes on to consider, although there is good evidence that social workers are subject to violence and threats from service users (Robson et al, 2014), this was not cited as the primary reason for struggling within the work context. Direct work with service users was more likely to be cited as one of the key satisfactions and sources of meaning in their working lives.

'Safety' in the broad sense of the term is the starting point of this chapter. It will also consider some of the organisational issues with which workers struggle. From this, it will discuss what social workers identified as important to their capacity to stay, and then draw conclusions from this as to what can support their ability to thrive and produce the best possible service for those with whom they work.

From the quantitative survey data gathered by *Community Care*, workers told us that – on average – 15 per cent experienced physical threat, verbal abuse or harassment between once a week and once a month, 22 per cent every few months, and 63 per cent less than once a year or never. In terms of emotional distress, 30 per cent experienced these at least once a fortnight, 22 per cent once a month or every few months, and only 19 per cent less than once a year. The survey question in relation to discrimination was phrased thus: 'I have never experienced discrimination during my work from my employer, managers or colleagues', to which 16 per cent disagreed, 18 per cent neither agreed nor disagreed and 65 per cent agreed. In other words, 37 per cent of workers experienced threat or abuse every year, but 63 per cent did not; 81 per cent of workers experienced emotional distress every year, but 19 per cent did not; 16 per cent of workers experienced discrimination at work, but 65 per cent did not: points that will be returned to later. It is worth noting that the categories were by no means discreet and considerable overlap was evident.

Thinking first about physical safety and verbal abuse: what observed from these statistics was reinforced in our 120 interviews? Physical safety was regularly commented on as the least of the social workers 'safety' problems. There was very little experience in relation to physical violence and few mentions of threat deemed by workers as significant. Where there were, good organisational support had usually been experienced in relation to clear-cut incidents. The workers expressed awareness but not a great deal of concern. Front line workers expressed less of a sense of safety, as one would expect. Instances of verbal abuse were generally perceived as: 'It's an inevitable part of the job.' However, there were noticeably inconsistent reports, even from the same offices, in relation to issues of physical safety. When asked specifically by the interviewer about one safety measure to protect them, 'Can you visit in pairs?', staff responses included: 'Yes', 'No', 'If you ask to' and 'It depends on your manager', the latter often being repeated in relation to a whole range of important safety issues.

Inconsistency was reported as a significant issue in relation to safety for workers. For example, and raised across several local authorities, was the worry around policies being inconsistently applied in relation to individual managers and individual staff interpreting what the policies really mean: cultures of 'usually people don't …' and safety policies available but not always used. 'You can …' but neither the organisation nor the individual worker *actually do*. There were also concerns expressed that asking for help would be interpreted as a reflection on one's ability. Also, not all social workers felt their concerns were taken seriously or valued, and this tended to be manager-specific. Again, there was inconsistency in relation to verbal abuse: not all organisations were reported as accepting that the verbal abuse of workers was threatening, and it was commented that – even in relation to racist abuse – there were not always clear policies and in some areas a sense that 'You just have to get on with it.'

The onus of responsibility for requesting policies to be actioned was commented on as prohibitive in itself: 'You have to actually ask to go out with another worker. You're not really going to ring your manager at home at 7.00 in the evening [as the policy states] to say you are back safe.'

A range of other issues connected to safety were reported as primarily an organisational matter. For example, inappropriate buildings – for example, separate from the main buildings and/or lacking alarms – were also a worry, as was the organisation itself compromising safety by failing to pass on information. One specific example given was of a man who, on being released from prison, had made threats to social workers who had not been informed of his release. Also, in relation to the responses – or lack of them – from the organisation was a slow reaction and unwillingness to change. For example, the sudden increase of knife crime in one London borough was seen to need a more rapid development of safety procedures for workers than the organisation had provided. A single but interesting comment considered whether the organisation should be proactively involved in addressing abuse from the public and other organisations. A more 'You don't get to talk about my staff like that' approach was suggested by the interviewee.

Physical safety and verbal threat, then, are certainly factors in social workers' dissatisfaction, with workers identifying that it could certainly be much improved within many social services contexts, and the responsibility for this being primarily organisational. However, issues of safety that produced far more anxiety and concern were expressed in relation to high workloads, fear of 'getting it wrong' and also of blame, while anxious, often quite destructive, states of emotional distress surfaced from the research data.

As we saw earlier, the statistics from the quantitative data collected in this research underline the regularity and ubiquity of emotional distress experienced by social workers. The qualitative interviews underlined just this situation and allowed us to understand the range and depth of feeling in relation to this.

Notably, and continuing this theme, the organisation itself was perceived as the space in which social workers' anxieties were generated, as well as identified as the context in which failures of care and support to ameliorate the stresses of the work were experienced.

The pressure faced by social workers from the political climate of austerity, necessitating local authority cuts that resulted in work overload (Grootegoed and Smith, 2018; Lavelette, 2019), or neo-liberal policy initiatives generating Ofsted inspections (Murphy, 2022) were experienced as exacerbated by the organisation's responses, or failure of responses, to these pressures. Ofsted in itself and, even more so, in the organisational changes that occur in some authorities in its aftermath, was identified as potentially hugely stressful when it lead to upheavals such as experienced key managers leaving and/or reorganisations. For example: 'I think we've been through a really rocky 18 months ... I think it's left a lot of staff absolutely traumatised ... I think turnover of staff was so fast that everybody's been left feeling insecure. And I mean, I've had 7 service managers in 15 months.'

In itself, inconsistency of managers and supervisors, including the breaks in relationships and in some cases the sheer unavailability of these potential support networks, were also generative of distress at work. Even while acknowledging that emotional distress is often unavoidable due to the impact of frequently working with traumatised children and struggling families, the key role of the supervisor is invariably underlined:

> We can't protect ourselves from emotional distress in this job because that's the nature of the work, and that's what the families are going through. It helps to talk about it.
> If we had regular time to offload all these things, because you are dealing with trauma day in day out ...

What happens in social work can generate distressing and/or vicarious responses in workers. What happens in the organisation after (and before) can contain and detoxify the anxiety generated and, in its absence, leave the worker distressed (Ruch, 2007).

Not all workers felt that they even had the space to attend regular supervision, because the pressures of work allocation – a bi-product of austerity and local authority cuts – increased the daily sense of stress and risk when there ws no time for key tasks: 'There is no time to offload the emotional fall-out from my work'.

Indeed, for some, supervision was identified as a source of stress in itself. Concern was expressed that the workers' performance might be judged if they were seen to be struggling emotionally, thereby leading to an analysis of the need for differentiating reflective supervision, which can offer some level of emotional support, from case management.

High levels of support for individuals in the face of distress, fear and anxiety, in the form of ordinary kindness, informal supervision and practical help, have been well-established as the benefits of a good social work team context (Tham, 2022). This will be discussed further shortly. What is perhaps most relevant here is the recognition from workers that the organisation can have an impact on the forming and sustaining of these supportive groupings. Conversely, where social work teams were undermined or simply lacked support from within the organisation, levels of distress experienced by workers were reported as increasing. Hot-desking, for example, was cited again and again as an example of organisational damage to teams and, during and after COVID-19, the organisation's role in proactively rebuilding teams was seen as a key element in social workers' 'recovery'.

The social workers we interviewed were asked questions about their caseloads (and their supervision) in a separate section of the questionnaire: one asking about support, rather than the 'emotional distress' aspects of feeling safe at work. However, there was a considerable overflow between these categories because the issues of feeling swamped by work, lacking support and feeling distressed tended to fuse with each other, often as an overwhelming feeling of anxiety. Also, caseload made a difference to how social workers coped with the emotional impact of the work (and vice versa).

Workloads were understood by some workers as an issue of safety: in themselves being 'unsafe' in the sense that their capacity to offer a sound and reliable service to service users might be compromised. Fear of making mistakes, blame, and then further emotional damage were highlighted. Pressures, particularly on front line workers, were expressed as both safety and 'blame' issues:

> If you're exhausted and you're working a 50-hour week, which lots are, you're not thinking straight. And that in itself is not safe. By Friday I'm just a zombie.
>
> I felt that I wasn't able to recognise some of the risks because I didn't have time to read through everything in as much detail as I would have wanted to, and things like that then cause risk.
>
> And I think that [high caseloads] are obviously damaging to your well-being because people start to feel inadequate and they feel like they are not doing their job properly.
>
> They don't hear when we say we can't do any anymore. I was given 2 weeks to do an entire assessment 'cause (a colleague) basically hadn't done it. I spent all nights, all evenings, all weekends working on it, to the point that I actually made myself unwell.

Another front line worker commented: 'If they came to you and said, "I know you are absolutely inundated; drowning in work, but just try and prioritise the important things", it would take some pressure off me because there's some constant, "You're not good enough. It's your fault it doesn't get done"'.

The lack of acknowledgement and recognition is pinpointed here as adding a level of emotional distress, suggestive of shame, self-doubt and/or moral injury (Frost, 2016; Haight et al, 2017; Frost, 2022). Work overload then (although seen by some as a current 'occupations hazard'), was also acknowledged as rendered tolerable if a level of emotional support, usually supervision, was available. Fear of being blamed and shamed was identified as part of the damage from high caseloads and not being 'able to do everything'. Workers pointed out that there were fears of 'doing it wrong' and 'of being publicly hauled over the coals'. Another commented that 'as a social worker anyway there's a tendency to blame oneself'.

Issues of discrimination and equal opportunities – also in our research question section on 'safety from' – were reported relatively infrequently. The quantitative findings produced the following stats: *Statement: I have never experienced discrimination during my work from my employer, managers or colleagues*: 16 per cent disagree; 18 per cent neither agree nor disagree; 65 per cent agree. In other words, 16 per cent of workers have experienced discrimination at work; 65 per cent have not.

Issues of gender were the most prevalent in the qualitative interviews on discrimination and equality – for example, in relation to organisational inflexibility around hours and family caring responsibilities. However, as I have argued elsewhere (Frost, 2022), the recognition and reporting of discrimination and equal opportunities issues are complex, particularly in relation to racial discrimination within what Obasi (2021) identifies as 'cultures of invisibility', in which being a worker of colour is either ignored or over-emphasised. As workers from black and minority ethnic groups commented:

> It's one of those things that's really difficult to pinpoint... a culture of bias... things are done in a very subtle way: even when this man's [colleague] instinct tells him there's racism at work, he repeats again and again, 'It's difficult to really pin it down.'
>
> In the very subtle way that it's difficult to really pinpoint discrimination directly in that sense. And so you can get used to those things and somehow get round it and move on for your own sanity.
>
> It's very subtle. You know that racism is going on ... we do have a high percentage of black and African Caribbean workers ... well, you can see who is where and how people get promoted and who gets what ... And I think it's always been that way.

So far, then, the chapter has set out key sources of pressure – the contemporary challenges that social workers are experiencing in local authority child and family work. Other issues, raised less frequently or forcefully, were connected to:

- the lack of presence/visibility of senior managers;
- the lack of inclusion in, and transparency of, organisational decision-making;
- an absence of recognition of their work (see later);
- slow or non-existent positive interventions if social workers do experience threat or public criticism; and
- an absence of opportunities for career progression.

Also, there were organisational annoyances such as parking issues and computer failings reported. There were surprisingly few comments about pay or conditions, with the exception of differential rates of pay: for example, when bonuses or retention payments applying to only some groups of staff were in place. Then it became evident that 'who gets more' was freighted with symbolic meaning and experienced as an issue of recognition or the lack of it, undervaluing and of unfairness, and productive of considerable resentment. It was also described as demotivating. Having such bonuses did convey to the workers awarded them that they were valued in the organisation. A 'motivation payment' given by one local authority to front line workers was cited as both 'useful' and 'divisive'.

Thinking now about social workers wanting to stay, rather than go: nearly a decade ago, I undertook a pilot study, with colleagues from Sweden and Italy, to look at retention and job satisfaction with front line child and family workers in our three somewhat diverse European countries. We had considered the question of 'Why do people leave …' in relation to which a huge body of retention literature already existed, and abandoned it in favour of the less addressed 'How do people remain?' in these demanding jobs (Frost et al, 2018). Somewhat to our surprise, we discovered that people stayed for reasons that were mostly not the reverse of those that people expressed when they left. For example, when workers explained what supported them in remaining in the job, the issues of meaning and values, of having good work teams and ongoing access to reflective spaces, were often the focus, not caseload size or salary levels (although this is not to suggest caseload size or remuneration are not related to how work is experienced).

Retention of workers, including the question of 'how might workers be persuaded to stay' in UK social work, has undoubtedly become a high-profile concern over the past years, with the numbers of workers leaving seeming to suggest that the working life of a child and family social worker may have become more difficult to sustain. The year 2023–2024 has been the first since 2017 that the rate of social workers in child and family work leaving the profession has slowed after several extremely worrying years (GOV.UK Children's Social Work Workforce, 2025). The post-COVID-19 increase was particularly notable, and high year-on-year rates of workers leaving between 2020 and 2022 were particularly concerning with, for example, a 21 per cent rise in vacancies, a 13 per cent rise in agency workers and, even more troubling, 31 per cent of workers leaving after only two years and 77 per cent of those who left not returning to children's services in that time period (Kulakiewicz et al, 2022).

This chapter now turns to offering an analysis of what makes staying in social work possible, or more likely, for social workers now. In other words, from the nearly 2,000 voices represented in our research data, what did social workers themselves identify as being able to improve current working conditions and increase their overall satisfaction with the work? Three important areas were identified as the key: the space and time for reflective thinking; the level of emotional support; and the context of a supportive, reliable and friendly work team. Issues of meaning and values also pay a significant part, as this chapter will consider briefly. Securing space and time, guaranteeing regular, consistent, reflective support, and strengthening teams, as strategies for improving the working life of social workers, seem profitable areas for the improvement of social workers' professional lives, and it is to these areas that this chapter now turns.

Thinking first about the issue of 'time'; where and by whom is this to be addressed, and in what ways? As discussed earlier, contemporary social workers feel under enormous pressure in their working existence: the product of increasingly unviable caseloads, exacerbated by an identified (or inconsistently offered) lack of support and recognition in relation to stresses, generated from this. That the political context of now long-term austerity has savaged local authority spending power is well-understood by practising social workers. Local authorities are not in a position to escape the regular rounds of 'cuts' and some fall out from this will invariably have an impact on their work. For the most part, social workers understand this while struggling with ever-increasing caseloads and the levels of anxiety these generate, so high as to be considered (see earlier) a safety issue.

It is easy to assume that there is little that can be done about case overload, but the responses of social workers in different local authorities registered some very different practices in relation to the management of the issue. As well as the matter of emotional support for the stress and distress this generates (see later), how it is handled within the council, the department and individual social work teams is by no means standard, and examples of differently valued organisational responses that could help or make matters worse were discussed in the interviews undertaken.

Drawing on social workers' traditional investment in cooperation and teamwork, two different authorities were piloting differential forms of case-holding as a way of sharing and de-stressing workloads. Joint case holding and, in a different authority, team case-holding were cited by workers as overwhelmingly beneficial in situations where workload had been oppressive.

Thinking about time per se could also produce innovations appreciated by most workers. An approach that seemed to be helpful was in relation to emphasising time away from work: for example, the concept of a nine-day working fortnight with a guaranteed day off per two weeks, as implemented in a West Country authority to cope with the stresses of the incursions of work into home and private life.

Less money going on locum positions and more on permanent staff was another area of change that workers felt strongly would improve the working situation in many teams for reasons of overload and team stability. Attempts at this re-balance seemed to be under way in some of the local authorities we worked with.

A range of smaller but significant improvements that could loosely be described as 'sensitivity' and/or 'attitude' were identified. Workers raised recognition issues and the need for a more validating attitude. They outlined how much better one could feel about one's work if it seemed to be of significance – to matter to the management – and that going the extra mile was somehow less onerous if it were genuinely and personally recognised within 'a community of value' to use Axel's Honneth's phrase from his 1995 work on recognition theory. In other words, recognition from those who know and understand what is involved in your work and whose opinion is relevant (Honneth, 1995; Houston, 2016):

> There is quite a lot of kind of, 'Well done,' kind of thing going around. But there's also quite a lot of, 'Why haven't you done this? Why haven't you done that?'
>
> And sometimes for me, that recognition, that thanks, can mean a lot. Especially when you've worked really hard with a very challenging family on a very challenging case and you know that you've done a good job. It would be nice to get that. But what we get instead is, 'You sent this email to the wrong inbox and it needs to go to this inbox.'

One of the strongest messages from social workers was 'don't add to our overload unnecessarily'. Workers across all local authorities were clear that working with service users was the foundation and key to why they entered and stay in the profession, and they expressed frustration at the organisations' seeming lack in supporting this. For example, one Home Counties' authority was seen as making this unnecessarily harder by its internal policies. A front line worker reported that: 'We have to see children in need every 10 working days, which is not statutory guidance but it's what XXX want as a policy. But then they haven't re-looked at the caseloads again with that.'

Several organisations were seen as generating other time-consuming activities that only exacerbated the sense of overload. Extraneous paperwork, inappropriate tasks and frequent changes in management and management systems were offered as examples. As similar research has also noted, there was a strong sense that there has been a move towards a 'stat-led', 'tick-box' culture, 'where all that matters are following processes and hitting performance markers'. For the workers, this underlines their concern that it increases workload without benefiting children. Even supervision, which is usually assumed to reduce levels of stress, can, if tied into excessive bureaucracy, exacerbate it: 'And there are times which … it does feel pretty unmanageable because again, the supervision forms take hours to fill out.'

In relation to work overload, then, in the research undertaken, we were aware that, even if workloads were increasing, there were still ways an organisation could think creatively and find ways of ameliorating the problem. Workers were clear that their capacity to undertake what they saw as the point of their job – the direct work with service users in the bigger context of supporting families and protecting children – could, and was in some places, be assisted by organisational approaches.

'Reflective spaces' was the second key issue advocated by the social workers we interviewed. The literature on the need and value of such spaces, for groups and for supervision, is steadily accruing in UK social work writing (Cooper, 2018; Ferguson, 2018), and local authorities in some areas are incorporating such a perspective into their organisational practices.

As the late Andrew Cooper (2018, p 26) reinforced:

> Relationship-based practice is not something you can practise in isolation. The power of case dynamics requires organisational attention, in particular the provision of reflective supervision as a standard part of agency life.

It was clear from the majority of workers from whom we collected data that an absence of reflexive spaces – reflective groups, peer groups/supervision groups; some elements of training, informal reflective conversations with colleagues and reflective supervision rather than simply supervision (which could be task-centred or, as mentioned earlier, seen as a site of more stress) – had an impact on their levels of emotional stress.

This was summarised thoughtfully by a worker in an Outer London area:

> [XXX Borough] is good about accepting people need to take sick leave, compassionate leave, that if they become stressed and they need to take time off it's [ok], but shutting the door after the horse

has bolted: the damage is done: reflective supervision predicts who is becoming overloaded – and that's mostly thin on the ground.

And a team leader/supervisor in the same area also connects up reflective supervision with emotional distress and what people worry about. Her section of the service has monthly reflective supervision to look at worrying cases, and then she offers one-to- one supervision. When anything is particularly emotional or aggressive, 'they come back and talk those sort of things through... they use each other and me quite a lot'. This also serves to underline how, even within the same organisation, there can be considerable variation in practice and, as many responses to many questions in our survey and interviews underlined: 'It depends on your supervisor'. Even the issue of whether supervision contains elements of the reflective or not, or is even reliable and empathetic, is regularly identified as personality- (of the supervisor) driven, not a dependable tool for emotional support and reflection. Contrasting comments from interviewees are indicative of this kind of inconsistency:

> I would say that has been really well responded to by my line manager ... I know my manager would have found time for me, even if she was up to her eyes in anything else.
> It's too dependent on the individual manager and on the individual being able to articulate that [reflective support].
> I've also had the experience of basically being told, 'I'm too busy. I'll kind of come back to you later.' ... there are a lot of times when you can feel quite emotionally isolated.'
> Perhaps some managers forget what it's like to be new and less experienced?

Flipping this from 'what's wrong' to how the situation could be improved, the mandatory training of supervisors in reflective supervision, and the organisational guarantee of protecting space in which this could be delivered, would seem to offer a good way forward. As the workers themselves identify, stable, consistent, reflective and well-trained supervisors are a fundamental tool for identifying, alleviating and – most importantly – preventing the emotional distress of social workers.

Reflective group supervision, differently named in different contexts (for example, as 'peer group supervision' or 'case presentation groups'), was also for the most part valued by the workers from whom we collected views, although notably 'I don't have time to go' was a not infrequent response.

The context of the group in itself may be part of what the workers value in these collective reflective sessions. The third issue raised in the research was that the source of emotional support most highly valued (for work 'atmosphere', informal advice and even recognition) was the social work team.

The team context of social work has often been prized highly above any other single factor in social workers' responses to questions around well-being and retention (Frost, 2025). Overall, in the surveys from 2018–22, 89 per cent of workers praised their friendly and helpful colleagues. When asked 'What could managers do to improve and promote the friendliness of my workplace?', 39 per cent suggested ways in which the teams could be supported. As well as registering that hot-desking and case overload (allowing no time for group engagement) were detrimental to team well-being, a range of positive changes that the organisation could effect were mooted, including the fundamental principle that teams should be kept together. Actions advocated included making time for peer supervision and actively team-building through the instigation and delivery of regular team days, team workshops and team socials. It is worth noting that there were 315 comments in the surveys on building the team: clearly an issue that was on the minds of these respondents.

The qualitative interviews similarly demonstrated the high value placed on work teams and groups, and the peer support that in many situations was where workers turned for a whole range of beneficial interactions within symbiotic work relationships. These groupings in the workplace were identified by workers as 'safe spaces', physical and psychological spaces of trust:

> Yeah, absolutely. You know when to not have conversations if there are people around if you don't know who they are. There are shared spaces, we've got pods that we can go into, little offices that we can go into if you need to have a bit of a debrief on something.
> That is very definitely our safe spaces. We trust all the individuals in there, we disclose very personal details, talk about feelings, how a situation made us felt, what we learnt from it. It's a really, really supportive team.

Teams were for informal supervision, reflective dialogue, shoulders to cry on, practical help and sharing work, advice and simply listening, and generally of great value: 'I think the biggest tool for a social worker is the people around them and having that camaraderie.'

It was evident in the later data collection in the survey, both during and after the pandemic, that the loss of the physical presence of the team was highly significant and highly challenging. Policies could lead to workers feeling isolated and disconnected from their team:

> I still feel quite isolated, even now. So I can go into the office now if I want to, but I predominantly work from home. And people are in and out but you often don't see many other people around.

You know, none of us were used to working at home. It was very isolating and horrible.

From the research, then — and agreeing as it does with other contemporary findings in relation to this (Tham, 2022) — getting workers back into the office, re-establishing teams and supporting teams in the various ways they identify are important aspects for increasing the satisfaction of workers and their capacity to remain responsive and supportive in order to increase the satisfaction of service users.

Overall then, time and space, reflexivity and team membership, as outlined earlier, are seen by workers to deeply affect their capacity to offer an optimum service, and their consciousness of how organisationally the situation could be improved is evident. As they reminded us again and again, having the time and resources to put into their work with service users was not just social workers' primary aim but also their source of meaning underpinning their commitment and professional identities. In the survey and the qualitative data collected, the level of passion for ethical, inclusive practice with experienced experts was underscored. For too significant a number, the organisations in which they practised were perceived as failing to support this.

The question of values, and whether local authorities shared them with workers, produced some thoughtful responses with quite profound implications as to what might be addressed at a fundamental level in order for social workers to thrive, and this resonant view from a front line worker seems worth quoting in full:

Interviewer: Do you think the organisation shares your values?

Respondent: No. No, I think the traditional social work values have got lost in local authorities. I don't know other local authorities, but in terms of things like advocacy for clients and making sure they know their rights for financial support and things that they are entitled to, you are made to feel as a social worker that you'd be wrong in sharing that information, and you'll get asked, 'Why did you tell that client those things that they were entitled to?' And I will say, 'But that is social work. That is what I trained in.' And if you go back to what they would say, these are the things that we're working towards, you know, our registration ... You're having to point out, 'No, this is what social work is about. This is social work.'

You know, about equality and making sure people are given all their information, and it's not for me to decide then what happens with that in a way. But making

> sure people, clients, are given equal opportunity with information and entitlements, it's very, I would say, resource-driven. It takes priority in terms of the saving ... finding ways to save money might impact on actually clients' rights, and I don't think... it doesn't feel like it did when I qualified in terms of the values that you brought to the job.

Organisation-wide discussions about values and meanings, about what local authorities' children and family departments are really invested in, and how the professional ethics and personal commitment of social workers align with these, could make a valuable starting place for a positive shift in workers' and organisations' trust, mutual recognition and commitment.

## Conclusion

This chapter set out to consider the voices of social workers in English child and family work over the period 2018–22 in relation to how they experience their current working lives. Local authorities' child and family departments commissioned Community Care and I to look in detail at these workers in the context of pressing concerns around retention. The surveys and interviews only focused on workers who were managing to stay (not those who had left), and what their struggles and satisfactions were in their roles. Led by their primary concerns across the findings, we have foregrounded issues of safety and support, caseloads and recognition, time, reflection and the team context. Their suggested ways in which a local authority could improve support in these areas, facilitating their primary focus – direct work with families and children – offer some positive ideas to inform considerations of not just retention but also the well-being, resilience and job satisfaction of the contemporary workforce.

## References

Collins, S. (2016) 'The commitment of social workers in the UK. Committed to the profession, the organisation and to service users?', *Journal of Social Work Practice*, 28(3): 159–79.

Cooper, A. (2018) *Conjunctions: Social Work Psychanalysis and Culture*, Karnac.

Ferguson, H. (2018) 'How social workers reflect in action and when and why they don't: the possibilities and limits to reflective practice in social work', *Social Work Education*, 3(4): 415–27.

Frost, L. (2016) 'Exploring the concepts of recognition and shame for social work', *Journal of Social Work Practice*, 30(4): 431–46.

Frost L. (2022) 'Psychosocial thinking for social work: the example of shame', in S. Frosh, M. Vyrgioti and Walsh, J. (eds) *The Palgrave Handbook of Psychosocial Studies*, Palgrave, pp 775–94.

Frost, L. (2025) 'The social work team post-COVID: why workers are still in recovery', *Journal of Social Work Practice*, 39(1): 101–3.

Frost, L., Hojer, S., Campanini, A., Sicora, A. and Kullburg, K. (2018) 'Why do they stay? A study of resilient child protection workers in three European countries', *European Journal of Social Work*, 21(4): 485–97.

GOV.UK (2025) *Children's Social Work Workforce*. Available from: https://explore-education-statistics.service.gov.uk/find-statistics/children-s-social-work-workforce/2024

Grootegoed, E. and Smith, M. (2018) 'The emotional labour of austerity: how social workers reflect and work on their feelings towards reducing support to needy children and families', *The British Journal of Social Work*, 48(7): 1929–47.

Haight, W., Sugrue, E. and Calhoun, M. (2017) 'Moral injury among child protection professionals: implications for the ethical treatment and retention of workers', *Child and Youth Services Review*, 82: 27–41.

Hingley-Jones, H. and Ruch, G. (2016) 'Stumbling through? Relationship-based practice in austere times', *Journal of Social Work Practice*, 30(3): 235–48.

Honneth, A. (1995) *The Struggle for Recognition* (trans. J. Anderson), Polity.

Houston, S. (2016) 'Empowering the "shamed" self: recognition and critical social work', *Journal of Social Work*, 16(1): 1–19.

Kulakiewicz, A., Foster, D., Danechi, S. and Clark, H. (2022) 'Children's social care workforce', House of Commons Library. Available from: https://commonslibrary.parliament.uk/research-briefings/cdp-2022-0142/

Lonne, B., Higgins, D., Herrenkohl, T. and Scott, D. (2020) 'Reconstructing the workforce within public health protective systems: improving resilience, retention, service responsiveness and outcomes', *Child Abuse & Neglect*, 110(3): 104.

McLaughlin, H., Scholar, H., McCaughan, S. and Pollock, S. (2023) 'Should I stay or should I go? The experience of forty social workers in England who had previously indicated they would stay in or leave children and families social work', *The British Journal of Social Work*, 53(4): 1963–83.

Murphy, C. (2022) 'If it's not on the system then it hasn't been done. "Ofsted anxiety disorder" as a barrier to social work discretion', *Child Abuse Review*, 31(1): 78–90.

Obasi, C. (2021) 'Black social workers: identity, racism, invisibility/hypervisibility at work', *Journal of Social Work*, 22(2): 1–19.

Robson, A., Cossar, J. and Quayle, E. (2014) 'Critical commentary. The impact of work-related violence towards social workers in children and family services', *The British Journal of Social Work*, 44(4): 924–36.

Ruch, G. (2007) 'Reflective practice in contemporary child-care social work: the role of containment', *The British Journal of Social Work*, 37(4): 659–80.

Tham, P. (2022) 'Not rocket science: implementing efforts to improve working conditions of social workers', *The British Journal of Social Work*, 52(4): 1896–1915.

Trevithick, P. (2011) 'Understanding defences and defensiveness in social work', *Journal of Social Work Practice*, 25(4): 389–412.

# 4

# Participation and decision-making

*Hayley Pert*

## Introduction

It has been well-documented that the numbers of children in receipt of social care services (as children in need, in need of protection or children in care), have risen over the past decade (Rogowski, 2024). This increase has coincided with international calls made in research to restructure these systems and services (MacAlister, 2022; Saar-Heiman and Gupta, 2024). Critiques of current social care systems generally centre around two key issues: inequity of experience by those who use services or, more broadly, ineffective or inefficient systems and processes. These critiques have focused attention on the experiences of those in receipt of those services and the level to which they are able to meaningfully engage in decision-making processes to which they are part. This is especially pertinent to social work as a profession given the core value base that focuses on empowerment, commitment to self-determination and the eradication of oppression. Social work is inherently concerned with power – its own and that of those it strives to work for. As the previous chapter outlines, the tension for workers, then, is to practise in a relational manner while operating within systems that are adversarial, complex and professionally conceptualised.

Theoretical ideologies that inform the discussion around 'participation' in social work have been outlined in Chapter 1. Typically, participation is, in social work, focused on the involvement of service users in their care. A more radical stance is offered by some and is led by a desire for participation in child welfare services to incorporate influence in policy and leadership, as well as service delivery, both for children (Walker, 2011) and parents (Saar-Heiman and Gupta, 2024). This chapter provides an outline of current challenges and barriers for participation in terms of involvement in services. Later chapters within this book offer opportunities and remedies to this approach, offering innovations that seek to transform the way in which participation is viewed and the inherent inequalities within the child welfare system.

In the context of child welfare services, there is not only a moral imperative to involve children and their parents in decisions about their lives, but a protective one. Without child and parent voices, social workers lose an important qualifier of progress and risk reduction – how their care and lives have improved, or not (Falch-Eriksen, 2021). Who better to provide an accurate measure of success than those who are living the reality of the plan and the interventions delivered within it. More importantly, there is recognition that the very groups served by statutory social workers experience need and therefore, most pressingly, require efficient, equitable and efficacious services (Toros, 2020). Importantly here, need does not, and should not, equate to powerlessness. Family-driven services shift positioning children, or indeed parents or carers, from being objects of concern to being experts, both in their own lives and in their experiences of professional intervention (LaBrenz and Fong, 2016; Brady et al, 2024, Petersen et al, 2025). Research has shown that, when families are viewed as such and not denied opportunities to effectively participate in decisions that affect them, there are tangible additional benefits for service delivery (Berrick et al, 2015; Van Bijleveld et al, 2019) for parents (Saar-Heiman and Gupta, 2024), for children and young people (in terms of self-esteem and confidence) (Diaz, 2020) and for trust in adults and processes (Bouma et al, 2018).

This chapter will consider these themes and issues in more depth within the context of UK legislation, policy and social work practice. What follows is a discussion of the current innovations in participatory social work practice set alongside examples from practice and research to illustrate the practicalities and challenges of person-led approaches.

## Legal frameworks supporting participation
### International frameworks

The participation of children in decisions about their lives is not a new concept in terms of contemporary social work practice. It is outlined in legislation and practice guidance as a requirement. The United Nations Committee on the Rights of the Child (UNCRC, 1989) provides a foundation for understanding the importance of the participation of children and young people. Although the term 'participation' is not referred to directly, under the UNCRC, children's rights include being heard and having their views considered in all decisions about them and their lives (UNCRC, 1989). Indeed, in its General comment no. 12 (2009), the UNCRC (2009, p 5) specifically defines participation as: 'ongoing processes, which include information-sharing and dialogue between children and adults based on mutual respect, and in which children can learn how their views and those of adults are taken in to account and shape the outcome of such processes'.

Importantly, this does not mean that these views or wishes must be acted on or that they determine outcomes, rather that young people should understand *how* they can contribute to decisions (Schofield and Thoburn,

1996). The emphasis shifts towards relationships and mutual respect with presumption placed upon children and young people being heard and shaping how services are delivered. The UNCRC is accepted as a baseline standard for participation reflected in national laws internationally, including the UK, although, as this chapter discusses, the fidelity to the originally proposed baseline standard in practice is questionable and inconsistent.

While the UNCRC 1989 remains the most influential global framework for children's participation, other international instruments exercise influence on the global understanding of participation. For example, Article 7 of the Convention on the Rights of Persons with Disabilities (United Nations, 2006) addresses the rights of children with disabilities. Echoing the sentiment of the UNCRC, the rights of disabled children to express their views on matters that affect them are reinforced. In practice, this, alongside disability activism, encourages nations to creatively develop systems that ensure that the voices of children with disabilities are heard in decision-making processes, regardless of ability.

## *Legislation in England and Wales*

In England and Wales, Section 1 of the Children Act (1989) places duties on agencies working with children to hear the 'wishes and feelings' of children and to take them into account. Specific provision is also made for the inclusion of Children in Care's views in decision-making and the review of care plans (Section 22, the Children Act, 1989). Given the context in which Children in Care are situated (subject to numerous decisions and decision-making forums beyond those of their peers), additional legislation and guidance are offered to support practice. Under the Adoption and Children Act, 2002, local authorities are required to ensure that every child in care has an Independent Reviewing Officer (IRO) tasked with, among other responsibilities, ensuring that the child is able to play a meaningful part in their care plan review process. This is the forum by which changes to their care plan, and so decisions about their care, can be formally enacted. However, this mechanism has been criticised. In *R v Rochdale Metropolitan Borough Council [2008] EWHC 3282 Fam*, ineffective IRO practice was found to have breached the human rights of a child in care. The judgement pointed to inadequacies within the review process including failures to ascertain, understand and consider the child's views. Despite this, the IRO role remains entirely unchanged. It is notable that it has always been temporary, initially planned for review itself in 2015 and known at the time as the 'sunset clause'. This came and went and the role stayed in place, unchanged. In the independent review of childrens social care, its author, Josh MacAlister, called for the abolition of the role. For now, the government has not adopted this and has instead opted to review the role with the objective of potentially strengthening it.

## Practice implications

These legislative provisions reflect a shift in how children are viewed: from 'objects of concern' to citizens, with rights (Pert et al, 2017). There has been focus within childcare social work practice upon listening to the voice of the child (Le borgne and Tisdall, 2017). In part, this has also been driven by tragedy and serious case reviews investigating child deaths have time and time again raised that children were not seen, not heard or not consulted. This phenomenon, often referred to as 'the invisible child' highlights the tension in practice of amplifying the voices of children, not merely seeing or consulting with them (Ferguson, 2017). In her review of the child protection system following the death of Peter Connelly, Eileen Munro (2011) highlighted the challenges that arise when amplifying the voice of the child. This has been captured in studies since, in which social workers' skills in including children in decision-making (Pert et al, 2017), time to build relationships (Caldwell et al, 2019) and staff turnover (Kennan et al, 2018; Diaz et al, 2020) all have an impact on how able children are able to exert their expertise, or how far they are impeded in doing so. There are additional challenges in doing so for children with special educational needs and disabilities (SEND) and studies have repeatedly highlighted the additional harm that this group can come to in light of this (Jones et al, 2012).

These structural challenges have resulted in a stagnation of development of practices to enable the participation of children in the child welfare context that has contributed to tokenism and a limited impact on decision-making remaining the status quo (Tisdall, 2015). By definition, a 'meeting' is an adult concept. Arguably, because the systems that govern (and regulate) social work practice have not changed, neither have the mechanisms that support it. While there is evidence that social workers may strive to adhere to the fundamental principles of the Children Act 1989, practical realities – such as excessive caseloads and administrative demands – limit the ability to engage children in meaningful dialogue (Diaz et al, 2019). The result for those children is all too often a superficial or tokenistic form of participation whereby children are consulted but not empowered to influence decisions in any significant way.

Aside from legal instruments to support children's participation, recent statutory guidance (Department for Education, 2023a) and the independent review of children's services (MacAlister, 2022) have interrogated the issue of how children are heard. Working Together statutory guidance (Department for Education, 2023a, p 3) specifically recommends 'empowering parents and carers to participate in decision-making by equipping them with information, keeping them updated and directing them to further resources'.

In the Independent Review of children's services, a manifesto pledge from the then sitting Tory government, its author Josh MacAlister (2022) makes specific mention of the need for independent advocacy for children, especially those who are care experienced, to be an opt-in, rather than an opt-out service. The need for advocacy and more consistent access to information and advice for children, young people and their families when encountering children's services has also been highlighted by the Children's Commissioner whose recent report on the state of advocacy services for children and young people in England (2023) highlighted significant and alarming gaps in provision with, on average, only 5 per cent of children entitled to an advocate referred to one. There are obvious complications in taking a statistic such as this on face value.

However, it is reasonable to assert that advocacy could play a crucial role in enabling children to engage meaningfully in decisions about their care. Its limited availability means that most children are left without this essential support and it is representative of a culture or attitude in which a child is not considered an equal voice in discussions about their care or how services could and should be delivered. This is reflected in wider research in which children in care face considerable barriers in complaining about the service they receive (Diaz et al, 2020), with one notable barrier being the denial of advocacy to which they are entitled.

The government's new vision to transform children's social care, 'Stable Homes Built on Love' (DfEb, 2023) sets out proposed reforms emphasising the need to upskill the child protection workforce including encouraging 'adults who work in children's social care to make sure they listen more to children' (DfEc, 2023).

These recent reports, published in quick succession, mark a recognition that returning to the fundamentals of the value base of the profession, of sharing power and positioning families as valuable alongside the skills necessary to support better partnership working, is necessary. However, without financial investment to make the systemic changes necessary to enact these recommendations – across all areas of social work practice and education – real reform remains aspirational.

## Children and young people

Much attention has been paid to amplifying the voices of children and families in statutory social work, both in research (Ferguson, 2017; Caldwell et al, 2019; Van Bijleveld et al, 2019; Richardson Foster et al, 2021; Cuevas-Parra and Tisdall, 2022) and in policy and statutory guidance (DfEa, 2023). However, despite efforts to strengthen practice, findings from research over the past decade consistently point towards a system in which children and young people, and their families, have not benefited from these efforts (Le Borgne and Tisdall 2017; Toros, 2020). Children often remain unable to participate in decision-making processes with their voices either being undervalued or ignored (Toros, 2020). The current picture is one in which professionals make decisions, determine risks and, importantly, also determine what information is shared with children, when and how (Kennan et al, 2018). The implications of this are wide-ranging. When children and young people are involved in decisions about their lives, this has the potential to improve the decisions themselves and their outcome. But what holds social workers back from enabling – indeed, promoting this? It is a question I asked myself as a newly qualified front line social worker some years ago. I found myself satisfying 'the system': inputting data into the IT system to show that I was meeting 'timescales'. There was no real interrogation of my practice – who I was with children and families. My employer wanted visits/meetings and so on done: doing these well was never a consideration. Whether I enabled children to engage in decisions did not feel like a priority at all.

In her paper in which children were interviewed about their experiences of decision-making over 20 years ago, Eileen Munro (2001) defined this kind of practice as 'practitioner gate keeping'. Children defined their experiences of decision-making forums as being 'talked about' rather than 'talked to'. This dynamic, although not universal, has proven difficult to shift. Research shows that social care systems remain adult-centric with children feeling invisible, 'just another person in the room' (Diaz et al, 2018), facing barriers complaining about poor service (Diaz et al, 2020) or feeling unheard and ignored (Falch-Eriken et al, 2018).

When considering the specific groups of children who will receive a service from social workers, the picture remains stagnant. Studies centring around participation within child protection conferences suggest that inclusion of children's voices is showing signs of improvement, although not all children are able to participate in conferences and their experiences vary (Richardson-Foster et al, 2021). What this also does not account for is how far or whether children are involved in re-designing these meetings to better suit their needs. Similarly, children's participation in the family court decisions remains limited. Research with young people has shown that they feel excluded and poorly informed during proceedings (Roe, 2021).

This is exacerbated by complexities of the wider system that can be confusing and alienating. Several studies have found that children subject to care proceedings want greater direct involvement in the process (Cashmore et al, 2023). This has prompted pilot projects in the North of England, such as the Young Peoples Participation Project, which aims to enhance young people's involvement in proceedings. The results are not yet published.

However, it is indicative of an understanding of the need by funders, local authorities and the courts, to explore more inclusive and child-led practices. The concept of 'child-friendly justice' has gained traction in recent years with the judiciary in England and Wales being pressed to reform, given that so many within it have called for change (Stalford and Hollingsworth, 2020). Judges are being encouraged to write more child-friendly judgements, particularly within private law proceedings and some directly to children, so that the focus becomes the child's experience and not the adults' needs.

Looked-after children, by virtue of being cared for by the state, are subject to a greater number of decision-making forums than their peers. One such forum is a Looked-after child review in which changes to the child's care plan should and can be made. A core function of this meeting is to hear the views of the child (Department for Children, Schools and Families (DCSF, now DfE) 2010), thereby making it an ideal opportunity for meaningful participation. However, research over many years in this field highlights that children and young people often do not feel that they participate meaningfully in their reviews (Pert et al, 2017; Diaz et al, 2018; Thomas, 2002).

There are significant structural challenges in balancing meaningful participation with the state's responsibility to protect children. The child welfare system typically intervenes in moments of crisis for a family or child, when the welfare of the child is at risk and the dominant discourse then defines them as 'vulnerable' (Le Borgne and Tisdall, 2017). Taken alongside a lurch towards risk adverse practice (Munro, 2018), this position can be stubbornly resistant to proposed changes to practice, particularly in terms of promoting participatory practices. How children are conceptualised within children's services strongly influences how involved they are (or feel they are), in decision-making forums. This tends to fall into two categories: either children are viewed as vulnerable, passive objects of concern or as active participants with views and expertise in identifying their own concerns and solutions (Le Borgne and Tisdall, 2017).

The desire to protect children from 'difficult' conversations often leads professionals to decide what information they should know, when they should know it and how much they are allowed to contribute to decisions about their care. For social workers being part of decisions that affect the lives of children (and their families) is complex. These decisions are augmented by uncertainty. This is compounded by external factors such as agency pressures, staffing and a rise in referrals to children's social care following a lull pre-pandemic (Department for Education and Skills, 2023c) This squeezes services, stretches staff capacity and affects morale. While this context is important to consider in terms of finding solutions, it does not – and should not – detract from the experiences of those children who may have opportunities to participate denied by such practices.

Challenges for childcare practitioners are also personal. While it is recognised that including children in decisions is to be preferred, there is no specific guidance available for practitioners on *how* to do this. A theoretical understanding of – and even commitment to – child participation and application of this in practice are not the same (Kennan et al, 2018). In a study by Diaz and colleagues (2018), social workers and IROs expressed a lack of training and understanding of what meaningful participation looked like. Definitions of 'participation' often differ between individuals. The IRO handbook (DCSF, 2010), a core guidance document for those supporting children in care, encourages participation of children in their meetings, but offers little practical guidance as to how this should be achieved. In their study, Polkki et al (2012) found that, while children expressed a desire to be part of decision-making forums, they did not always want to attend meetings – an understandable position given that a 'meeting' is an entirely adult concept. Less explored is how to reframe or redesign decision-making forums to be less adult-centric. Choice in how to participate, in what manner and when is known to be an essential component of meaningful participation (Pert et al, 2017). Non-engagement is also a valid choice but one that should not be confused with a lack of opportunity to participate.

In social work, child participation not only means the opportunity to express wishes and feelings but also to have them heard, and the weight by which this is considered can fall to individual practitioners (Van Bijleveld, 2019). The confines of practitioner skill, confidence and the emotional toll of the work will have a disproportionate impact on children's experiences of participation, resulting in inequitable services for said children. For children with Special Educational Needs and Disabilities (SEND), practitioners' skill and views of ability become key enablers or barriers for participation (Olli et al, 2012). The SEND code of practice (DfE and DoH, 2015) explicitly requires those working with disabled children to involve them in decisions. However, research shows that children with SEND are often the least listened to within education, health and social care settings (Kennedy, 2015). This could be due to a range of factors, not least that, for some disabled children, their preferred or primary method of communication may not be speech. The fact that this is a barrier at all highlighs the urgent need for individual practitioners and their leaders to transform their approaches to inclusion within services.

The voices of disabled children are also more absent than those of their peers in research. Studies that consider interventions necessary to support disabled children in school and within social care are most often drawn from the views of adults around them (Annan et al, 2013). The views of these children are alarmingly absent. Given that children with SEND and their families interact with a wide range of services simultaneously, the need for less adversarial, more inclusive services is critical. This issue has been highlighted in the recent SEND review (DfE and DoHaSC, 2022), which ambitiously aims to deliver change for children and families and to improve parental confidence in statutory services.

## Parent and professional partnerships

Parents have often reported child welfare systems to be adversarial, confusing and disempowering (Bekaert et al, 2021). This complex interaction between parents and social workers, tasked with protecting or offering services to children in need or in care, is often characterised as one riven with adversary (Lalayants and Merkel-Holguin, 2024). Parents often perceive child and family social workers as being critical of them and can find child protection conferences – in particular – to be disempowering and oppressive (Corby et al, 1996; Gibson, 2015; Muench et al, 2016; Diaz, 2020). In a similar vein, child protection support has specifically been singled out as widening the power differential between parents and the professionals within the system, alienating parents who feel blamed and shamed by a system and profession that should do the very opposite (Dumbrill, 2006). It goes without saying that meaningful and sustained change in this circumstance would be difficult to achieve.

Despite services, and legislation, supporting the notion of partnership working, for many parents involvement with children's social care is neither voluntary nor welcome (Lalayants and Merkel-Holguin, 2024). Contextually, this is important. Social workers must navigate complex systems, processes, key performance indicators and regulatory expectations that can, but shouldn't, compromise building relationships with families (Harris, 2012). It is safe to say that child protection and welfare services are guided by professionally driven and fueled procedures, expectations and language. This results in some parents feeling 'engulfed by a confusing, complicated system that they know can regulate their life' (Lalayants and Merkel-Holguin, 2024, p 3). The enormity of this requires social work, as a profession, to seriously consider its focus and impact on parents.

This procedural focus has a profound and negative impact on professional practice. As highlighted in Munro's Review of Child Protection in England (2011), the emphasis on proceduralism over relationship-building creates a growing tension within the system, which can lead to compassion fatigue, whereby practitioners exhibit 'very little recognition or awareness of the stresses experienced by families as a result' (Devine and Parker, 2015, p 2). Instead of fostering partnerships, developing individual and collective agency of parents and, in doing so, challenging the oppression that these processes can perpetuate the system, often places parents in an adversarial position – reinforcing, rather than reducing, the power imbalance between families and professionals.

I was struck recently in a teaching session in which scenarios were put to social work students. In one (a real-life example), a man called his social worker to say that he could not make it to the child protection case conference that week because his own father had just received a cancer diagnosis that he was distressed about. Asked what their responses would be, almost all those in the room felt the meeting *had* to go ahead regardless. Rationales for this included timescales, deadlines and a lack of social worker power to make the decision to postpone alone. These responses highlight the procedural pressures that can overshadow the purpose of such meetings. The aim of a child protection case conference (or any meeting children's services would convene) is to identify and reduce risk, meet need and review it. Without the family present, the question I ask myself is 'How can this really be achieved?'. Logically and morally, it would be better to postpone in order to involve the family at a better time when they were more emotionally able to engage. The barriers to doing this would, as the students themselves identified, be procedural and professional: availability of social workers and other professionals at short notice, the meeting being 'out of timescale', even availability of rooms would come before promoting the engagement of the parents. Described as 'muscular authoritarianism', Featherstone et al (2014) criticise this approach, which, they argue, prioritises directing parents, rather than capturing their thoughts, feelings and expertise in order to offer the best-needed and wanted support available.

Parents' distrust of child protection systems remains a critical issue. In their recent study, Saar-Heiman and Gupta (2024) found parents' views of child protection systems, in particular, to be ineffective or even corrupt. This centred around a mistrust of the system, which was considered intentionally oppressive, punitive and coercive. One parent considered the agency to be politically and financially motivated to maintain a level of control over people within society, with social workers 'part of the system' (p 3). This echoes previous research in which parents described limited understanding of systems and meetings frightening (Muensch and Diaz, 2016). More recent studies confirm that these tensions remain with parents feeling distrustful, isolated and with few supports to help them navigate confusing systems (McLean et al, 2020; Metzger et al, 2023).

One of the recommendations of the recent *Independent Review of Children's Social Care* in the UK was the need for parental advocacy (MacAlister, 2022). The review highlighted the importance of independent representation for parents and recommended that all families working with children's social care should be offered parental advocacy. International research supports this with parental advocacy in child welfare systems found to support behaviour change, engagement and relationships between parents and services (Better Care Network and IPAN, 2020). However, parental advocacy services, delivered in England today, are most often time-limited or one-off events rather than being embedded into the fabric of systems, meetings and service delivery.

## Inclusive practices

The picture presented within this chapter may well appear challenging. Practice will vary and differ across and within local authorities. The diverse range of social work education programmes, especially within childcare practice, means that individual practitioners will adopt differing approaches to partnership work. While there is no one right way, what the evidence from families served by this variation in practice tells us is that, all too often, they feel powerless (Toros, 2020; Bekaert et al, 2021). The evidence within this chapter indicates that drastic change is needed at both political and local levels in order to deliver services that emphasise a more humane and rights-based approach to child welfare.

There are approaches and models that do attempt to bridge the gap between protecting children and working in partnership with their parents, carers and families. These include peer parental advocacy (PPA; Fitz-Symonds et al, 2024), children chairing child-in- care reviews and Family Group Conferences (FGCs; Frost et al, 2014). What follows is a brief overview of these innovations, their role in supporting meaningful participation and the challenges of implementing them in practice today.

### *Family Group Conferences*

While children's services are often guided by principles of holistic and systemic thinking, practice can remain stubbornly restricted to the individual or nuclear family. Views of extended family can be sought, or even a family friend, but that can be where this exploration stops. Sometimes this may be the right thing to do, but there is a challenge to doing so that limits opportunity to explore vulnerability and need in a more social and holistic way. FGCs encourage practice that involves, more intentionally, wider networks around the child and is derived from a repositioning of families as experts who share decision-making and therefore power. It thereby reframes the role professionals have in social work intervention. This will be explored in much greater depth in Chapter 6 and so what follows is a brief overview.

FGCs were famously developed in New Zealand. At the time, Māori children were more likely to enter state care than their peers. It is now enshrined in law in New Zealand that an FGC referral must have been made before a child can be taken into care (Wood et al, 2024) Since the 1990's, the practice has gained traction in the UK and is now widely used as a mechanism to empower families to collectively find the best solutions for their child/ren, drawing upon the wisdom, knowledge, resources and expertise in their own family.

Drawing upon Māori culture in which community meetings are important, the conference itself is a structured one that involves everyone relevant and important to the child/ren. It is not limited to immediate family and can involve friends or other relatives. A key principle is that if – or once – wider family or friends are more aware of the challenges faced by the child/ren, they will be best suited to identify solutions, thereby reducing the need for state intervention (such as care proceedings). The FGC is facilitated by an independent facilitator who 'guides' rather than 'chairs'. Crucially, each child should be viewed as part of a community, rather than as an individual. This community collaboratively creates a plan to support and protect the child, which is then presented to the social worker. Research generally supports the positive experiences of families involved in the FGCs (Forrester, 2024), although evidence that they reduce risk or keep children at home is limited (Nurmatov et al, 2020). However, a more recent randomised controlled trial in England found that FGCs offered at pre-proceedings resulted in fewer children entering care (Taylor et al, 2023).

In practice, FGCs may diverge from this model, which could have implications for their effectiveness and role in empowering families and sharing decision-making. This also presents challenges for researchers in assessing the efficacy of FGCs (LaBrenz and Fong, 2016).

### *Peer parental advocacy*

PPA is a form of peer advocacy whereby parents with lived experience of the child protection system support other parents navigating it in real time (Tobis et al, 2020). Proponents of PPA argue that it counters professionally driven structures and processes that drive children's services and inherently redistributes power between professionals and families (Diaz et al, 2023). One key benefit of PPA is the increased level of shared decision-making afforded by such an approach, as well as improved relationships between social service professionals and families (Rockhill et al, 2015; Bohannan et al, 2016; Trescher and Summers, 2020). Indeed, the use of PPA in Camden was recently highlighted by the Independent Review of Children's Social Care (MacAlister, 2022) as an example of innovative practice. However, there is limited research regarding PPA in the UK, not least because there are still relatively few PPA services there. Much of the research undertaken on PPA has been in the US, which has been shown to reduce the need for children to enter state care (Tobis, 2013; Tobis et al, 2020). This will be explored in greater depth in Chapter 7.

*Children chairing reviews*

This chapter has outlined the IRO role and spoken of the importance of Children in Care (CIC) Reviews as a potential vehicle for participation. Ten years ago, I carried out a research project (Pert et al, 2017) in which I interviewed children and young people in care about their experiences of their reviews. The findings were bleak. They described their reviews as 'boring', 'done to them' and ineffective. However, one exception stood out. A young boy, passionate about football, had a more positive experience after his IRO met with him beforehand to discuss how the meeting would be structured and what he wanted it to focus on. After the review, the IRO created a visual representation of the meeting's action points: a football goal with footballs – each with a key action: flying into a goal. The child found this engaging and empowering but, most importantly, he knew what the adults around him were now going to do for him.

This was in 2014 when children chairing their reviews was beginning to take traction in the UK. When I went to networks and forums to speak about this, I got mixed responses. Some IROs seemed excited, some skeptical: Wouldn't that mean two separate meetings? How would the 'adult issues' be discussed? While the boy in my example had not, strictly speaking, chaired his review, it was the closest I had seen to a child having meaningful input into how a meeting was arranged and carried out, and in this sense it was *his* meeting. This example highlights how children can feel more involved when they have a say, even if they are not formally chairing the meeting.

Chairing the review might not appeal to all young people, but it is encouraged 'where appropriate', in the IRO Handbook (Department for Education and Skills, 2010). A child chairing their own review is not tantamount to their taking full responsibility for the process. This could feel overwhelming. Instead, chairing-in part- can be considered. A key finding from young people interviewed about their experiences of CiC Reviews was that those who had chaired their own reviews felt more positive about the review process overall. Those who had not chaired reported feeling frustrated and bored during reviews (Diaz et al, 2018). Other factors such as relationships with social workers and, importantly, IROs made a tangible difference to young people's participation in this forum. Although still under-researched, the practice of children chairing their own reviews has enormous potential to empower young people, shift existing structures that position professionals (and adults) as experts and foster better engagement in decision-making processes.

## Conclusion

A focus upon partnership working and participation requires us to examine individual practice as well as the systems and processes that govern social work. It challenges social workers, as well as regulators, policy makers and academics to move beyond procedural approaches to delivering and quality assuring social work. While there is no simple solution, it is as complex as it is difficult to understand that the very fundamental principles of a profession, its very values, can become lost within processes that do not privilege the voices of those at its centre. Whether this is deliberate or accidental, it highlights an ethical dilemma that demands attention.

Policy changes at the national level, such as those discussed in the Independent Review of Children's Social Care (MacAlister, 2022), are a step in the right direction. However, neither the outgoing Tory government that commissioned this report, nor the current Labour government, have indicated a desire to enact these recommendations. True transformation requires not only policy shifts but also a cultural change within services. For leaders, exploring and promoting new, innovative frameworks and processes is meaningfully designed around the needs of the individuals they serve. For individual practitioners, greater creativity and ambitious practice within the systems in which they operate would allow for more collaborative practice with children, young people and families. Social work should be built on relationships, empathy and understanding; yet it too often becomes entangled in bureaucratic processes that diminish these principles. Outside front line practice, academics have an important part to play in driving this change by producing evidence-based insight into what works, and by involving and amplifying the voices of children and families on this issue.

This chapter has sought to tease together these challenges and to present back what the impact of this is upon those who use these services. The fact that children and their parents consistently tell researchers that they do not feel heard, or even feel oppressed, is not only alarming but must also be a call to action. It is clear that there is a need to reimagine how social work services engage with families. In this way, participation can become more than a tick-box exercise and instead a genuine, impactful process that respects the input of those it involves. New innovations or practices that are increasingly being adopted, such as PPA or children chairing reviews, are encouraging and there will be more examples not discussed within this chapter. These approaches return social work to its values with people, and not procedures, at the centre of practice.

**References**

Adoption and Children Act (2002) 'Local authority foster parents', Ch. 38. Available from: https://www.legislation.gov.uk/ukpga/2002/38/section/38

Annan, M., Chua, J., Cole, R., Kennedy, E.K., James, R., Markusdottir, I. et al (2013) 'Further iterations on using the problem analysis framework', *Educational Psychology in Practice*, 29(1): 79–95.

Berrick, J.D., Dickens, J., Pösö, T. and Skivenes, M. (2015) 'Children's involvement in care order decision-making: a cross-country analysis', *Child Abuse & Neglect*, 49: 128–41. Available from: https://doi.org/10.1016/j.chiabu.2015.07.001

Better Care Network and IPAN (2020) *International Review of Parent Advocacy in Child Welfare: Strengthening Children's Care and Protection Through Parent Participation*, Better Care Network and IPAN.

Bohannan, T., Gonzalez, C. and Summers, A. (2016) 'Assessing the relationship between a peer mentoring program and case outcomes in dependency court', *Journal of Public Child Welfare*, 10(2): 176–96.

Bouma, H., López López, M., Knorth, E.J. and Grietens, H. (2018) 'Meaningful participation for children in the Dutch child protection system: a critical analysis of relevant provisions in policy documents', *Child Abuse & Neglect*, 79: 279–92. Available from: https://doi.org/10.1016/j.chiabu.2018.02.016

Brady, B., Devaney, C. and Jackson, R. (2024) 'Participation in practice in child welfare: processes, benefits, and challenges', *European Journal of Social Work*, 1–11. Available from: https://doi.org/10.1080/13691457.2024.2424938

Caldwell, J., McConvey, V. and Collins, M. (2019) 'Voice of the child – raising the volume of the voices of children and young people in care', *Child Care in Practice*, 25: 1–5. Available from: https://doi.org/10.1080/13575279.2019.1552447

Cashmore, J. (2002) 'Promoting the participation of children and young people in care', *Child Abuse & Neglect*, 26: 837–47.

Cashmore, J., Kong, P. and McLaine, M. (2023) 'Children's participation in care and protection decision-making matters', *Laws*, 12(3): 49.

Children Act (1989) Chapter 41. Available from: https://www.legislation.gov.uk/ukpga/1989/41/data.xht?wrap=true

Children's Commissioner (2023) The state of children and young people's advocacy services in England. Available from: https://www.childrenscommissioner.gov.uk/resource/the-state-of-children-and-young-peoples-advocacy-services-in-england/

Corby, B., Millar, M. and Young, L. (1996) 'Parental participation in child protection work: rethinking the rhetoric', *British Journal of Social Work*, 26: 475–92.

Cuevas-Parra, P. and Tisdall, E.K.M. (2022) 'Investing in activism: learning from children's actions to stop child marriage', *Childhood: A Journal of Global Child Research*. Available from: https://doi.org/10.1177/09075682221117295

Department for Children, Schools and families (2010) Independent reviewing officers' handbook: Statutory guidance for independent reviewing officers and local authorities on their functions in relation to case management and review for looked after children. Available from: iro_statutory_guidance_iros_and_las_march_2010_tagged.pdf

Department for Education and Department of Health (2015) Special educational needs and disability code of practice: 0 to 25 years. Available from: SEND_Code_of_Practice_January_2015.pdf

Department for Education (2023a) Working together to safeguard children: a guide to multi-agency working to help. Protect and promote the welfare of children. Available from: Working together to safeguard children 2023: statutory guidance

Department for Education (2023b) Children's social care: stable homes, built on love. Government Consultation Response. Available from: https://assets.publishing.service.gov.uk/media/650966a322a783001343e844/Children_s_Social_Care_Stable_Homes__Built_on_Love_consultation_response.pdf

Department for Education (2023c) Guide for children and young people: stable homes, built on love. Available from: Guide for children and young people: Stable Homes, Built on Love - GOV.UK

Department for Education and Department of Health and Social Care (2022) SEND review: right support, right place, right time. Available from: https://www.gov.uk/government/consultations/send-review-right-support-right-place-right-time

Devine, L. and Parker, S. (2015) ESRC evidence briefing: rethinking child protection strategy: child protection and assessment. Available from: https://www.semanticscholar.org/paper/ESRC-evidence-briefing%3A-Rethinking-child-protection-Devine-Parker/5e36cb3dfdc7c6f79e2975114120eb1ca918e086#citing-papers

Diaz, C. (2020) *Decision Making in Child and Family Social Work: Perspectives on Children's Participation*. Policy Press.

Diaz, C., Pert, H. and Thomas, N. (2018) '"Just another person in the room": young people's views on their participation in child in care reviews', *Adoption and Fostering*, 42(4): 369–82. Available from: https://doi.org/10.1177/0308575918801663.

Diaz, C., Pert, H. and Thomas, N.P. (2019) 'Independent reviewing officers' and social workers' perceptions of children's participation in children in care reviews', *Journal of Children's Services*, 14(3): 162–73. Available from: https://doi.org/10.1108/JCS-01-2019-0003

Diaz, C., Pert, H., Aylward, T., Neill, D. and Hill, L. (2020) 'Barriers children face complaining about social work practice: a study in one English local authority', *Child and Family Social Work*, 25(2): 460–8. Available from: https://doi.org/10.1111/cfs.12702

Dumbrill, G.C. (2006) 'Parental experience of child protection intervention: a qualitative study', *Child Abuse & Neglect*, 30(1): 27–37. Available from: https://doi.org/10.1016/j.chiabu.2005.08.012

Falch-Eriksen, A. and Backe-Hansen, E. (2018) 'Child protection and human rights: A call for professional practice and policy'. In A. Falch-Eriksen and E. Backe-Hansen (eds) *Human Rights in Child Protection. Implications for Professional Practice and Policy*. Palgrave, pp 1–14. Available from: https://doi.org/10.1007/978-3-319-94800-3_1

Falch-Eriksen, A. and Toros, K. (2021) 'Children expressing their views in child protection casework: current research and their rights going forward', *Child and Family Social Work*, 26(3): 485–97.

Featherstone, B., White, S. and Morris, K. (2014) *Re-imagining Child Protection: Towards Humane Social Work with Children and Families*. Policy Press.

Ferguson, H. (2017) 'How children become invisible in child protection work: findings from research into day-to-day social work practice', *British Journal of Social Work*, 47(4): 1007–23. Available from: https://doi.org/10.1093/bjsw/bcw065

Fitz-Symonds, S., Evans, L., Tobis, D., Westlake, D. and Diaz, C. (2024) 'Mechanisms for support: A realist evaluation of peer parental advocacy in England', *The British Journal of Social Work*, 54(1): pp 341–62. Available from: https://doi.org/10.1093/bjsw/bcad200

Forrester, D. (2024) *The Enlightened Social Worker: An Introduction to Rights-Focused Practice*. Policy Press.

Gibson, M. (2015) 'Shame and guilt in child protection social work: new interpretations and opportunities for practice', *Child & Family Social Work*, 20(3): 333–43.

Gilligan, R. (2004) 'Promoting resilience in child and family social work: issues for social work practice, education and policy', *Social Work Education*, 23(1): 93–104.

Harris, N. (2012) 'Assessment: when does it help and when does it hinder? Parents' experiences of the assessment process', *Child & Family Social Work*, 17(2): 180–91. Available from: https://doi.org/10.1111/j.1365-2206.2012.00836.x

Jones, L., Bellis, M.A., Wood, S., Hughes, K., Eckley, L., Bates, G. et al. (2012) 'Prevalence and risk of violence against children with disabilities: a systematic review and meta analysis of observational studies', *The Lancet*, 380: 899–907.

Kennedy, E.K. (2015) The Revised SEND Code of Practice 0–25: effective practice in engaging children and young people in decision-making about interventions for social, emotional and mental health needs. *Support for Learning*, 30: 4.

Kennan, D., Brady, B. and Forkan, C. (2018) 'Supporting children's participation in decision making: a systematic literature review exploring the effectiveness of participatory processes', *The British Journal of Social Work*, 48(7): 1985–2002.

LaBrenz, C.A. and Fong, R. (2016) 'Outcomes of family centered meetings for families referred to Child Protective Services', *Children and Youth Services Review*, 71: 93–102. Available from: https://doi.org/10.1016/j.childyouth.2016.10.032

Lalayants, M. and Merkel-Holguin, L. (2024) 'Navigating the child welfare system: the role of enhanced parent advocacy supports in child protection', *Journal of Public Child Welfare*, pp 1–23. Available from: https://doi.org/10.1080/15548732.2024.2315133

Tisdall, E.K.M. and Le Borgne, C. (2017) 'Children's participation: questioning competence and competencies?', *Social Inclusion*, 5(3): 122–30.

MacAlister, J. (2022) *The Independent Review of Children's Social Care*. Department of Health and Social Care. Available from: https://assets.publishing.service.gov.uk/media/640a17f28fa8f5560820da4b/Independent_review_of_children_s_social_care_-_Final_report.pdf

Metzger, I.W., Moreland, A., Garrett, R.J., Reid-Quiñones, K., Spivey, B.N., Hamilton, J. et al. (2023) 'Black moms matter: a qualitative approach to understanding barriers to service utilization at a Children's Advocacy Center following childhood abuse', *Child Maltreatment*, 1(4): 648–60. Available from: https://doi.org/10.1177/10775595231169782

McLean, K., Clarke, J., Scott, D., Hiscock, H. and Goldfeld, S. (2020) Foster and kinship carer experiences of accessing healthcare: A qualitative study of barriers, enablers and potential solutions. *Children & Youth Services Review*, 113: 104976. Available from: https://doi.org/10.1016/j.childyouth.2020.104976

MacAlister, J. (2022) *The Independent Review of Children's Social Care*. Department of Health and Social Care. Available from: Independent review of children's social care - final report

Muench, K., Diaz, C. and Wright, R. (2016) 'Children and parent participation in child protection conferences: a study in one English local authority', *Child Care in Practice*, 23(1): 49–63. Available from: https://doi.org/10.1080/13575279.2015.1126227

Munro, E. (2001) 'Empowering looked-after children', *Child & Family Social Work*, 6: 129–37.

Munro, E. (2011) *The Munro Review of Child Protection: Final Report – A Child-Centred System*. Department for Education.

Munro, E. (2018) 'Decision making under uncertainty in child protection: creating a just and learning culture', *Journal of Child and Family Social Work*, 24: 123–30.

Nurmatov, U., Foster, C., Bezeczky, Z., Owen, J., El-Banna, A., Mann, M. et al (2020) *Impact of Shared Decision-Making Family Meetings on Children's Out-of-Home Care, Family Empowerment and Satisfaction: A Systematic Review*. What Works Centre for Children's Social Care. Available from: https://orca.cardiff.ac.uk/id/eprint/132949/1/WWCSC_Shared_Decision-making_Family_Meetings_systematic_review_Feb2020.pdf

Olli, J., Vehkakoski, T. and Salanterä, S. (2012) *Facilitating and Hindering Factors in the Realization of Disabled Children's Agency in Institutional Contexts: Literature Review*. Routledge.

Pert, H., Diaz, C. and Thomas, N. (2017) 'Children's participation in LAC reviews: A study in one English local authority', *Child & Family Social Work*, 22: 1–10.

Petersen., Križ, K., Shier, H., Lotan, H., Schwartz-Tayri, T.M., Naddeo, L., … Vigevani, D. (2025) 'Children and young people's participation in child protection: outcomes of transformative participation in international contexts', *European Journal of Social Work*, pp 1–15. Available from: https://doi.org/10.1080/13691457.2025.2482889

Pölkki, P., Vornanen, R., Pursiainen, M., and Riikonen, M. (2012) 'Children's participation in child protection processes as experienced by foster children and social workers', *Child Care in Practice*, 18: 107–125. Available from: https://doi.org/10.1080/13575279.2011.646954

*R v Rochdale Metropolitan Borough Council* [2008] EWHC 3282 Fam

Richardson-Foster, H., Barter, C., Stanley, N. and Churchill, H. (2021) 'How child focused are Child Protection Conferences?', *Child Abuse Review*, 30(5): 458–72.

Rockhill, A., Furrer, C.J. and Duong, T.M. (2015) 'Peer mentoring in child welfare: a motivational framework', *Child Welfare*, 94(5): 125–44.

Roe, A. (2021). *Children's Experience of Private Law Proceedings: Six Key Messages from Research*. Nuffield Family Justice Observatory. Available from: https://www.nuffieldfjo.org.uk/resource/childrens-experience-of-private-law-proceedings-six-key-messages-from-research

Rogowski, S. (2024) *Critical Social work with Children and Families: Theory, Context and Practice*, 2nd ed. Policy Press.

Saar-Heiman, Y. and Gupta, A. (2024) 'Beyond participation: parent activism in child protection as a path to transformative change', *Children and Youth Services Review*, vol. 157, article 107443.

Schofield, G. and Thoburn, J. (1996) *Child Protection: The Voice of the Child in Decision Making*. IPPR.

Stalford, H. and Hollingsworth, K. (2020) ' "This case is about you and your future": towards judgments for children', *The Modern Law Review*, 1–29.

Taylor, T., Blackshaw, E., Lawrence, H., Stern, D., Gilbert, L. and Raghoo, N. (2023) *Randomized Controlled Trial of Family Group Conferencing at Pre-Proceedings Stage*. Foundations.

Thomas, N. (2002) *Children, Family and the State: Decision Making and Child Participation*. Macmillan, Policy Press.

Tisdall, E.K.M. (2015) 'Children's rights and children's wellbeing: equivalent policy concepts?', *Journal of Social Policy*, 44(4): 807–23. Available from: https://doi.org/10.1017/S0047279415000306

Tisdall, E.K.M. and Le Borgne, C. (2017) 'Children's participation: questioning competence and competencies?', *Social Inclusion*, 5(3): 122–30.

Tobis, D. (2013) *From Pariahs to Partners: How Parents and Their Allies Changed New York City's Child Welfare System*. Oxford University Press.

Tobis, D., Bilson, A. and Katugampala, I. (2020) *International Review of Parent Advocacy in Child Welfare*. Available from: https://bettercarenetwork.org/about-bcn/what-we-do/organizations-working-on-childrens-care/international-parent-advocacy-network-ipan

Toros, K. (2020) 'A systematic review of children's participation in child protection decision-making: tokenistic presence or not?', *Children and Society*, 35(3): 395–411.

Trescher, S. and Summers, A. (2020) *Outcome Evaluation Report for Washington State's Parents for Parents Program. Capacity Building Center for Courts*. Available from: https://www.courts.wa.gov/CWCIP/docs/Parents%20for%20Parents%20Phase%20II%20Evaluation.pdf

United Nations (2006) *Convention on the Rights of Persons with Disabilities*. Available from: https://www.ohchr.org/en/instruments-mechanisms/instruments/convention-rights-persons-disabilities

United Nations Committee on the Rights of the Child (UNCRC) (1989) *The United Nations Convention of the Rights of the Child*. Available from: https://www.unicef.org.uk/wp-content/uploads/2010/05/UNCRC_united_nations_convention_on_the_rights_of_the_child.pdf

UN Committee on the Rights of the Child (UNCRC) (2009) *General Comment No. 12: The Right of the Child to be Heard*. Available from: https://digitallibrary.un.org/record/671444?ln=en&v=pdf

Van Bijleveld, G.G., Bunders-Aelen, J.F.G. and Dedding, C.W.M. (2019) 'Exploring the essence of enabling child participation within child protection services', *Child & Family Social Work*, 25(2): 286–93. Available from: https://doi.org/10.1111/cfs.12684

Walker, G. (2011) 'Child rights, social justice and exclusion'. In Jones, P. and Walker, G. (eds) *Children's Rights in Practice*. Sage, pp 32–43.

Wood, S., Scourfield, J., Meindl, M., Au, K.M., Evans, R., Jones-Willams, D. et al. (2024) 'Family group conference provision in UK local authorities and associations with children looked after rates', *The British Journal of Social Work*. Available from: https://doi.org/10.1093/bjsw/bcae019

# PART II
# Advocacy and family participation

# 5

# Family Drug and Alcohol Courts

*David Westlake and Melissa Meindl*

## Introduction

The way court proceedings are conducted in the UK is changing and 'problem-solving' courts are increasingly found in different areas of the justice system (Mentzou and Mutebi, 2023). Central to this shift is the idea that the court arena can serve as a forum for change in cases where there are entrenched social problems. The approach these courts adopt is underpinned by the principles of person-centered care, which means individuals' circumstances, strengths and needs are kept at the forefront of proceedings. By operating within existing courts, problem-solving courts can couple the authority of the court with necessary services to help families, with judges at the centre of rehabilitation and active agents in this process (Bowen and Whitehead, 2015).

The Family Drug and Alcohol Court (FDAC) is one example of such a court that has been established in the UK family justice system. FDACs aim to enable children to safely remain or be reunited with their birth parents, in cases where the parents are misusing drugs or alcohol (Tavistock and Portman NHS foundation Trust [2018] FDAC information for professionals leaflet). It does this by offering an alternative form of care proceedings that differs in several key respects, including the type and nature of hearings, the professionals involved and how they practice, and the level of support offered. More fundamentally, FDAC re-orientates court proceedings to foreground a problem-solving approach to help parents overcome their complex needs and problems associated with their substance misuse.

This chapter will consider how FDAC does things differently to promote positive outcomes for children and families affected by parental substance misuse. We begin with an overview of the FDAC model, including its origins and aims, key principles and components, before outlining how it has continued to develop in the UK. We will then explore FDAC's evidence base, providing an overview of the key research findings on the effectiveness of this approach and some detail from an evaluation we have recently completed. Building on this, we hone in further on the evidence about how FDACs work more meaningfully with families, particularly through the relationships that are developed with the FDAC team and judges. We close out the chapter by examining the practical implications of the FDAC approach for child and family social work practice. The lessons around implementation serve as a resource to improve practice, support families and promote a collaborative and interdisciplinary approach both within FDAC proceedings and the wider field of child and family social work.

We have both been aware of FDAC for several years. At the time it was being developed in the UK, David Westlake (one of the authors of this chapter) spent several weeks gathering data for a study of care proceedings (Masson et al, 2008) at the Wells Street Family Proceedings Court – the cradle of FDAC in London. There was a buzz around the idea, aided in no small way by the wisdom and charisma of the late Judge Nick Crichton who pioneered the model in its early years. It was clear that many people involved felt it was a better way of going about care proceedings than the traditional approach.

A decade after the first pilot began, Melissa took a deep dive into FDAC, conducting a small review of the available FDAC evidence in 2018 and leading a rapid realist review of the model in 2019. More recently, we worked together to evaluate the first FDAC pilot in Wales, which ran from 2021 to 2023. Before we say more about all of this, let's clarify what FDAC is, how it came about in the UK and how it differs from standard care proceedings.

## Origins and aims of the Family Drug and Alcohol Court

In the mid 1990s, an alternative to traditional family courts was developed in the US family justice system to address the high number of child abuse and neglect cases involving parental substance misuse. The specialised, problem-solving court, called 'Family Drug Treatment Court', was modelled after adult drug courts. They adopted elements of adult drug courts considered effective in helping individuals with substance misuse problems, increasing drug treatment completion, reducing positive drug tests and lowering drug-related crimes. Elements included regular court hearings and judicial monitoring, frequent drug testing, specialist treatment and other support services, and rewards and sanctions surrounding compliance.

Using a problem-solving, multidisciplinary, collaborative, family-centred approach, family drug treatment courts were designed to address parental substance misuse and improve parenting skills. Their main goals were to reduce child maltreatment, expedite permanent decisions for children, help keep families together, and balance the rights and needs of both parents and children. Towards these goals, they helped parents engage with treatment services and motivated them to stay in treatment so that more were able to be reunited with their children. Research on family drug treatment courts showed that parents entered treatment for substance misuse faster, stayed in treatment longer and were more likely to a) successfully complete treatment and b) be reunified with their children. In instances where parents did not engage, this was taken into account and the court arrived at quicker decisions to establish a permanent alternative for the children, meaning that the children who were not reunified found themselves in permanent placements more quickly (Green et al, 2007).

Inspired by this encouraging evidence, Judge Crichton wanted to develop a similar problem-solving approach in the UK and pioneered FDAC as an adapted version, tailored to the needs and structures of the UK court and social care systems. Preparations over a few years in the early 2000s led to the first pilot at the Wells Street Inner London Family Proceedings Court (FPC) between 2008 and 2012, and then an enduring presence at this court.

Similar to family drug treatment courts in the US, the purpose behind developing FDAC in the UK was to tackle a problem that would be familiar to many working in the sector – the high proportion of cases presenting in family courts with issues of drug and alcohol misuse threatening the safety and well-being of children. This was a growing problem that was being felt acutely by the family courts in the first decade of the 2000s, and estimates from the time suggest that between 1 in 10 and 1 in 14 children were affected by parental alcohol or drug use (Forrester and Harwin, 2011). Indeed, substance misuse contributes in no small part to the unrelenting upward trend in care applications that continues currently in the UK (MacAlister, 2022).

## A team, a judge and a trial (for change): principles and components of the Family Drug and Alcohol Court

As with family drug treatment courts, FDACs assume that the optimal outcome is for families to overcome their substance misuse and related difficulties so that they can safely raise healthy, well-adjusted children. When this is not the case, the aim is to find alternative long-term placements quickly (Centre for Justice Innovation, 2019). A key principle of FDAC is that parents are given a genuine opportunity to overcome the concerns that pose a risk to their children. This materialises in an offer of an intensive, co-developed, personalised package of support and interventions during what is known as a 'Trial for Change'. This is a structured yet flexible period during which a parent is given an opportunity to demonstrate their ability to address their substance misuse and other related issues. It is designed to facilitate an assessment of whether parents can make the necessary changes quickly enough to safely care for their child, and to afford parents the best chance of doing so.

Throughout the Trial for Change, parents are supported by a multidisciplinary FDAC team, one of whom will be their keyworker throughout their proceedings. The composition of the team varies for each FDAC site, but guidance on getting started from the FDAC national partnership proposes a number of key staffing positions. These include a team manager, who should be a qualified social worker or clinical psychologist; a social worker and senior social worker, one of whom should have a domestic abuse specialism; a specialist substance misuse worker; a parent mentor co-ordinator; a clinical nurse; a post-proceedings worker; an administrator; a clinical lead; and an adult psychiatrist. The team co-ordinates and provides intensive therapeutic treatment and support, and is trained in problem-solving and 'trauma-informed' approaches to working with parents.

Throughout the 26 weeks of court proceedings, the team facilitates weekly testing of parents' substance use. Parents are also supported by a specially trained judge, who provides ongoing monitoring, encouragement and accountability across the duration of the parent's FDAC proceedings. In addition to more traditional court hearings with lawyers present, parents have 'non-lawyer reviews' (NLRs) every fortnight with the same judge. These reviews are informal and judges make deliberate efforts to engage differently with parents by speaking to them directly rather than via legal representatives.

## Development in the UK and the contemporary picture of the Family Drug and Alcohol Court

After being established in the Wells Street FPC in London, FDAC performed well in early evaluations, which suggested that it may reduce drug and alcohol misuse and the need for children to be in care (Harwin et al, 2014; Bambrough et al, 2018; Harwin, Alrouh et al, 2018). These positive appraisals boosted its profile and helped it spread to other courts over the course of the next decade or so. At times, the number of sites grew to more than 16 operating across the UK. Currently, there are 13 specialist FDAC teams, working in 19 courts and serving families in 35 local authorities.

As part of our research on FDAC in Wales, we consulted all FDAC sites that were operational at the time in order to learn how FDAC had continued to develop in the UK since it was first introduced. This exercise showed that, while all the current FDAC sites still reflect the core model developed and evaluated during the London pilot, various adaptations have been made locally in the years since. This has mostly stemmed from a need to tailor the FDAC service to meet local needs, and/or to ensure that the FDAC site is operationally viable, sustainable and has the best chance for successfully helping families. Not all FDACs had made changes to the core model, but the adaptations that had been made were generally to do with (1) the range of specialisms within the team, (2) the way the service was funded, and (3) the relationship between the FDAC and the local authority or authorities it served.

## Expanding the service

Several FDACs had expanded their team or service by adding specialisms to improve their capacity to work with specific issues. The most common issues that demanded extra input were domestic abuse and mental health support, and many FDACs either recruited specialists in these areas or provided training on these topics for existing team members. And, at a broader level, all FDAC sites have received additional training on specialist domestic abuse intervention in recent years.

Another way in which several FDACs have expanded their service reflects the findings of previous evaluations, which noted the potential value of offering parents post-proceedings support. This is essentially a continuation of support from the FDAC team after the final FDAC recommendation and the nature of this varies. It might be as informal as a series of coffee mornings, or more intensive help that is more akin to the within-proceedings offer, which gradually reduces for up to a year after the conclusion of the case. Offering a post-proceedings service has been deemed necessary by some FDACs to reduce the risk of setbacks immediately after the intensive period of proceedings ends – which may include relapse, further abuse or neglect, or placement breakdowns.

Given that this book is about empowering families, the provision of a peer mentor within an FDAC is worth discussing. Peer-mentoring schemes are generally considered successful by FDAC teams. However, many have generally found it difficult to offer parents in FDAC proceedings peer mentors, even though the core model does recommend that this role is included in core FDAC teams. This seems to be due to lack of funding and difficulty finding suitable volunteers. When we reviewed the current situation in 2022, five FDACs had parent mentors and two others who had previously had mentors hoped to reintroduce them. Where mentors were available, some were assigned to specific parents while others provided more ad hoc and flexible input when it was needed (such as during drug testing or in court hearings). We heard positive comments about mentoring when it was available – with stories of high demand being supported by the fact that there was a waiting list for mentors at one site.

There is also a range of other specialisms or roles that have been added to respond to local needs. Some examples of these include programme managers to assist FDACs in planning, decision-making and collaborating in addition to systemic family therapists, Family Group Conference workers, health visitors and services for employment, education and housing.

## Funding

As with many interventions in children's social care, funding for FDACs is a powerful determinant of the nature and extent of what can be delivered.

In our study, it was described as shaping the scope and remit of sites, and it has clearly become a significant factor in the long-term viability of FDACs. As FDAC has grown in the UK, the way it has been funded has diversified. Variability in funding FDACs is ultimately linked to the different ways in which they are commissioned. There are currently three ways they tend to be set up:

1. as a new independent service, run, for example, by a charity or health trust;
2. through expanding an existing local service;
3. by building a new stand-alone team, using seconded staff from other parts of the service.

How any given FDAC site is funded and structured can also change during its lifespan, particularly if the sources of funding change. The London FDAC pilot, for instance, was funded by central government but is now commissioned by the local authorities it serves.

The expansion described earlier has been possible for some FDACs due to additional funding through a different commissioning structure, and the timing of changes is closely linked with funding. Similarly, others have faced restructures, downsizing and service closures when funding has ceased or reduced. Some FDACs have secured more reliable and long-term sources of funding through links with local authorities, although this has had drawbacks such as one FDAC team only being able to focus a proportion of their role/caseload on FDAC work with the remainder taking on other roles, thereby making them more indispensable to the local authority.

Many FDAC team members we spoke to expressed continual concerns and uncertainties around funding, which had a significant and lasting influence on the work the teams undertook. Instability of funding has been shown to create recruitment problems, instability in teams, constrained services and/or site closures.

## Links with local authorities

Related to the funding and commissioning structures of FDACs, another important factor for them is the relationship teams have with the local authorities they serve. All FDACs are independent from local authorities although in practice, as commissioning structures have changed, they have varied in how closely they work with local authorities and how independent they feel. Some FDACs have developed more separation from local authorities (for example, have no shared funding, data, or working sites), while others have closer ties (for example, shared resources, data and staff). With benefits and downsides being shared about both, we have not been given the impression that one style of relationship is better than another.

## The evidence base and Family Drug and Alcohol Courts' effectiveness in the UK

Evaluations suggest that FDACs are more successful in achieving and maintaining results compared to standard proceedings (Harwin et al, 2018; Allen et al, 2021; Neo et al, 2021; Shaw, 2021). The initial FDAC pilot in London was evaluated in two studies. In the first (Harwin et al, 2014), all 146 families (149 children) in the pilot were compared with similar cases in standard care proceedings (that is, families [n=101] who were involved because of parental substance misuse). The second study (Harwin et al, 2016) tracked 140 families from the pilot (90 of which were included in the previous study) in a five-year follow-up study, comparing outcomes with cases heard in standard care proceedings in the same Family Proceedings Court, at the same time the pilot was running. The studies showed that the FDAC was more successful than the standard care proceedings in helping parents to overcome the substance misuse that placed their children at risk of significant harm. They also found that a) more FDAC mothers than mothers in the comparison group were reunited with their children, although this did not reach statistical significance and could therefore be by chance, and that b) a higher proportion of FDAC mothers both stopped misusing substances and were reunified with their children. At the 5-year follow-up, the risk of substance misuse was found to be significantly lower for FDAC mothers reunited with their children, with a higher proportion of FDAC mothers sustaining cessation than comparison mothers. In addition, a significantly higher proportion of FDAC families, reunited at the end of the proceedings, did not experience any disruption, indicating that family reunification via FDAC is more durable than in the comparison cases.

While there are potential issues with the study design here – notably the possibility that the comparison groups used are somehow different and destined to have different outcomes anyway – these are all positive indicators. Moreover, research on the London pilot also started to demonstrate FDACs' benefits for parents who did not stop misusing substances or who were not reunified with their children, as well as cost savings associated with FDACs through shorter hearings, fewer expert witnesses and fewer hearings with lawyers present.

As FDAC has grown from the original pilot, a number of other research studies have looked into how it works and whether it has appeared to achieve its aims, including mixed-methods studies of individual sites and several qualitative studies. Many of these studies supported the findings that families in FDAC proceedings are significantly more likely to both retain care of their children and cease substance misuse, compared to those in standard proceedings (Harwin, Alrouh et al, 2018; Harwin, Ryan et al, 2018; Zhang et al, 2019; Allen et al, 2021; Neo et al, 2021; Shaw, 2021).

Over the past couple of years, some of the largest and most ambitious evaluations of FDACs have taken place, using a range of methodologies to measure their impact, test new iterations of the model, and capture how it is implemented and experienced. Most recently, the National Centre for Social Research conducted the most comprehensive study of FDACs to date. The study compared data on families in FDAC care proceedings from 13 FDAC sites with similar families in standard care proceedings. In line with what other researchers had found previously, they concluded that – again compared to standard care proceedings – parents and primary carers in FDAC proceedings had more positive outcomes:

- They were more likely to be reunified with their children.
- A higher proportion of FDAC parents ceased to misuse drugs or alcohol.
- FDAC had lower proportions of contested hearings and use of external expert witness assessments.
- The children in FDAC proceedings had a lower probability of being placed in local authority care.

These successes have been attributed to several aspects of the FDAC model. These include the way FDACs work with families and the relationships that are built with the multidisciplinary team, the collaborative way of working with parents and professionals, the role of the judge and the less adversarial nature of court. Researchers have also noted the way parents have reported being more involved in co-produced goals and plans, and feeling more respected by the professionals involved. This is particularly apparent in the case of judges, who are clearly perceived differently in FDACs (Harwin et al, 2018; Allen et al, 2021; Mason and Wilkinson, 2021).

Alongside these studies of the impact of FDACs, there have also been attempts to understand the cost-effectivenes of the model. Given the relatively high costs of care, interventions that are able to reduce the need for children to be removed from their birth families only need to have a modest effect in order to prove cost-effective. This is especially true if children who would otherwise be placed in specialist or residential placements are able to remain safely within their birth families, such is the cost of those placements.

It is therefore no surprise that the economic modelling exercises of FDACs' costs and savings that have been carried out to date are also positive. These suggest that FDACs can yield savings for both local authorities and other statutory agencies, compared to standard care proceedings (Whitehead and Reeder, 2016; Centre for Justice Innovation, 2021, 2024). As well as making these savings through increased reunifications, avoided recurrent care proceedings and care placements (Allen et al, 2021; Centre for Justice Innovation, 2021), resources are also saved through avoided or reduced call-outs of emergency and police services for substance misuse-related issues (Allen et al, 2021), fewer contested hearings (Harwin et al, 2011; Papaioannou et al, 2023) and reduced need for externally commissioned expert assessments (Papaioannou et al, 2023). Projections for scaling up the FDAC model through central government funding suggest that – by reducing legal costs, keeping children out of care and helping parents to cease substance misuse – FDACs produce £3 of savings to the state for every £1 invested and that these benefits would be increased in line with investment.

This combination of promising findings about the impact of FDAC, and encouraging signs about how those involved perceive and experience it, makes for a good foundation for testing FDAC more thoroughly and in new places. More rigorous comparative studies, which use either randomisation to produce reliable comparison groups or high-quality quasi-experimental designs, are yet to materialise, although such a study is a logical next step if the model is to be tested at a large enough scale. However, the expansion of FDACs into the devolved jurisdiction of Wales provided us with an opportunity to test the intervention in a different setting.

## Overview of the Welsh evaluation

After observing the development of FDACs from across the River Severn, the Welsh Government was persuaded that it was worth piloting FDAC in a single location in Wales. The pilot was set to run for two years, starting in 2021, in the Cardiff and Vale of Glamorgan region. Our evaluation looked at whether it was feasible to implement FDAC in this new setting, explored how the pilot was experienced by key people involved, including parents and professionals, and examined any signs of potential within the constraints of the relatively small number of families involved. We also explored whether the pilot resembled the core model and what was being done in existing sites in England, with a view to determining whether this was coherent and sufficiently well-defined to scale up further into other parts of Wales.

We collected data in a number of ways in an attempt to understand how FDAC worked from different perspectives and for different stakeholder groups. Much of the data we collected – for instance, using interviews and focus groups – was qualitative in nature, as were the insights gathered through the time we spent observing court sessions, meetings and the wider activities of the FDAC team. We also analysed some quantitative data that was gathered by the service, which helped show how the pilot fared in relation to processes and outcomes for children and families.

Some of our analysis took what is known as a 'realist' approach, which seeks to identify key drivers of change and the mechanisms through which change might occur. This meant that we were able to describe some of the key pathways through which FDACs seem to lead to the outcomes that other researchers have documented (as well as some which had not been documented previously). Here we focus on a few of the findings that seemed most relevant to the topic of this book regarding relational-based change.

## How do family drug and alcohol courts appear to empower families and create relationships?

As we have already discussed, FDAC has some fundamental features that distinguish it from standard care proceedings, and much of this has to do with the way it prioritises relationship building and gives parents the autonomy to make positive changes. Standard care proceedings are often seen merely as a legal process that takes place after an often long period in which social workers and other agencies have tried to bring about change, so it is not surprising that families may feel powerless to change the outcome: and that they have reached an endpoint. FDAC, on the other hand, sees change as something that can happen even at the relatively late stage of court proceedings. By gauging the motivation of parents, creating processes of support and accountability, and keeping a close eye on how the situation develops, FDAC supports parents who have the motivation and ability to change even if they have not managed it previously. The following aspects of FDAC are arguably the key facilitators of this.

### Keyworkers

Many parents who experience the family court are isolated, and part of any successful change process is going to involve trusting professionals and accepting help. The range of different people involved, including the judge, the members of the FDAC team and other professionals, such as legal representatives, means that there are opportunities to trust and accept help from a range of sources. However, the relationships parents develop with their keyworkers are perhaps the most important, and facilitate much of the other work done by the FDAC team. The keyworker is usually from a therapeutic background and works with parents intensively, sometimes seeing them several times a day. This safe, trusting and mutually respectful relationship parents build with their keyworker is important because it results in parents feeling able to be vulnerable with their worker and the wider the FDAC team. This enables them to be open and honest – for example, about their substance misuse – which, in turn, helps the team personalise the support they receive.

Keyworkers use a range of skills that can be thought of as exemplifying the therapeutic problem-solving approach of FDAC teams. These determine how they communicate with parents, such as using normal words instead of jargon, listening without judging, being interested in the wider experience of the parents beyond the problems they are dealing with, focusing on their strengths and resources, and using humour to lighten the mood. When this is done well, parents feel that the professionals are working *with* them rather than *against* them. They feel empowered to take responsibility for what has happened in the past and to change their substance misuse for a better future. Crucially, they also feel hopeful about change and worthy of support.

## Regular drug testing

While the use of drug testing may feel somewhat draconian, many parents were positive about it. Two things seemed important here – the way the testing was handled by the team and what it represented. Like other aspects of FDAC, the testing was designed to make parents feel actively involved and not passive recipients of the court process. Parents were able to choose their own test pot and taught how to interpret the results – and they felt this brought the process more within their control. Another aspect of testing that made them feel like active participants, rather than passive observers, was the fact that the results were instant. This meant that they had the opportunity to show the professionals that they were making progress, sticking to the plan and overcoming their difficulties. For those who were abstaining from drugs and/or alcohol, this gave them proof that they were on the right track. This increased their hope and self-confidence that they could beat their substance misuse and be reunified with their children.

While the parents involved in our study did not frame this as empowering in itself, one can argue that this aspect of FDAC may have been experienced as empowering for those who saw drug testing as a means of proving to others that they were persevering. More generally, some professionals noted the increased agency that parents had through FDAC – right from the point where they chose whether to sign up for it, which gave them 'choice' and 'options', which they would not have in standard proceedings. One of the Children's Guardians commented that parents are given 'the opportunity to understand that actually they have some power in all of this, and actually they have the ability to change the outcome, whereas you don't get that focus [in standard care proceedings]'.

The main process for this within FDAC is the fortnightly NLRs mentioned earlier. These provide a forum for the judge and professionals to set goals, delegate and agree ownership of tasks and responsibilities, and review progress, without the formality or detachment of communicating via legal representatives. During the NLR, everyone relevant to the care plan is given a chance to speak to the judge and others present, which means that a parent feels they are an active participant with a voice that can be heard.

There was a sense that it was helpful for parents and professionals to be clear about what needed to happen in the next fortnight, and the fact that professionals were also held accountable by the judge was appreciated by parents. They felt this made the process fairer and more transparent, and in the longer term this seemed to increase parents' trust in the process and in authority more generally. The process was also credited with the lower rates of contested final hearings because parents were more accepting of decisions when they felt that they had been given a fair chance to change.

Another function of these sessions, which is facilitated by the way judges operate, is that the expectations of parents are demystified. Speaking directly to them, often in the 'well' of the court rather than from behind their desks, judges give parents clear and consistent messaging about what they need to be working on throughout proceedings in order to be reunified with their child(ren) and feedback on progress is given. This includes affirming and celebrating what has gone well, and highlighting what needs more work. This way, parents develop a clear picture of what changes are expected or required of them and the potential consequences if they do not make changes. This increases their motivation to address their substance misuse and other barriers to reunification.

Several aspects of this are designed to facilitate change by increasing the parent's motivation, hope, confidence and resolve, as well as reducing their anxieties about the court process or potential outcomes. The strengths-based approach of the judge and the other professionals is important, and manifests in the use of communication skills training to acknowledge positives and empathise while being clear about what still needs to change and what risks remain. The absence of lawyers to filter this communication means that it feels more personal and less like the parents are caught up in a formal process that is out of their hands. The physical positioning of the judge further reinforces the notion that the boundaries between the formality of the court and the legal system it represents are softened, at least partially, in order for meaningful change to be given a chance.

These are subtle but important aspects of FDAC that create a more relaxed atmosphere in which parents can feel more comfortable. We observed this extending beyond the NLRs themselves because there was often a lot of informal discussion between parents and professionals both before and after hearings. This helps to distinguish the hearing from standard proceedings, create an openness that facilitates relationships and promote the change that often follows.

## Concluding thoughts

In the past few decades, the child protection system in the UK has been characterised by incremental rather than revolutionary changes. The family courts have operated in broadly the same manner for much longer than that, and changes to the core operating model of courts in general are very rare. However, the judges involved in the Welsh evaluation recognised the same problem in the present day that Judge Crichton identified back in the mid-2000s: that standard care proceedings do not give some families the best chance of success and that an alternative way is needed. Problem-solving courts represent a somewhat radical new approach, and FDAC clearly offers a distinctive and quite different way of going about care proceedings. Viewed in this way, it is remarkable that FDAC has grown across England and established itself as an interesting and promising alternative.

Along with the positive findings that have emerged from multiple evaluations of FDACs, which have been critical in supporting its development, this sense that something needs to change has arguably propelled FDAC to where it is today. Undoubtedly, if the various issues with funding and commissioning were easier to resolve, then we would see more FDACs operating across England and Wales – and perhaps further afield too.

The problem FDACs seek to address is no less urgent than it has ever been – the numbers of children being taken into care continue to rise. FDAC offers a unique combination of relational, strengths-based and intensive support, which is overseen by a judge and bounded by clear and consistent monitoring. Situating this within the court arena serves to further motivate parents who want to change, and provides a swift alternative route for children when this is not possible. All this considered, it seems to us that FDAC itself is worth making more widely available. Some of the principles and practices it involves – particularly around relationship-based change – may be applicable beyond the FDAC in other parts of children's social care.

## References

Allen, K., Paskell, C., Goder, R., Ryan, M. and Clery, L. (2021) 'Evaluation of Pan Bedfordshire FDAC Final evaluation report', *Research in Practice*.

Bambrough, S., Crichton, N. and Webb, S. (2018) 'Better outcomes and better justice: The Family Drug and Alcohol Court', in A. Foster (ed.) *Mothers Accused and Abused*, Routledge, 1st ed., pp 124–37.

Bowen, P. and Whitehead, S. (2015) *Problem-solving Courts: An Evidence Review*, Centre for Justice Innovation. Available from: https://justiceinnovation.org/publications/problem-solving-courts-evidence-review

Centre for Justice Innovation (2019) *Thinking About Developing a Family Drug and Alcohol Court FDAC? Guidance on Getting Started from The FDAC National Partnership*.

Centre for Justice Innovation (2021) *Rolling-out Family Drug and Alcohol Courts (FDAC): The Business Case*. Available from: https://www.justiceinnovation.org/publications/rolling-out-family-drug-and-alcohol-courts-fdac-business-case

Centre for Justice Innovation (2024) *Family Drug and Alcohol Courts (FDAC): The Case for Investment*.

Forrester, D. and Harwin, J. (2011) *Parents who Misuse Drugs And Alcohol: Effective Interventions in Social Work and Child Protection*, Wiley-Blackwell.

Green, B.L., Furrer, C., Worcel, S., Burrus, S. and Finigan, M.W. (2007) 'How effective are family treatment drug courts? Outcomes from a four-site national study', *Child Maltreatment*, 12(1): 43–59.

Harwin, J., Ryan, M. and Broadhurst, K. (2018) 'How does FDAC succeed with parents with substance misuse problems? Exploring relational practices within the English Family Drug and Alcohol Court', *Child Abuse Review*, 27(4): 266–79.

Harwin, J., Alrouh, B., Ryan, M. and Tunnard, J. (2014) *Changing Lifestyles, Keeping Children Safe: An Evaluation of the First Family Drug and Alcohol Court (FDAC) in Care Proceedings*. Brunel University.

Harwin, J., Alrouh, B., Broadhurst, K., McQuarrie, T., Golding, L. and Ryan, M. (2018) 'Child and parent outcomes in the London family drug and alcohol court five years on: building on international evidence', *International Journal of Law, Policy, and the Family*, 32(2): 140–69. Available from: https://doi.org/10.1093/lawfam/eby006

Harwin, J., Alrouh, B., Ryan, M., McQuarrie, T., Golding, L., Broadhurst, K. et al. (2016) After *FDAC: Outcomes 5 Years Later. Final Report.* Lancaster University.

Harwin, J., Ryan, M., Tunnard. J., Pokhrel, S., Alrouh, B., Matias, C. et al. (2011) 'The Family Drug and Alcohol Court (FDAC) Evaluation Project'. Final Report.

MacAlister, J. (2022) *The Independent Review of Children's Social Care: Final Report*. HM Government.

Mason, C. and Wilkinson, J. (2021) 'Services for parents who have experienced recurrent care proceedings: where are we now? Findings from mapping of locally developed services in England', Research in Practice.

Masson, J., Pearce, J. and Bader, K. (2008) *Care Profiling Study*. Ministry of Justice Research Series 4/08. Ministry of Justice and Department of Children, Schools and Families.

Mentzou, A. and Mutebi, N. (2023) Problem-solving courts. UK Parliament.

Neo, S.H.F., Norton, S., Kavallari, D. and Canfield, M. (2021) 'Integrated treatment programmes for mothers with substance use problems: a systematic review and meta-analysis of interventions to prevent out-of-home child placements', *Journal of Child and Family Studies*, 30(11): 2877–89.

Papaioannou, K., Kuo, T.-L., Dimova, S., Fugard, A., Sharrock, S., Roberts, E. et al. (2023) *Evaluation of Family Drug and Alcohol Courts*. Foundations.

Shaw, M. (2021) 'A proof-of-concept pilot for an intervention with pregnant mothers who have had children removed by the state: the 'early Family Drug and Alcohol Court model,' *Societies*, 11(1): 8.

Whitehead, S. and Reeder, N. (2016) Better Courts: the financial impact of the London Family Drug and Alcohol Court, Centre for Justice Innovation.

Zhang, S., Huang, H., Wu, Q., Li, Y. and Liu, M. (2019) 'The impacts of family treatment drug court on child welfare core outcomes: a meta-analysis', *Child Abuse & Neglect*, 88: 1–14.

# 6

# Strengthening families through Family Group Conferencing

## Lorna Stabler, Tim Fisher and Kar Man Au

This chapter is a collaborative endeavour drawing on the differing knowledges and experiences – lived, living and learned – of three people with their own perspectives of Family Group Conferencing (FGC).[1]

Kar Man is an experienced practitioner and parent who has taken part as a participant in an FGC and as an advocate for others during their FGC, and who is now a trained FGC co-ordinator. She has extensive experience of working along family members, practitioners and researchers in building an understanding of FGC and its transformative potential.

Tim is Principal Social Worker in East Sussex. He has been a social worker for nearly 20 years. He believes in the FGC model having worked with it since he managed to get a social work student placement on a project that organised FGCs in the community in Cardiff, South Wales. He also managed the FGC work in Camden for 12 years.

Lorna is a researcher who is passionate about the empowerment of children and their families in a social work context, and the potential of FGC to do this. She comes to this work with her own experiences of foster and kinship care, and a personal understanding of the value and need for community for young people and adults alike.

## What is Family Group Conferencing?

In the most straightforward way, an FGC is a structured meeting where extended family members come together to make decisions and plans

---

[1] Generally, 'FGC' is the abbreviation for both the overarching term for the practice of Family Group Conferencing and an individual Family Group Conference. When 'FGCs' are mentioned here, this is referring to more than one Family Group Conference Meeting. Foundations (2025): *Rapid evidence review: Families' Experiences of Family Group Conferences*, available at: https://foundations.org.uk/wp-content/uploads/2025/06/families-experiences-of-family-group-conferences-rapid-evidence-review.pdf

for children and young people in need of support. This collaborative approach empowers families to use their collective wisdom and resources to find solutions, emphasising the strengths of the family unit rather than focusing on deficits. This section explores the history and key components of the model.

## History
### Māori origins of the Family Group Conference

The FGC model has its roots in the Māori community of New Zealand (Love, 2000). It was developed as a response to the disproportionate number of Māori children being placed into care. The Māori community has a rich tradition of collective child-rearing, where the responsibility for children's upbringing is shared among extended family members rather than being confined to a nuclear family model. This approach was not being recognised or respected by the prevailing social work practices, which treated families as isolated units.

The Māori community's anger at the high rates of child removal led to the development of the FGC, drawing on their cultural strengths and practices. The community had a history of coming together in shared conversations to address problems and create plans in a communal setting. This tradition of collective decision-making and problem-solving provided a strong foundation for the FGC model.

---

**Box 6.1: Tim's reflections on Family Group Conferences**

Tim reflects on what is special to him about FGCs: 'As someone who trained to be a social worker and has a background in community organising and campaigning, I was drawn to FGC early in my career. I remember being in a seminar where FGC was presented, and it immediately resonated with me as a paradigm shift in decision-making. The idea of families making decisions during private family time appealed to my sense of progressive, community-based work.

I managed to secure a placement in an FGC project called Family Circle during my social work course. The project had a welcoming environment and actively involved young people and parents in its development. This experience stood in stark contrast to my previous placement in adult services, where I often had to deliver bad news about care eligibility. FGC, by contrast, was about empowering families at crucial times, making decisions collaboratively and widening the circle to include the community.

This method felt more aligned with my values, as it involved working with families rather than imposing solutions on them. The FGC approach of collaboration, community involvement and shared decision-making continues to inspire my practice, demonstrating a different, more inclusive way to address child protection and family support.'

## Introduction and development in the UK

FGC was introduced to the UK by social workers from North America who had studied the practice in New Zealand (Nixon et al, 2005). They recognised its potential to address similar issues within the UK context, where many communities were also experiencing challenges related to child welfare and social work interventions.

The first FGC in the UK took place in Wales (Marsh and Crow, 1998). Since then, the model has spread across various regions, becoming an important part of the child welfare system. The drivers for adopting FGCs in the UK included the need to empower families, share decision-making power and position professionals differently within the intervention process.

## Legislative framework in the UK

The Children Act 1989 and other legislative frameworks in the UK provided a conducive environment for the adoption of FGCs. These laws emphasised the importance of involving families in decision-making processes and ensuring that interventions were supportive rather than punitive. The experience of communities in the UK, where people often felt disempowered by traditional social work practices, highlighted the need for an approach that respected and harnessed family strengths (Morris and Connolly, 2012).

FGC's potential to empower families, share power and position professionals as facilitators rather than directors of the process made it an appealing model for the UK. The approach aligned with the legislative emphasis on family involvement and the broader goals of the child welfare system.

Through FGCs, families in the UK have been able to come together, share their collective wisdom and create plans that support the well-being of their children. The model continues to play a crucial role in strengthening families and ensuring that children receive the support they need within their communities.

The emphasis on family-led decision-making, transparency and inclusion reflects Māori cultural values, which hold the family as the central unit of support. The evolution of FGC into different cultural contexts, including the UK, shows its adaptability to various family dynamics while maintaining the same focus on collaboration and empowerment.

## The Family Group Conference process

The FGC process consists of several stages:

1. *The offer:* the process begins with a conversation between practitioners and families about why an FGC might be helpful. This stage involves exploring how the FGC would look for them and getting families to the point of wanting to say 'Yes'.
2. *Preparation:* leading up to the FGC, everyone involved thinks about their responsibilities, what they want to bring to the plan and how they want to respond to the professionals' concerns.
3. *Information sharing:* on the day of the FGC, professionals share their concerns and the family responds, asking for clarifications as needed.
4. *Private family time:* this is the pivotal stage where the family has the opportunity to discuss and create its own plan without professionals in the room. This paradigm shift allows the family to take control of the decision-making process.
5. *Agreeing the plan:* professionals rejoin the meeting to agree on the family's plan. The principle here is that the professionals share their concerns clearly enough for the family to understand them, and the family's plan is agreed upon without major changes.
6. *Review and monitoring:* after the meeting, it is crucial to keep the plan alive. This involves ongoing review and adaptation to reflect changing needs and risks within the family. It ensures that the plan remains relevant and effective, even if circumstances change.

## What does a Family Group Conference look and feel like?

An FGC can be a transformative experience for families facing difficult situations. It can provide a refreshing alternative to being directed by authorities, allowing families to explore solutions that work for them.

### *Atmosphere and setting*

An FGC typically involves the extended family and other key supporters of the child or young person. These meetings are often held in a comfortable location, such as a community centre or family home. This is different from where social work meetings are usually held – often within large buildings that are not a place that families would enter in their day-to-day lives (Bernheim et al, 2025).

The atmosphere is welcoming and supportive, with food provided to create a relaxed environment. This setting helps put families at ease and encourages open, honest communication. At its heart, an FGC should resonate with (and

**Figure 6.1:** Painting by Family Group Conferencing researcher and artist Alankrita S reflecting on the special environment of a Family Group Conference

reflect) a family's cultural life – a way that they would want to be together to discuss their hopes, dreams, fears and plans.

An often overlooked but crucial aspect of FGCs is the role that food and environment play in the process. The choice of venue – whether it is the family home or a community space – and the inclusion of food are essential elements that contribute to the atmosphere of the FGC. Offering food during the meeting not only creates a relaxed and welcoming environment but also promotes bonding and facilitates open communication. Sharing a meal together is a universal human practice and, in the context of an FGC, it serves as a symbolic gesture of unity and cooperation (Dunbar, 2017). This small but significant detail helps set the tone for the meeting, encouraging participants to feel more comfortable and open to sharing their perspectives (see Figure 6.1).

## What is important about Family Group Conferencing?

FGC stands out from other collaborative ways of working between families and professionals because of its core principles and the profound impact it can have on everyone involved in the process. It embodies empowerment, shared decision-making, and recognising the strengths and knowledge within families.

For many families, an FGC feels empowering. It allows them to take control of their situation, using their knowledge of family dynamics and networks to create a plan that fits their unique circumstances. Instead of being told what to do by someone who does not fully understand their lives, families have a chance to say what is right for them and to receive support tailored to their needs.

> **Box 6.2: Kar Man's reflections on Family Group Conferences**
>
> As Kar Man highlights: 'Trust is a cornerstone of the FGC process. Being offered an FGC in a difficult situation can feel like a second chance, an opportunity to demonstrate your capacity to solve problems with the support of your network. It boosts confidence and helps overcome the shame associated with needing help.
>
> The FGC process is transparent, putting all concerns and worries on the table and focusing on the issue at hand rather than individual egos. This transparency helps overcome shame and encourages seeking help, revealing that there is a supportive network willing to assist. It's a transformative process for both individuals and their relationships with others. One family described the FGC process as a 'breath of fresh air'. It gave them the opportunity to take the lead, see the bigger picture, and find solutions knowing they had support. This approach not only addressed their immediate crisis but also helped them grow and develop new skills, turning a difficult situation into a transformative learning experience.
>
> For professionals, FGC is also a learning experience. Every family is different, and professionals can enrich their knowledge and practice through these diverse interactions. The impact of FGC extends beyond resolving immediate issues; it fosters a method of collaboration and problem-solving that can be applied to various aspects of life.
>
> FGC is not just a tool to address immediate concerns but a long-term transformative process for families and professionals alike, promoting continuous learning, collaboration, and community involvement.'

## *Empowerment and shared power*

Traditionally, families involved with social services often feel they have no agency. They are seen as needing intervention because they have problems. However, FGCs help families rediscover their agency and confidence. By participating in the FGC process, families can realise that they have the power to shape their own lives and find solutions that work for them. This empowerment is a key aspect of the FGC, transforming it into a powerful tool for positive change.

At the heart of the FGC is the principle of empowerment. It enables families to take control of their situations, make informed decisions, and create plans tailored to their unique circumstances. Unlike traditional approaches whereby decisions are often imposed by authorities, the FGC shares power between families and practitioners. This collaboration respects the family's expertise in their own lives and encourages professionals to value the family's input.

## Recognising families' strengths and knowledge

The FGC shifts the focus from viewing families solely as sources of risk to recognising them as sources of safety and support. It draws on the family's inherent strengths and knowledge, building on their capacity to find solutions that work best for them. This approach respects the family's insights and acknowledges their critical role in the well-being of their children.

## Creating a framework for involvement

The FGC provides a structured framework for involving families in decision-making processes. While everyone agrees that families should be central to these decisions, traditional professional processes often overshadow this ideal. The FGC ensures that families are genuinely involved, creating a level playing field for participation and collaboration. It is not just about putting people in a room: it is about giving them the right information, building their confidence and overcoming barriers to effective participation.

## Trust and relationship building

Trust is a crucial component of the FGC. The process begins with professionals offering families an FGC, which inherently involves trust in the family's ability to resolve their issues. This trust extends to gaining the family's trust in the FGC process. It is about creating 'good enough' trust, whereby both families and professionals believe in each other's commitment to the child's best interests. This mutual trust allows for more effective and empathetic collaboration.

## Changing perspectives

The FGC provides an opportunity for all parties to see each other in a different light. Families come prepared, having heard and understood the information beforehand, which reduces emotional overwhelm and defensiveness. Similarly, professionals can focus on the family's strengths rather than being confined to their reports and legal obligations. This new perspective fosters a more productive relationship and collaboration.

## A tool for relationship repair

---

**Box 6.3: A Family Group Conference as a tool for relationship repair**

As Kar Man explains: '[An] FGC is not just a pragmatic tool; it is a relational act that helps build and repair trust and understanding. The restorative nature of FGCs allows families to not only address the issues at hand but also repair relationships and foster healing. FGCs allow families to have open, honest conversations about their challenges, which leads to greater understanding and ultimately to more sustainable solutions. This process of collective problem-solving and shared responsibility is a hallmark of the restorative nature of FGC.

In summary, FGC embodies a strengths-based, culturally sensitive, and restorative approach to family support and decision-making. By empowering families to take control of their own lives, FGCs foster trust, collaboration, and lasting change.'

---

An FGC can also serve as a vehicle to break through barriers and repair relationships between families and social services. It restores a sense of collaboration that should inherently exist, allowing for genuine, productive partnerships. FGCs provide a platform for families to collectively acknowledge the impact of past events, explore the underlying issues and work together to create a plan for moving forward. This restorative approach is future-oriented, focusing on healing and creating positive outcomes rather than assigning blame.

The restorative elements in FGCs are essential for fostering a sense of unity within the family. By addressing harm in a supportive and non-adversarial environment, families can repair their relationships and move towards reconciliation. The model's flexibility and adaptability ensure that it can meet the unique needs of each family, creating a space where families can grow, learn and ultimately thrive together.

## Restoring natural instincts

FGCs work with the natural instincts of family and community, offering a genuine collaboration opportunity for families to plan and protect a child's life. Professionals should be prepared for the FGC to yield results they might not anticipate, embracing the process as a genuine offer of collaboration rather than merely setting a test for the family.

In essence, the importance of an FGC lies in its ability to empower families, foster trust and create a collaborative environment where all voices are heard and respected. It is a transformative tool that aligns professional support with the family's natural capacity to care for their children, thereby resulting in more effective and sustainable solutions.

## The practicalities of delivering Family Group Conferences in the UK

Delivering FGCs in the UK involves various practical considerations, including the recruitment and training of co-ordinators, the structure of services and the perceived independence of these services from social care. There follows an overview of these key aspects.

### Family Group Conference co-ordinators

The role of the co-ordinator is crucial in maintaining the integrity of the process. Co-ordinators must be skilled in facilitating group dynamics, ensuring that all voices are heard and respected, while also allowing the family the autonomy to drive the conversation. The flexibility of the FGC as a model means that each conference is unique, adapting to the specific needs and cultural contexts of the family. This adaptability is one of the FGC's greatest strengths because it ensures that families feel empowered and supported within their own cultural framework.

---

**Box 6.4: The importance of community connections**

Tim's perspective on the importance of community connections of FGC co-ordinators: 'In London, Family Group Conference co-ordinators are mostly freelance, forming a large practice community of professionals who speak different languages and come from diverse cultural backgrounds. This gives London a unique environment for Family Group Conferences, resembling the approach seen in the Netherlands. This diversity within the co-ordinator community can unlock new possibilities and unlocks the cultural intelligence embedded n the heart of the model. This connection with the community brings an added layer of authenticity and relevance to the process.'

---

FGC co-ordinators come from diverse backgrounds. While some are social workers, many are not. They may come from the communities they serve or from other disciplines that involve family support and decision-making. Their varied backgrounds bring a range of skills to the FGC process, which is crucial for its success. Matching co-ordinators with families is also crucial.

The right match can significantly enhance the FGC's effectiveness, ensuring a smooth process and successful outcomes. Co-ordinators act as facilitators, helping families to plan their meetings and ensuring that everyone's voice is heard without bias or judgement.

A key aspect of the FGC is the independence of the co-ordinators. However, whether families perceive them as independent or not can be challenging. In the UK, FGCs operate in two main ways. One model involves external services provided by charities commissioned by local authorities. The other model has FGC teams employed directly by local authorities but operating independently of statutory services. Both models have their pros and cons. External services might be perceived as more independent but could lack a deep understanding of social services. In-house services might build better relationships with social workers but could be seen as less independent by families.

In some local authorities, a hybrid model is used. Freelance FGC co-ordinators are commissioned directly by local authorities, offering a balance of independence and integration. This model allows for matching co-ordinators with families based on culture, language and skills, thereby enhancing the effectiveness of the FGC process.

### Training and development

Training and development of FGC co-ordinators are crucial. Co-ordinators are trained to facilitate rather than assess, emphasising their role in helping families create their own plans. In London, efforts have been made to include co-ordinators who have personal experience with FGCs or have aged out of care themselves. This lived experience adds significant value to the process.

Training for FGC co-ordinators typically involves a three-day course provided by national organisations such as the Family Rights Group and Daybreak. Additional training options include a learning pathway in London and a postgraduate certificate offered by the Family Rights Group. An accreditation programme for FGCs also exists, although it was initially funded by the central government.

### Network and peer learning

A significant factor in the development of FGCs in the UK has been the network approach. National and regional networks of practitioners and managers facilitate peer learning and the exchange of best practices. This dynamic model mirrors the values of the FGC, promoting continuous improvement and support among those involved in the process. When these networks are active, they significantly enhance the practice of the

FGCs. However, when they dwindle, it can have a negative impact on the development and effectiveness of FGC services.

## Private family time and collective problem solving

The FGC model embodies the principles of reciprocity and collective problem-solving that resonate with the values of community. At its core, FGCs highlight how families, friends and broader community networks can come together to support each other in difficult times, demonstrating that solutions are not solely within the domain of professionals but are generated through the collective efforts of those directly involved. FGCs foster trust, transparency and empowerment – key elements in creating a thriving, interconnected community.

---

**Box 6.5: Kar Man's reflections on private family time**

As Kar Man explains: 'Private family time is the 'heartbeat' of the FGC process. It creates a safe, inclusive space where family members can speak without fear of judgment. Without external influence, family members can engage in meaningful conversations that transcend blame and past conflicts, focusing instead on the future and solutions. This setting nurtures trust, strengthens family bonds, and fosters a sense of ownership over the decisions made. It is here that families experience empowerment, as they are not passive recipients of professional solutions but active participants in shaping their own destinies.'

---

The practice of FGC provides an intentional space for families to take control of their lives by formulating their own solutions. The concept of 'private family time' is critical in this regard. During this phase, families are given the space to discuss their concerns openly and without the presence of professionals, which allows trust to flourish and authentic conversations to emerge. This time is where the real work of the FGC takes place, because family members use this moment to explore solutions and demonstrate their capacity to address issues together.

This dynamic shifts the power balance in a transformative way, as noted by Merkel-Holguin (2004), who describes FGC as a democratic experiment. By empowering families to take ownership of their decisions, FGCs challenge the traditional top-down model of decision-making, thereby creating a more collaborative and inclusive environment where solutions are family-generated and sustainable.

The role of the co-ordinator is critical in ensuring that private family time remains productive. It is important that co-ordinators adopt a flexible approach, recognising that each family brings its own unique dynamics and cultural values to the table. A successful FGC co-ordinator understands the need to carry some of the risk involved in the process, because the outcomes are never guaranteed. Yet, by maintaining an unwavering belief in the process, co-ordinators can inspire confidence within families, encouraging them to engage fully in the process and take charge of their future.

### The Family Group Conference as a model for expanding circles of support

The inclusive nature of the FGC brings in the wider relational network of the family, tapping into previously overlooked strengths and resources. It is essential that all relevant members of the family and community are invited into this process, allowing for broader participation and richer contributions to the discussion. A family is not simply the nuclear unit but a web of relationships that, when engaged collectively, can find solutions to complex issues. FGCs also emphasise the importance of emotional support within these networks.

Emotional statements and supportive aims, as part of the FGC plan, are vital elements. They not only ensure that practical solutions are in place but also strengthen relational bonds, which are necessary for long-term success. As Tim Fisher notes, these emotional connections and personal commitments from family members foster trust and accountability, ultimately leading to more effective and sustained outcomes.

### Professional growth through the Family Group Conference

For professionals, the FGC offers a reciprocal learning experience. Social workers and co-ordinators are challenged to relinquish some of the control they traditionally hold and to trust the family to lead the process. This creates a partnership rather than a directive relationship, thereby allowing professionals to learn from the insights and approaches that families contribute. Burns and Früchtel (2014) describe the FGC as a bridge between the 'life world' of families and the 'system world' of professionals, highlighting how the FGC connects formal services to the lived experiences of those they serve.

The impact of the FGC extends beyond just the immediate family members. FGCs are not just beneficial to the individuals directly involved but to the broader professional network as well. Professionals gain insight into the strengths and resourcefulness of families, shifting their perspectives from viewing families as recipients of services to partners in the decision-making process. The process creates a space for shared learning and mutual respect, whereby professionals are invited into the family's life-world, gaining a deeper understanding of their challenges, capacities and resilience.

> **Box 6.6: Challenges for research focusing on Family Group Conferencing**
>
> Lorna's grapples with some of the challenges for research focusing on FGC:
>
> 'One of the fascinating yet complex aspects of Family Group Conferencing is how it is described and understood by different people. Some view FGC as a process, encompassing various stages that families and practitioners go through to reach an outcome. Others see it as an intervention, a specific method to address problems like safeguarding concerns by bringing people together to formulate a plan. Another perspective is that FGC is a right, ensuring families are involved in decision-making about their lives.
>
> From a research standpoint, evaluating FGC as an intervention is more straightforward because it is relatively static, making it easier to measure outcomes and understand costs and benefits. When viewed as a process, research becomes more challenging due to the variability in stages and the continuous nature of the process. Understanding when the process begins and ends can be ambiguous, especially since the impact of the family plan can extend far beyond the immediate concern.
>
> Considering FGC as a family right introduces different research challenges. One major controversy in the UK is whether FGC should be subjected to randomized control trials (RCTs). RCTs can show the effectiveness of interventions but involve some families not receiving FGC, which raises ethical concerns. This debate is crucial because while practice wisdom suggests FGC's effectiveness, it may not be work in the same way for everyone.'

In summary, the FGC is not just a tool to address immediate concerns but a long-term transformative process for families and professionals alike, promoting continuous learning, collaboration and community involvement.

## What does the evidence say about Family Group Conferencing?

'Evidence' can have different meanings to different people. Within research, evidence can relate to proving or disproving a hypothesis using evaluative research methods. This can lead to categories regarding the quality of evidence. In this section, we explore what people think about how FGCs work and then some of the research evidence. We feel a focus on evidence is helpful in some regards – it can help us to understand how FGC might work in relation to some set outcomes that are a necessary consideration – but not in others as the hierarchical nature of evidence privileges certain types of knowledge over others. Therefore, in this section, we refer to evidence in a broad sense and try to give voice to different types of knowledge.

## How is Family Group Conferencing used in the UK?

One study of FGC in the UK – Family VOICE[2] – carried out a comprehensive survey of UK local authorities (Wood et al, 2022). The survey had strong participation rates, especially from Wales (86 per cent), Northern Ireland (80 per cent) and England (69 per cent), with 160 local authorities taking part in total. The survey indicated a significant increase in FGC use since 2016.

While most FGC services are funded and delivered by local authorities, there are notable regional variations. For instance, England tends to have more in-house services while Wales relies more on purchased agency services. Scotland, on the other hand, often contracts out FGC services. Interestingly, non-profit organisations play a more significant role in Wales, Scotland and Northern Ireland than in England, highlighting the collaborative nature of FGC implementation. FGC co-ordinators are typically independent (94 per cent) and often trained (50 per cent +) by the Family Rights Group.

The scale of FGC delivery varies widely, with annual conferences ranging from 5 to 800 per local authority. Interestingly, Wales has the highest rate of FGCs per child population despite having the lowest total number. FGCs are typically offered during pre-care proceedings (96 per cent) or when creating child protection plans (96 per cent). They are also commonly used for reunification plans (84 per cent) and early help (71 per cent). Most local authorities use FGCs for cases involving child abuse or neglect (98 per cent), and domestic abuse (96 per cent). Children are always (51 per cent) or sometimes (48 per cent) invited to FGCs and are usually offered an advocate. Almost all families (99 per cent) are given private family time during the process.

The theoretical approaches underpinning FGC practice include restorative practice (n = 14), signs of safety (n = 9), systemic practice (n = 9), and strength-based approaches (n = 9). Most FGC services (92 per cent) collect data on family satisfaction and offer follow-up reviews (94 per cent). However, only a third have formally evaluated their services.

During the COVID-19 pandemic, FGC services demonstrated adaptability by moving online or using hybrid models (76 per cent). While this transition was initially challenging, most services successfully adjusted to the new format. The most important feature of private family time was ensured, even during virtual meetings, highlighting the respect for family privacy and the adaptability of FGC services.

The survey indicates that FGC use is expanding and becoming more widespread across the UK, with services evolving to meet changing needs and circumstances.

---

[2] Available from https://orca.cardiff.ac.uk/id/eprint/171051

## What do people seek from Family Group Conferences?

FGCs are designed with the well-being of the central person or family in mind. The desired outcomes that participants aim to achieve through FGCs include:

### Well-being and support

At the heart of every FGC is the goal of enhancing the well-being of the central person. Everyone involved hopes that the process will lead to the individual receiving the right support, thereby ensuring that their physical, emotional and social needs are met. The family members involved are usually committed to seeing positive changes in the lives of their loved ones.

### Creating a tailored plan

Another critical outcome is developing a plan tailored to achieve the goals identified during the conference. This process involves identifying the central person's needs and circumstances, discussing potential solutions and agreeing on a plan of action. The plan should be actionable, realistic and aligned with the needs and circumstances of the central person. The collaborative nature of FGCs helps craft a plan that reflects everyone's shared intentions and resources.

### Empowerment and participation

FGCs are a platform for empowerment. They empower the individual at the centre, their family members and other participants. The process fosters participation and boosts confidence, encouraging individuals to voice their concerns, contribute ideas and make decisions. Moreover, families often learn new skills through this engagement, which can be helpful beyond the conference itself.

### Building a support network and strengthening relationships

The long-term outcome sought in FGCs is establishing or reinforcing a solid support network. The process aims to strengthen relationships that provide ongoing support by bringing together family members, friends and professionals. The network becomes a safety net for the central person when facing challenges and maintaining their well-being over time.

## What do families say about their experience?

FGCs are not necessarily easy for families. In the same early study (Marsh and Crow, 1998) described earlier, it was reported that families found the meetings emotional and stressful, but that the majority would choose to deal with future issues in the same way.

Families are the experts in their family network. They know their cultural background. When participating in an FGC, they often have a wealth of insights to share about their experiences. These reflections highlight both the strengths and challenges of the process:

*The need to be informed*

Families emphasise the importance of being fully informed about the purpose of the FGC before they accept the offer. Understanding what to expect and the potential benefits allows them to make a more confident participation decision. Without this clarity, families may feel uncertain or reluctant to engage in the process.

*The role of the co-ordinator*

The role of a passionate and skilled FGC co-ordinator is often cited as crucial to the conference's success. Families agreed that a skilful and passionate co-ordinator can make the process feel more accessible, ensuring that everyone's voice is heard and that the plan developed is truly reflective of the family's needs and strengths.

*The vulnerability of participation*

Participating in an FGC can be a vulnerable experience for families. Sharing personal stories and concerns in a group setting can be intimidating, especially when discussing sensitive issues. However, it is essential to understand that this vulnerability is a necessary part of the process. It can lead to deeper connections, a more substantial commitment to the agreed-upon plan and a sense of empowerment from having your voice heard and your concerns addressed.

*Having a voice*

Families felt that one of the most significant aspects of the FGC experience was the opportunity to have a voice. The process allows them to express their concerns and ideas, and to demonstrate their capacity to support the central person. This empowerment ensures that the family feels valued in the plan's success.

*Feeling respected and valued*

Families often felt their confidence increased when they felt respected, valued and trusted during the FGC process. This sense of respect often comes from being listened to and having their contributions taken seriously, which can significantly affect how they perceive the experience.

## Hope

One of the most critical aspects of the FGC experience for families is the sense of hope that it brings. Hope gives families another option in their situation – a chance to find a way forward that suits them better than being told what to do by force. The collaborative nature of FGCs allows families to explore solutions they believe in, thereby providing a sense of agency and possibility even under challenging circumstances.

## Change in relationships

Another positive outcome that families often mention is the positive change in their relationships – with their support network and the professionals involved. The FGC process can facilitate open communication and mutual understanding, which helps to mend strained relationships and build new ones based on trust and cooperation.

## The transformational nature of Family Group Conferences

Some families said that the FGC process is transformational and can lead to meaningful and lasting change when done properly. The key lies in how the process is handled: if everyone approaches it with genuine intent and care, the outcomes can be profound and enduring. FGCs, when carried out effectively, can do more than address immediate concerns: they can transform relationships, perspectives and lives.

## The effectiveness question

**Box 6.7: Lorna's reflections on evidence**

Lorna emphasises:

'Evidence comes in different guises and different types of evidence are needed for different purposes. For me, some of the stories I have heard from families who have had Family Group Conferences have had the most impact on my thinking about how FGC can improve outcomes. However, the Randomised Control Trial carried out by Coram and Foundations which reported that when families had an FGC in pre-proceedings, their children were less likely to enter care, has had a huge impact for FGC services who could use this evidence to argue for more resources. This kind of evidence, which can also show potential of FGCs to divert costs from child removal to preventative services, is also so important. When researching FGC, we need to ensure that the evidence that is produced serves these different purposes.'

FGC has much in common with other approaches that have been introduced in many different contexts globally, such as Family Team Decision Making, Family Involvement Meetings and case planning (Thørnblad et al, 2016). Because of this, the international evidence base for FGCs is difficult to summarise. A systematic review published in 2020 (Nurmatov et al) focused on all types of shared decision-making meetings internationally. The findings of this review indicated mixed results and evidence that was not classed as methodologically rigorous to answer questions about effectiveness.

However, there has been a move to carry out bigger-scale evaluations of FGCs in the UK. The largest study – a randomised control trial in England (Taylor et al, 2024) – focused on the use of FGC when families were in pre-proceedings (ahead of court proceedings to remove children from their parents). The study reported positive results, including that FGCs were cost-effective, with children in referred families significantly less likely to go into care. Twelve months after the pre-proceedings letter, children whose families were referred for an FGC were 8.6 percentage points less likely to go into care. Moreover, among children in families referred for FGCs, 36.2 per cent were in care; among children in families not referred for FGCs, 44.8 per cent were in care.

**Box 6.8: Reflections on the role of practitioners**

Tim acknowledges the important role of practitioners in creating, sharing and using evidence:

'Practitioners and managers within FGC services are alert to research and evidence, which tends to percolate through the network. Coordinators, managers, researchers, and others connected to FGC form a well-networked community that actively practices the values they promote, maintaining strong connections where ideas and insights about FGC ripple through effectively.

There is also significant focus on cost savings and the cost-benefit of conducting an FGC – this remains a consistent theme in practice networks and the FGC community. This is important but I think it is good when other messages about the benefits also are part of the Conversations. A recent example is the work by Lorna and Bekkah Bernheim, which explores the role of place and the importance of the setting where an FGC is held. Such insights hold value not only for those directly involved in FGCs but also influence social workers who practice within these frameworks. Over time, the weight of evidence supporting the effectiveness of FGCs may positively impact how local authorities and other organisations perceive and prioritise FGC, subsequently affecting individual practitioners.

Furthermore, FGC advocates within local authorities can use key research findings to promote FGC, sharing impactful messages and research highlights directly with social workers who may be making referrals for FGCs.'

---

Currently, this is the only evaluation of its kind in the UK. The results indicate that FGCs can have an impact on outcomes that are important to local authorities. It does not, however, tell us much about the other outcomes, such as empowerment, involvement and improved relationships, that some people associate with FGCs.

### Do practitioners think Family Group Conferencing works?

Social workers have been reported to have an overwhelmingly positive attitude to FGC (Sundell et al, 2008). Arguably, one of the reasons that the FGC has become so well used in the UK is that it 'makes sense' to practitioners. To put families at the heart of decisions and making plans about their own lives fits with the value base of social work (Parkinson, 2018).

From the very first pilots of FGCs in the UK, professionals have recognised their many benefits. For example, Marsh and Crow (1998) carried out an evaluation of the early implementation of FGCs. Eighty conferences, involving 99 children from 69 families, were part of the study. Data was collected from social workers and co-ordinators one year after the FGC took place. In 74 of the conferences, participants were able to reach full agreement with most plans combining elements of family help and some agency support services. Professionals reported that they were generally very impressed by the family plans for their creativity. Moreover, 67 per cent of social workers thought that plans were likely to result in better protection for the child than they would otherwise have. Half of the social workers participating stated that they had improved their relationships with families.

This positive regard for FGCs from the perspective of practitioners who might work with families who access FGCs is likely one of the key reasons for its increasing use throughout the UK.

## Next steps for Family Group Conferencing in the UK

As we have discussed, FGC is becoming increasingly widespread in the UK. In this section, we will discuss some of the recent developments that we are most excited about.

Lorna: Family Group Conferencing replacing professional-led decision-making

'I see the potential of Family Group Conferencing within children's social care to transform or replace some of the professional, risk led processes for decision making that have proliferated over the last few decades in the UK. There is increasing recognition that we need to be looking to families for the answers – if children need support and care, it is children themselves and the people who love them who know what is best. However, Family Group Conferencing in the UK has continued to be an add on to professional processes which exclude and shame families. I've had the pleasure of leading a project that explored the potential of Family Group Conferencing to replace the much maligned (by practitioners and families alike) child protection conference. Although there are huge barriers in practice and policy to making these changes in a sustainable way, whether they are successfully introduced, they have the potential to truly shift power to families and communities.

However, it is important that a move to empowering families is not a way to just place a burden on overstretched family networks without the accompanying re-allocation of budgets to support community development and family support.'

Tim: Community ownership and self-referrals

'I have been inspired by our discussions with colleagues from the Family Group Conference network in the Netherlands, particularly from Eigen Kracht Centrale, where the approach is deeply rooted in the community. The FGC facilitators in their model are residents of the community, which is a significant aspect of their approach. In London, Family Group Conference co-ordinators are mostly freelance, forming a large practice community of professionals who speak different languages and come from diverse cultural backgrounds. This gives London a unique environment for Family Group Conferences, resembling the approach seen in the Netherlands. This diversity within the co-ordinator community can unlock new possibilities and unlocks the cultural intelligence embedded in the heart of the model. This connection with the community brings an added layer of authenticity and relevance to the process.

We've had some loopbacks and ripples from the Family Group Conference work that have been nice, and I think opening up to self-referrals for people to claim a Family Group Conference for themselves on their own initiative has allowed for some of that. Two examples stand out. One member of the Family Advisory Board in Camden had a Family Group Conference about her child when the child was little, and social workers were worried about her ability to care for the child. She had a really great Family Group Conference and became involved with the parent group and many of our subsequent initiatives. Ten years later, she utilised Family Group Conference again for an issue her child had in school, and it had a positive result. Similarly, another member had a Family Group Conference for her child when she was struggling with leukaemia, and later used it to plan for her grandmother's care. These examples show how the future potential of Family Group Conferences can perhaps be best harnessed by citizens.'

**Kar Man:** Family Group Conferencing in adult social care

'Working on research on Family Group Conferences (FGCs) across child and adult services, I've observed differences in how these meetings are applied in each context. Although empowerment, family involvement, and a strength-based approach are at the core of both, the legal context, network composition, and focus often vary significantly between children's and adult services.

Adult services have only recently started using FGCs. The Care Act 2014 places a duty on local authorities to safeguard adults at risk of abuse and neglect, promoting their independence and well-being through coordinated support from multiple agencies. Within this framework, adult FGCs focus on the person's right to self-determination, helping them to shape their own care plans with dignity.

Children's services operate under a different legal framework, mainly the Children Act 1989 and the Children Act 2004. These acts allow local authorities to intervene and even remove children from their homes if needed to ensure their safety and well-being. Both the Care Act and the Children Acts aim to provide multi-agency work to protect the person at the centre of the process. However, the main difference is that adults aren't at risk of being removed from their families, even in cases where safeguarding concerns exist.

From my observations, families in children's services often prefer to devise their plans without relying heavily on additional services. There's a sense that seeking help could be seen as a reflection of their ability to keep their children safe, and families may hope that demonstrating their capability will reduce social services involvement. This process can help families realise their agency and resilience, a significant and unique form of empowerment. In adult services, however, families tend to welcome support and stay connected with services since that support helps the centre person access the care they need.

The networks involved in adult FGCs are also a bit different. They often include not only family members but also friends, neighbours, and even professionals who are involved in the individual's life. This reflects the adult's broader social connections beyond just their immediate family. Plus, service support in adult FGCs is comprehensive and longer-term, providing a deep level of care compared to children's FGCs.

Children's FGCs are primarily focused on ensuring the safety of the child at home with family support, which is a unique and crucial aspect. This contrasts with adult FGCs, which give the person at the centre a chance to shape their care plans with input from a diverse network, focusing on their independence and quality of life while still meeting their care needs.

In adult FGCs, I've noticed that sometimes the co-ordinator is asked to stay during private family time to keep things on track, but they don't participate in the actual discussions or decisions. There are also cases where the FGC aims to support the whole network, not just the central person, recognising that those who provide care often need some support themselves.

In both children's and adult services, FGCs aim to empower the individual and their support networks, but each service's approach reflects the unique legal context, network composition, and primary focus. With adult services, the emphasis on self-determination and broad support networks – including friends and professionals – shapes a different but equally meaningful way of using FGCs. This model really shows potential for tackling a range of social issues in human services, offering a flexible, family-centred approach to support.'

## Final words

All three authors bring very different experiences and perspectives on FGCs. However, they have a shared commitment to shifting power into the hands of families and communities, and see the potential of the FGC to do this in the UK. No approach is a silver bullet; no single way will work for all families and all issues. The UK context presents many challenges to the FGC reaching its potential for families and communities. But we are heartened and excited about the developments in practice and research in this area, and look forward to the next decade of FGC.

## References

Bernheim, B., Fisher, T., Marquez, L. and Stabler, L. (2025) 'The power and potential of space and place in family group conferencing: reimagining the role of the venue in child protection practice', *Qualitative Social Work*, 24(4): 355–72.

Dunbar, R.I.M. (2017) 'Breaking bread: the functions of social eating', *Adaptive Human Behavior and Physiology*, 3: 198–211.

Love, C. (2000) 'Family group conferencing: Cultural origins, sharing, and appropriation – a Maori reflection', in G. Burford and J. Hudson (eds) *Family Group Conferencing: New Directions in Community-Centered Child and Family Practice*, Aldine de Gruyter, pp 15–30.

Marsh, P. and Crow, G. (1998) *Family Group Conferences in Child Welfare*, Blackwell Science.

Morris, K. and Connolly, M. (2012) 'Family decision making in child welfare: challenges, opportunities, and outcomes', *Child & Family Social Work*, 17(1): 1–9.

Nixon, P., Burford, G., Quinn, A. and Edelbaum, J. (2005) *A Survey of International Practices Policy & Research on Family Group Conferencing and Related Practices*, American Humane Association & FGDM Project.

Nurmatov, U., Foster, C., Bezeczky, Z., Owen, J., El-Banna, A., Mann, M. et al (2020) *Impact of Shared Decision-Making Family Meetings on Children's Out-Of-Home Care, Family Empowerment and Satisfaction: A Systematic Review*. What Works Centre for Children's Social Care (Project Report). Available from: https://orca.cardiff.ac.uk/id/eprint/132949

Parkinson, K. (2018) 'The theoretical context for FGCs', in *Family Group Conferences in Social Work*, Policy Press, pp 15–34.

Sundell, K., Vinnerljung, B. and Ryburn, M. (2008) 'Social workers' attitudes towards family group conferences in Sweden and the UK', *Child & Family Social Work*, 6(4): 327–36.

Taylor, S., Blackshaw, E., Dorsett, R., Lawrence, H., Stern, D., Gilbert, L. et al (2024) 'Impact of family group conference referrals at pre-proceedings stage on child outcomes: a randomised controlled trial', *The British Journal of Social Work*, 54(6): 2358–77.

Thørnblad, R., Strandbu, A., Holtan, A. and Jenssen, T. (2016) 'Family group conferences: from Maori culture to decision-making model in work with late modern families in Norway', *European Journal of Social Work*, 19(6): 992–1003.

Wood, S., Scourfield, J., Au, K., Evans, R., Jones-Williams, D., Lugg-Widger, F. et al (2022) *A UK Wide Survey of Family Group Conference Provision* (Project report). CASCADE. Available from: https://orca.cardiff.ac.uk/id/eprint/171051

# 7

# Parent activism in child welfare in high-income countries

*David Tobis and Fae Rowley*

## Introduction

Parents with lived child welfare experience, grandparents and other kin are playing decisive roles in reforming child welfare systems in several high-income countries. These parents and family members, experts by experience, are trained and work as parent advocates providing peer-to-peer support to other parents. Some are also activists for policy, programme and system change.

In this chapter, peer-to-peer advocacy is referred to as 'parent advocacy'. Parents working to change child welfare policies, programmes or systems beyond helping an individual, is referred to as 'parent activism'. Many parents are involved in both advocacy and activism, and sometimes the boundaries between advocacy and activism overlap. Peer-to-peer advocacy informs and helps build a base for activism.

Research has documented the efficacy of peer-to-peer advocacy in child welfare (Slettebo, 2013; Tobis et al, 2020; Diaz et al, 2021; Devine et al, 2023; Fitt et al, 2023; Cocks et al, 2024). Much less attention, research and funding have focused on child welfare parent activists working to reform child welfare policies and systems. Although some academic literature (Tobis, 2019; Castellano, 2021; Saar-Heiman et al, 2024) and grey literature (*Rise Magazine*, 2016; Monkman, 2019; CBC News, 2001; McGowan, 2022; Swan, 2024) describe the participation of parents with lived child welfare experience at a policy level, little research has documented the impact of parent activism on policy and system reform.

This chapter begins to fill that gap. It is based on a scoping review that looks at the emerging range of activities and research by and about parents who have worked to change child welfare policies and systems in eight high-income countries where parent advocacy and parent activism have taken root: Australia, Canada, England, Finland, Norway, Scotland, the United States and Wales. Although parent advocacy and activism in child welfare is also beginning to emerge in other high-income countries, they have not been reviewed for this chapter.

This chapter focuses on the origins, growth and spread of parent activism through high-income countries. It only focuses on peer-to-peer parent advocacy to the extent that that work laid the foundation for parent activism. This chapter identifies 11 domains in which parents with lived child welfare experience are involved in activism for policy and system reform with a few illustrative examples. A longer description of parent activism in these countries is available online (Tobis, 2024a).

The conclusions are based on a scoping review including a review of academic and grey literature, interviews with parents and their allies, and site visits. The methodology is available online (Tobis, 2024b). The information should be seen as illustrative and anecdotal as a comprehensive assessment of parent activism in each country was beyond the scope of this review. More parent advocacy and activism are occurring in child welfare than has been identified in this review. Generalisations should be made with caution.

## Origin of parent activism in child welfare
### Indigenous resistance

The first documented instances of collective parent activism against child separation began with Indigenous, enslaved and formerly enslaved peoples who organised as communities against colonialism, slavery, genocide, stolen children, Indian boarding schools, deracination, and deculturation of their children and communities in Australia, Canada, New Zealand and the United States. The practices, laws and institutions of so-called child welfare systems were used to carry out these genocidal policies (CBC News, 2001; Haskins and Jacobs, 2002; Commission des droits de la personne et des droits de la jeunesse, 2009; Jacobs, 2016; Jacobs, 2020; Briggs, 2021; Ahuriri-Driscoll et al, 2023; Levitt et al, 2023).

Historically, child removal and family disruption, and the emergence of colonial child protection systems, sparked resistance. In this early period, before the current child welfare systems developed, parents were often part of organised movements by Indigenous and enslaved communities' rights movements more generally, rather than specifically focused, on child welfare. Into the late 20th century, instances of Indigenous parents resisting child removal or advocating for reunification with their children occurred sporadically, often in localised clusters. However, there is insufficient documentation of parents acting as a unified force driving systemic change in child welfare policy. Research beyond the scope of this chapter is needed to document the role of parents working to reform, transform or abolish the genocidal use of child welfare systems against Indigenous and enslaved people.

### Māori Family Group Conferences

Parents first became involved in a significant way in child welfare decision-making at the case level among the Māori of New Zealand and then spread to other high-income countries. In the early 1990s, when the Māori concept of Family Group Conferences (FGCs) spread to the United States, parents had not been involved in child welfare policy or system reform. Although parents in child welfare had fought back individually to prevent removal of a child or to press for reunification with their children (Gordon, 1988), it appears that parents had not previously organised in child welfare to be a force for policy or system reform until the 1990s in New York City (Tobis, 2013).

Initially, parent participation in child welfare decision-making in the United States and in other high-income countries was focused at the case level. Parents with lived child welfare experience were trained to provide peer-to-peer support at initial child safety conferences, in FGCs, as visiting coaches for parents while children were in care, in parent support groups and as part of interdisciplinary legal teams representing individual parents. The peer-to-peer support was provided initially to parents immediately before children were removed (initial child safety conferences), while children were in care (to promote reunification) and less frequently after reunification or in home when there was a risk of removal.

*Peer-to-peer support programmes*

Peer-to-peer advocacy in child welfare helped create an environment in which parent activism could take root. As of 2024, it is estimated that there are at least a hundred peer-to-peer parent advocacy programmes in child welfare in the eight countries reviewed for this chapter (Tobis et al, 2020). Most of these programmes are in the United States, primarily funded by government, either through contracts, grants or directly administered by government child welfare agencies. In addition, some peer-to-peer support programmes are based in social service or activist organisations.

## The development of parent activism

Parent participation in child welfare decision-making expanded in the late 20th century from peer-to-peer support to include policy activism. New York City was the jurisdiction in which parent activism first developed and became a movement. That story has been told elsewhere (Tobis, 2013).

*Growth and spread of parent advocacy and activism to high-income countries*

Since the development of a movement of parent activism in child welfare in New York City, parent activism has grown in number, types of activities and militancy. It is estimated that hundreds of parents with lived child welfare experience work in programmes that seek policy and system change in the countries reviewed for this chapter. Hundreds of additional child welfare affected parents use social media to critique and reform child welfare systems in high-income countries. And thousands of child welfare affected parents are involved in the work of these groups. Whereas parent activists initially sought to reform child welfare, activists now include parents who want to transform or abolish child welfare systems. These parent activists and their allies prefer the term 'family policing' or 'family regulating' systems rather than 'child welfare' or 'child protection' systems to better capture the nature of their relationship to those systems (Rise Staff, 2022; JMAC for Families, 2024; Movement for Family Power, 2024).

### Reasons for the spread of parent advocacy and activism

Many underlying and proximal factors contributed to the growth and spread of parent advocacy and parent activism at the end of the 20th and the beginning of the 21st centuries. Underlying factors include crises in child welfare with increasing numbers of children in care in Australia, Canada, England, Finland, Northern Ireland, the United States and Wales (Ensign, 1990; Australian Institute of Health and Welfare, 2002; Hélie et al, 2022; Scottish Government, 2024); models existed of successful parent participation that could be studied and replicated (Tobis, 2013); the United Nations Committee on the Rights of the Child (UNCRC, 2021), which came into force in 1990, and the United Nations Guidelines for the Alternative Care of Children (2009) provided a legal framework for youth and parent participation; the Black Lives Matter movement and the MeToo movement that began in the second decade of the 21st century created a more receptive environment for both grassroots activism and government action to address issues that oppress people of colour, particularly women.

Proximal factors also contributed to the spread of parent activism, including the emotional resonance and persuasiveness of parents with lived child welfare experience; allies who travelled throughout their own countries and to other countries, speaking on panels with parents; and several foundations providing seed money and technical assistance to develop, evaluate and spread parent advocacy and activism.

One issue is why parent advocacy took root in high-income Anglophone countries rather than elsewhere. The answer lies in the nature of the heavy-handed, colonial and post-colonial approaches of their child welfare systems, often violating parents' rights, offering minimal family support and intruding deeply into family life. The harm caused by the systems sparked advocacy and activism for change.

### Parent leadership

The degree of parent leadership is important. *Rise Magazine*, a parent-led organisation, defines child welfare organisations as parent-led, parent-influenced or parent-supported although the boundaries between these categories are not always precise (Rise Staff, 2022):

- *Parent-led:* Refers to organisations in which parents with child welfare experience have power and lead the organisation. The organisation creates a sense of safety, belonging, trust and connectedness for parents.
- *Parent-influenced.* Refers to organisations in which parents are actively involved in shaping the organisation's parent advocacy programme. However, allies act as gatekeepers to the levers of power and decision-making.
- *Parent-supported.* Refers to programmes in which allies hold institutional power. Parents act at the pleasure and around the priorities of more powerful people. A parent-supporting organisation may be tokenistic.

## Domains of parent activism in child welfare

Parent activism in child welfare is beginning to develop in the eight countries under review. These activities are relatively widespread in the United States but are less developed in the other countries. Although the boundaries between activist activities are not always precise, this chapter groups parent activism into 11 domains. Space limitations allow only a few illustrative examples of parent activism (Tobis, 2024a):

1. Programme design
2. Training and technical assistance for parent advocates and activists
3. Training social workers and lawyers
4. Conducting research
5. Participating on government-administered advisory panels
6. Parents writing their stories
7. Working with media and social media
8. Plaintiffs in impact litigation
9. Participating in legislative campaigns
10. Grassroots and community organizing
11. Creating and working in parent advocacy and activist networks

These are discussed further in the sections that follow.

### 1. Programme design

In addition to working as peer-to-peer advocates within child welfare agencies, parents also work at the programme level in several high-income countries to design, plan, develop, evaluate, conduct research and strengthen programmes. The programmes are often parent-influenced rather than parent-led. In Australia, for example, Family Inclusion Strategies in the Hunter (FISH, 2022) held a 'Listening Campaign' in which parents and peer workers talked to senior managers from government agencies and service providers. The information from parents and other family members informed social workers, administrators, government officials and FISH itself about changes to be made in practice, programmes, policies and the system (FISH, 2022).

In addition, the presence of parents working in child welfare programmes has influenced the culture of the agencies in which they work (Dogan, no date; Rauber, 2010; Huebner et al, 2017; Lewis-Brooke et al, 2017;. One study found that family mentors changed the workplace, community culture and attitudes (Huebner et al, 2010).

### 2. Training and technical assistance for parent advocates and activists

Parents are involved in training parents to be peer-to-peer advocates and policy activists. One of the first examples of parents working with allies to train parents to be advocates and activists was the Parent Leadership Training Curriculum and training course developed by the Child Welfare Organizing Project in New York City in 1998 (CWOP, 2008). The training curriculum was developed and delivered jointly by parents and allies. The assessment of the CWOP training focused on the impact of the training on those who were trained.

Cumulatively, over 50 per cent of the Curriculum's graduates have secured employment as peer outreach workers, advocates, and/or organisers at over 20 foster care, preventive, legal and community service agencies. Over 70 per cent of the Parent Leaders who had a child in foster care when they began the Curriculum had reunited their family by its conclusion (CWOP, 2008).

When CWOP ended in 2018, *Rise Magazine*, a parent-led organisation, became the main programme in New York City to train parents to be activists through its Rise & Shine Parent Leadership Program. The training programme includes a writing workshop, public speaking, community-building and reflection sessions, a mini-project and knowledge-building workshops. It includes 10 hours of interactive learning via 'shadowing' and participation in advocacy and organising opportunities outside Rise & Shine programme hours.

Rise also has a contract with the New York City Administration for Children's Services (ACS), the city's public child welfare agency, through which Rise deploys parents to train social work staff and parent advocates in all New York City foster care agencies to provide peer-to-peer support to parents whose children are in foster care.

Parents in at least three other groups in the United States train parents with lived child welfare experience to be activists. JMAC for Families, also based in New York City and also parent-led, focuses its training and policy initiatives on protecting parents' rights (JMAC for Families, 2024). Movement for Family Power (MFP) has an explicitly abolitionist perspective. The organisation mainly supports grassroots activists who have an abolitionist framework. MFP supports 'systems-impacted activists by providing technical assistance, including skills-based training, fundraising, and leadership development' (Movement for Family Power, 2024). A third group, the Birth Parents National Network (BPNN), a Casey Family Program initiative, involves parents to provide information, training and technical assistance for activists who primarily work collaboratively with governments to bring about policy reform and practice changes (BPNN, 2024).

Most other training provided by parents with lived child welfare experience in the United States is narrowly focused on specific job requirements, such as to provide peer-to-peer support, to attend initial child safety conferences or to support parents in child welfare proceedings through interdisciplinary legal teams. Nevertheless, some of this task-focused training includes broader areas such as the history of the parent advocacy movement, parents' role in that history and how they can be involved in programme evaluation and improvement (Arsham, 2024).

Be Strong Families is a national US-based organisation that trains groups of child welfare involved parents, caregivers and their families in the Parent Café model that facilitates mutual support among parents (Be Strong Families, 2024). Be Strong Families deployed two trainers – one parent and one ally – to train parents in the Parent Advocacy Network (PAN) in Wales to lead Parent Cafés in Swansea and Anglesey (Tobis, 2024c).

In several local authorities in England, such as Southwark, Camden and Telford, parents have been trained to be peer-to-peer workers. In Southwark, for example, nine parents have been trained as advocates and six currently work as advocates (Cox, 2025). The advocacy module of the training is accredited by the Open College Network (Southwark Council, 2024).

In Australia, parents and allies in FISH provide comprehensive training for parents to provide peer-to-peer support. FIN (Family Inclusion Network) in South-East Queensland trains parents to work for policy and law reform. The Reily Foundation in Adelaide trains parents to work for policy change.

Formal training for parents to be policy activists in child welfare, however, has occurred only infrequently outside the United States such as in the United Kingdom by the Parent, Family and Allies Network (PFAN, 2022) and in Manitoba, Canada, by Zoongizi Ode Inc. (formerly Fearless R2W) (Zoongizi Ode, 2024). The limited capacity to train parent activists in high-income countries is a key factor constraining the growth of policy activism among parents with lived child welfare experience.

## 3. Training social workers and lawyers

Parents with lived child welfare experience began speaking in classes of social work in the late 20th century in several countries and in law school classes in New York City. Parents' presentation enables the next generation of professionals to better understand the perspective, experience and recommendations of parents. Trained parents now speak in law and social work classes in other American states and several other countries. In Helsinki, Finland, for example, parents from the Kasper Dandelion Parent Advocacy programme present their perspective to students in schools of social work and to other professionals throughout the country (Tobis, 2024d). In New South Wales (NSW), Australia, parents with lived child welfare experience who work with FISH regularly assist in teaching at the University of Newcastle.

Parents also train social work staff who work in child welfare agencies. The local authority in Telford, England, beginning in 2022, deploys parents to inform social workers about parents' experience and perspective (Tobis, 2024e).

Throughout Australia, for at least the past decade, reports have recommended that parents be part of the training for child protective service workers. In July 2024, FINseq (Family Inclusion Network, South-East Queensland) launched 'Parents as Partners', the first child welfare parent training for new government child safety officers. The mandatory training was co-written and co-delivered by parents and allies to 40 department staff in Queensland. The training may become a permanent feature of worker training (Whitworth, 2024).

In NSW, the Sydney Local Health District created the first Australian government-administered peer-to-peer support programme. It is targeted to expectant mothers with significant child protection concerns. The peer workers participate in panels, conferences and facilitated workshops for professionals (Lewkowicz et al, 2024).

## 4. Conducting research

Parents with lived experience are engaged in a) research initiated by academic allies of parents, and b) research initiated and carried out by parents themselves. In the first category, parents selected by allies to participate in the research have constrained influence. Their role as researchers is generally to refine rather than define the research that has been developed by allies. In research initiated by parents, where parents are leading rather than influencing, the parents set the agenda, define the research questions, carry out the research and develop the recommendations. Both types of parent involvement in research are described below.

*Research initiated by academic allies and government*

Parents with lived experience have been involved in many ally-initiated research projects. In the Nurturing Families study in Kentucky, 'parents join the project advisory committee to meet regularly at key decision points in the projects' (Pecora, 2024a). According to one of the principal investigators, 'parents make a big difference. We think through the research questions better. We have their insights on what the data means. And they make any presentations more compelling ...' (Pecora, 2024b).

In NSW, Australia, academics, practitioners and family members partnered to explore 'family inclusion from the perspectives of key people who are actively involved when children are removed from their parents' care' (Ross et al, 2023).

In England, the government undertook an Independent Review of Children's Social Care (McAlister, 2022). The review established an Experts by Experience Board and interviewed parents. Although the Board wrote 'We saw them [the research team] shift their thinking on some key issues and knew we were being listened to', the final report had no explicit reference to parents with lived experience playing a role in shaping child welfare policy or working in peer-to-peer support programmes (McAlister, 2022).

*Research initiated by parents*

*The Way Forward* is a report prepared by parents and allies in PFAN, a parent-led Network in the UK. The report (PFAN, 2024) uses strong language to critique the British government's Independent Review of Children's Social Care described earlier:

'Children's social care in England is currently not fit for purpose. It alienates families in communities, fails to protect children, and places older children at increased risk of involvement in gangs and sexual exploitation.'

Research reports in several other countries have been initiated and directed by parents with lived child welfare experience. One such report entitled *'An Unavoidable System: The Harms of Family Policing and Parents' Vision for Investing in Community Care'* was led and conducted by parents from *Rise Magazine* working with TakeRoot Justice, an organisation that 'provides legal, participatory research and policy support to strengthen the work of grassroots and community-based groups in New York City' (*Rise Magazine* and TakeRoot Justice, 2021). The study 'documents the harm of the family policing system and outlines how parents affected by the system believe families can receive care and support without the surveillance, control, trauma and loss inflicted by the current system' (*Rise Magazine* and TakeRoot Justice, 2021).

The International Parent Advocacy Network (IPAN) produced an online multi-source, multi-media Toolkit for Transformation (IPAN, 2024), the product of global collaboration between parents and allies. The Toolkit presents documents on the efficacy of parent advocacy, how to conduct legislative activism, how to create parent support groups; it also describes press conferences and ways to deal with the media to ensure that the voice of parents is present in child welfare news stories. The Toolkit enables parents to learn from each other's experiences to build the power of parent advocacy and activism. A focus on shifting the balance of power in child welfare is often a hallmark of parent-led work.

## 5. Participating on government-administered advisory panels

Government-administered advisory panels, including parents with lived child welfare experience, have been established in the United States and in several other high-income countries. In 2018, the U.S. Department of Health and Human Services (HHS), through its Administration for Children and Families, issued a memorandum that lived expertise should be incorporated into all agency efforts to improve policy and practice in child welfare (Milner, 2018).

Augsberger and Collins (2022) reported that 26 of the 50 states of America have child welfare advisory boards in which parents with lived experience are present. Most of these panels were created between 2011 and 2021.

Government child welfare agencies in other high-income countries also established child welfare parent advisory panels. In Norway, a consumer advisory board was established by the government a decade ago. The board of ten meets eight times a year and consists of foster parents, foster children, parents with lived child welfare experience, clients from the mental health system and others. The child welfare parent advocate on the board reported:

> Our voice isn't the strongest. I can't say there is a policy that we pushed through. We provide a reminder that the government should listen to parents ... I don't think we have power at the top at all. We try to work from the bottom with the workers in the field. (Loland, 2024)

In Queensland, Australia, in 2020, the Minister of Child Safety, Youth and Women, with assistance from Micah (a nonprofit organization providing services and supporting justice) and FIN created the first governmental parent advisory committee in Australia. This committee produced Australia's first Charter of Rights for parents involved in child protection in Queensland. The Charter of Rights is aspirational, not statutory (Whitworth, 2024).

In the UK, at least 12 local authorities in the past several years have established parent advisory panels in child welfare and/or are engaged in collaborative research with parents (Fisher, 2024).

No research, however, has evaluated whether any of these advisory panels in any of these countries improve the well-being of children and families. That research is needed as these advisory panels spread.

## 6. Parents writing their stories

From the beginning of parent activism in child welfare in the late 1990s in New York City, parents have written about their lives, their experiences with child protective services, and their recommendations. *Rise Magazine* provides classes for parents to learn to write and then to publish their stories. Rise runs writing groups at advocacy organisations, legal providers, foster care agencies and family support programmes. When Jeff Dannhauser was the executive director of Graham Windham, a private child welfare agency in New York City (he is currently the commissioner of ACS) he attended the graduation of parents from one of Rise's writing groups. He said:

> The Rise graduation was a fabulous moment. The parents read their stories, their families came out, and our staff listened and ate dinner with them. For our staff, it helped us be so much more aware of the full context of our parents' lives. Their children also saw their parents accomplish something important and saw that their parents were worthy of their esteem. (*Rise Magazine*, 2016)

Groups of parents in other high-income countries are now writing their stories and experiences with child protective services. In Wales, allies in the PAN work with parents to write and read their stories to other parents and social workers.

Parents' stories have been influential. They help the writers feel empowered. Other parents feel less alone reading stories similar to their lives. The stories help social workers understand parents' perspective and recommendations.

## 7. Working with media and social media

### Working with media

Parents who have been involved with the child welfare system work with the media in two ways. First, they are sources of information for journalists. They respond to journalists' requests for on-the-ground experience with child welfare. These journalistic inquiries are relatively new as, prior to the 21st century, journalists rarely or ever contacted parents involved with child welfare to learn of their experiences and views. Second, parents proactively approach reporters to promote reports their organisations have prepared or to pitch a child welfare-related story.

Richard Wexler, executive director of the National Coalition for Child Protection Reform (NCCPR, 2024), which monitors child welfare-related media activities around the United States, often connects parents with media preparing stories on child welfare throughout the country.

Parents in other high-income countries, particularly from Indigenous communities, are using media to present their perspective on child welfare. For example, CBC News in Canada carried a story 'Grandmothers walk in protest against child welfare system, proposed federal legislation' (Monkman, 2019). In NSW, Australia, Grand Mothers Against Removal (GMAR) organises and writes about the increased rate of removal of Aboriginal and Torres Strait Island children after a landmark national study ('Bringing Them Home') called for a decrease in Indigenous removals (University of Sydney, 2019).

*Using social media*

Individual parents who feel abused by child protection use social media (primarily Facebook as well as Instagram, Twitter/X, YouTube and Tik Tok) to expose the injustices of child protection systems and to rally support for demonstrations, legislation and campaigns. The posts reflect the rage that individuals experienced as a result of their treatment by child protection systems.

A dozen of these social media sites were identified and reviewed in the United States, the United Kingdom and New Zealand. It appears likely that hundreds, if not thousands, of other child welfare parent-led social media sites exist. The names of many of these sites reflect parents' anger and militancy: Fight CPS, 2024 (U.S.), Mad Angels Army, 2024 (U.S.), Legally Stolen Children, 2024) (U.K.) and Hands Off Our Tamariki, 2024 (New Zealand).

The use of social media by parents to fight child protection systems appears to have proliferated in the mid-2010s. Followers of these sites range from a handful to 21,300 for Fight CPS.

### 8. Plaintiffs in impact litigation

The United States has a long tradition of parents with lived child welfare experience participating as named plaintiffs in impact litigation (Nicholson v Scoppetta, 2004; Richardson, 2024). The Family Justice Law Center is the first legal center established with the purpose of bringing impact litigation against the child welfare systems on behalf of parents. One potentially transformative lawsuit represents parents who allege that ACS uses unconstitutional and 'coercive tactics' that 'traumatise the families it is charged with protecting' (Bromwich and Newman, 2024). In February

2025, a New York State Appellate Court found these practices illegal (Poggio, 2025).

Impact litigation brought by parents in child welfare is much less common in other high-income countries. In Australia, in one of the few such lawsuits, Shine Lawyers (a prominent Australian law firm), on behalf of First Nations families, is bringing a class action investigation against the Departments of Child Protection in South Australia and Victoria that alleges that families have been subjected to unlawful racial discriminatory practices (Shine Lawyers, 2024).

Impact litigation should be studied to determine the extent to which it has been used in child welfare, its impact and where it might be a viable advocacy tool.

## 9. Participating in legislative campaigns

Legislative campaigns, led or influenced by parents, have been part of the arsenal of parent activism in the United States and infrequently in other countries. In New York State, parents and their allies worked for years to successfully pass a law in 2023 to reform the State Central Registry of child abuse and neglect. The law, among other things, raised the standard to confirm a case of abuse or neglect from 'some credible evidence' to 'a preponderance of evidence' (*Rise Magazine*, 2020). The Parent Legislative Action Network (PLAN, 2024) and *Rise Magazine* (2024) (both parent-led organisations) worked closely with lawyers to define what to include in the legislation and to promote its passage (*Rise Magazine*, 2020).

In Washington State, parents were centrally involved in the passage of several pieces of legislation benefitting families and children (Selivanoff, 2024). Parents successfully championed the Keeping Families Together Act of 2023 to 'reduce the number of children placed into foster care, reduce racial disproportionality in the child welfare system, and support relatives to take care of children when they must be placed out of home to protect their safety' (Washington State Department of Children, Youth & Families, 2024). Another campaign led by parents and their allies in Washington State contributed to the passage of legislation that implemented a parent advocacy programme throughout the state.

Parents with lived child welfare experience were involved in a national legislative campaign in the United States. Parents testified in the U.S. Congress to successfully pass the Family First Prevention Services Act of 2018. Although the legislation has been criticised by allies and parents, it authorised new federal funding for prevention services for mental health, substance abuse and in-home parent skill-based programmes for children and youth at risk of foster care (Mack, 2021).

Legislative campaigns led or influenced by parents in other countries are far less common than in the United States. In NSW, Australia, several parent-influenced organisations (including FISH, Aboriginal Legal Services [ALS] and AbSec (NSW Child, Family and Community Peak Aboriginal Corporation) were active in the legislative campaign to repeal section 106A of the NSW Children Care and Protection Act. Section 106A allowed the Children's Court in NSW to remove a child merely because a previous child had been removed (Davis, 2019). As a result, many young children, particularly Aboriginal children, were removed at birth, contributing to Aboriginal children being 12 times more likely to be in statutory out-of-home care than the rest of the population (McGowan, 2022). The legislative changes in section 106A were very weak compared to what was proposed in a scathing criticism of the child welfare system in NSW (Davis, 2019; Children and Young Persons Amendment Act, 2022 No. 67).

## 10. Grassroots and community organising

Grassroots and community organising, particularly by Indigenous communities, is carried out in child welfare to build community power for families and communities who seek relief, justice and self-determination (Bobo et al, 2001; California Labor Federation, 2023). Grassroots community-organising groups in child welfare have several characteristics in common. The groups tend to be parent-led rather than parent-influenced. They are more militant, angry and demand more radical change than organisations that are engaged exclusively in peer-to-peer support or that work collaboratively with government. They work outside government to push government to change. They start out without money and work with volunteers, although several have gained foundation support and have become self-sustaining organisations.

Although some receive government support, most do not. Although some groups have received training to develop support groups or to deal with specific issues such as trauma or confidentiality, most grassroots activists have not been trained in the fundamentals of organising and have learned to organise through on-the-job training.

Grassroots community organising groups in general, and in child welfare specifically, use a variety of activities and tactics to develop power and exert influence on policy makers. In child welfare, these activities include webinars, reports, letter writing campaigns, working with the media, vigils, street demonstrations, legislative campaigns, lawsuits and cultivating allies and champions in government. These activities are often based on engaging and mobilising large numbers of people for action to raise consciousness about the problems of child welfare and to develop power to bring about specific policy and programme changes.

In the United States, prominent grassroots parent-led or parent-influenced organisations in child welfare include California Families Rise, JMAC for

Families, Movement for Family Power (supports grassroot parents) and Give Us Back Our Children (Philadelphia and Los Angeles). Movement for Family Power prepared a list of 20 grassroot activist groups in child welfare in 13 states, Washington DC and nationally (Cloud, undated).

Indigenous organisations in Australia that use grassroots organising to reform child welfare include GMARNSW (Grandmothers Against Removal New South Wales) (Swan, 2024), SNAIIC (National Voice for Our Children), and AbSec (NSW Child, Family and Community Peak Aboriginal Corporation). In Canada, Zoongizi Ode (formerly Fearless R2W) uses grassroot organising. In England, LAW (Legal Action for Women and, in Scotland, PAR (Parents Advocacy and Rights) are grassroot organisations that work with parents and allies.

One other development has begun to expand grassroots organising and participation of parents with lived child welfare experience. At least two global anti-poverty organisations and coalitions that mobilise the grassroots on issues of poverty and race are increasingly focusing on the overlap of poverty, child welfare and parent participation. The first, Global Women's Strike, is a coalition of many organisations including Give Us Back Our Children based in Philadelphia and Los Angeles (Global Women's Strike, 2024). The second, ATD 4th World, is an international anti-poverty and human rights organisation, working on five continents. It is increasing its focus in the United Kingdom and the United States on the overlap of poverty and child welfare (ATD 4th World, 2024). Both organisations work with parents with lived child welfare experience.

## 11. Creating and working in parent advocacy and activist networks

At least five child welfare parent advocacy networks have been established in high-income countries to support parents, parent advocacy and policy reform in child welfare. These include Birth Parents National Network (BPNN, 2024), Family Inclusion National Network Australia (FIN Australia, 2024), International Parent Advocacy Network (IPAN, 2024), Parent Advocacy Network (PAN, 2024) and Parent Family and Allies Network (PFAN, 2024). All but one of these networks was established in the past seven years, reflecting the recent growth of parent advocacy and activism in the United States, the United Kingdom and Australia.

All the networks are collaborations of parents with lived experience and their allies. They are either unfunded or have very limited budgets, except for BPNN that has funding from Casey Family Programs. The networks' activities vary as does the extent of parent leadership. One or more of the networks' programmes include support and referrals for individual parents struggling with the child welfare system; support groups for parents to share their experiences and gain comfort from each other; online information, literature and webinars; deployment of parents to speak at public forums; and campaigns to reform policy.

## Conclusion and recommendations

The following conclusions and recommendations are based on the scoping review and more than three decades working with parents and their allies to promote parent advocacy and activism in child welfare. The information and conclusions should be seen as illustrative and anecdotal rather than comprehensive. It is certain that more parent activism is occurring in child welfare than has been identified in this review. Generalisations should be made with caution.

### *Parent advocacy (peer-to-peer support) in child welfare*

Parents with lived child welfare experience are providing peer-to-peer support as parent advocates in child welfare systems in each of the eight high-income countries reviewed for this chapter. In the past three decades parent advocacy has spread throughout the United States and is taking root in the other seven countries reviewed for this chapter.

There are now more than 100 peer-to-peer parent advocacy programmes in child welfare in these countries (Tobis et al, 2020). The majority of the programmes are in the United States with England a distant second. Australia's Family Inclusion Networks and other parent advocacy programmes operate on a small scale in five states, each reaching only a small number of families (FIN Australia, 2024). The other high-income countries reviewed each has a few peer-to-peer support programmes in child welfare.

Parent advocacy has been embraced in only a very few jurisdictions in the countries in which it exists. In those countries, relative to each country's system, generally only a few parents with children in foster care receive peer-to-peer assistance. For example, in Wisconsin, U.S., only about 4 per cent of the families of children in care are assisted by a trained parent advocate working in the state's child welfare agency though additional parent advocates are employed in some county offices (Wisconsin Department of Children and Families, 2024). In Iowa, U.S., 48 per cent of parents with children in care utilised a parent partner for peer mentoring. Iowa appears to be the state with the highest percentage of parents with a child in care who utilise a parent advocate (Malone, 2024). Washington state also has a high percentage of parents who work with a peer advocate though its programme helps parents navigate the juvenile dependency court system (Casey Family Programs, 2021).

New York City and Washington State are the only jurisdictions in high-income countries in which peer-to-peer support reaches a majority of the families in the system.

## Parent activism (policy and system change) in child welfare

Dozens of programmes and as many as a thousand parents, are involved in child welfare policy activism in high-income countries. The majority of these programmes are located in the United States though policy activism also occurs in other high-income countries.

In the United States, parents are training parent activists and social workers (for example, Rise in New York City), participating in legislative campaigns (for example, JMAC for Families and PLAN (2024) in New York State; Keeping Families Together, Washington State); are named plaintiffs in class action law suits (Family Justice Law Center, NYC), mobilising grassroots activists (for example, California Families Rise, Movement for Family Power (national), Give Us Back Our Children in Philadelphia and Los Angeles). and conducting research (for example, Rise and Casey Family Programs).

Parent activism for policy reform is also developing and expanding in England. The organisations and activities include the Parent, Family and Allies Network (PFAN) (webinars, reports that critique the system, and parent support groups), Legal Action for Women (demonstrations outside the Central London Family Court and policy campaigns), Family Rights Group (public forums and policy input), and advisory committees and research involving parents at local authorities (most prominently in Camden and Southwark and in seven other local authorities).

Parent activism for policy and system reform is less organised and systematic in the other countries except among Indigenous communities in Australia, Canada, New Zealand and the United States (Monkman, 2019; University of Sydney, 2019. McGowan, 2022; Swan, 2024).

## Impact of parent activism

Research has documented the positive effects of peer-to-peer support in child welfare. The strategies and impact of parents working as activists for policy and system reform in child welfare have rarely been studied and evaluated. One prominent exception are reviews and evaluations of the parent activism movement in New York City (Tobis, 2013; Tobis, 2019; Castellano, 2021; Rise staff, 2022).

New York City is the only jurisdiction in a high-income country in which a robust parent advocacy and activist movement has developed. Parent activism in New York has reached a critical mass with reinforcing synergy. Some of the elements in that movement are:

- Rise Magazine is a parent-led activism, training and information centre for parents, social workers and students.

- JMAC for Families and PLAN, both parent-led, provide grassroots organising for legislative and policy change.
- At least a hundred parents are employed in dozens of child welfare agencies, including foster care, preventive services and ACS itself, the government child welfare agency. Most of these positions are funded by ACS.
- Specially trained lawyers in four law firms use interdisciplinary legal teams (including a lawyer, a social worker and a parent advocate) funded by government to represent parents in child welfare proceedings.
- New York University, Columbia University and CUNY law schools have family defence clinics that train lawyers to defend child welfare-involved parents.
- Several academic and research centres informed by parents evaluate parent advocacy programmes (for example, Marina Lalayants, Hunter School of Social Work) and critique various aspects of the child welfare system (Family Policy Project).
- The Family Justice Law Centre has brought major litigation on behalf of parents against the public child welfare agency.
- Major media outlets now regularly seek out the perspective of parents with lived child welfare experience.
- Financial support for parent advocacy is provided by several foundations and the public child welfare agency.

These individuals and organisations in New York City constitute a countervailing force that pushed government to support and fund parent advocacy and to better meet the needs of children, parents and families (Tobis, 2013). Washington State and Philadelphia have different elements of a movement, but do not yet have full reinforcing synergy as in New York City.

Among other high-income countries, England has gone farthest in developing different elements of parent advocacy and activism which include:

- A dozen local authorities with small but expanding peer-to-peer parent advocacy programmes.
- A network co-led by parents and allies providing information and policy activism (PFAN).
- Parent advisory panels in several local authorities.
- Grassroots organising (Legal Action for Women and PAR).
- NGOs providing peer-to-peer support and policy activism (Family Rights Group).
- Parent support groups (in NGOs and several local authorities).
- Several academic research centres that critique child welfare, conduct research with parents and evaluate parent advocacy programmes. Simon Haworth at the University of Birmingham, for example, worked with parents as researchers and interviewees, to produce the Children and

Families Truth Commission report. The study was launched at the House of Lords in London in 2024 at a meeting chaired by Baroness Grey Thompson (Phillips, 2025).
- An international anti-poverty organisation, ATD 4th World, is beginning to focus on child welfare and parent participation.

These activities and organisations are scattered throughout England and the UK, limiting collaboration among groups and the development of an integrated movement.

## Legislative impact

Other indicators, besides formal evaluation research, reflect the significant impact of parent activism. Legislation, for example, has been enacted with pressure brought by many groups including parents with lived child welfare experience and their allies. The Families First Prevention Services Act (2018) was enacted in the United States with support from parents who testified in Congress. In New York State, parents and their allies led the successful legislative campaign to raise the standard of what constitutes abuse and neglect. In Washington State, parents led a successful legislative campaign to fund the Parents for Parents programme statewide and to pass E2SHB 1227 to reduce the number of children placed into foster care. Reviews of these legislative reforms show mixed results. Whereas the Parents for Parents programme in Washington State has been found to be effective, the Family's First Preservation Services Act has fallen far short of its promise (Trescher and Summers, 2020; Mack, 2021).

Although most parent-involved successful legislative campaigns have occurred in the United States, several child welfare reform campaigns have succeeded in other high-income countries. In NSW, Australia, legislation supported by parents, made it more difficult for the child welfare system to automatically remove a second child (Davis, 2019; Children and Young Persons Amendment Act, 2022 No. 67).

## Changing the child welfare debate

Parent activism has changed the debate around child welfare reform in several high-income countries. Parents in many jurisdictions have influenced the child welfare policy debate to include parents' perspective. Parents have helped shift the locus of discussion in two significant ways: away from child removal toward increased support for families; and toward increased parent participation in decision making at both the case and policy levels. Parents with lived child welfare experience present at conferences, speak on panels and webinars, sit on government advisory panels, write about their experiences with protective services, participate in research as informants, advisors and researchers, campaign for legislative and policy reform, are named plaintiffs in impact litigation and regularly present their perspective to the media.

In some jurisdictions in the United States, particularly with large, urban child welfare systems, parents and their allies have shifted the policy debate to include a discussion of child welfare as the Family Policing System and have introduced calls for the abolition of the current child welfare system (Roberts, 2022; Movement for Brown and Dasgupta, 2024; Family Power, 2024; *Rise Magazine*, 2024). These more radical positions and discussions have been present among Indigenous communities in other high-income countries but have not reached non-Indigenous communities there in a significant way.

Few evaluations have been conducted of the tactics, strategies and impact of policy activism by parents in child welfare. That research is needed to expand and deepen the positive changes parents have helped bring about.

### *The role of government in parent advocacy and activism*

Governments in high-income countries other than the United States, that have supported parent participation, have primarily funded small scale, pilot peer-to-peer support programmes. These government-run or government-funded peer-to-peer programmes are often parent-influenced or parent-supported rather than parent-led. In the United States, federal, state and local governments have supported and funded larger scale peer-to-peer parent advocacy programmes.

Some local authorities, counties, states, provinces and countries have also created advisory panels which include parents with lived child welfare experience. These government-administered advisory panels tend to be parent-supported in which non-impacted people hold institutional power. Many of these parent advisory panels have used parent input to develop materials that may be more accessible to parents or have organised periodic 'fun' events for parents and their children; few of these panels involve parents to review and significantly change policies. In Southwark, London, parents on the local authority's advisory panel play a role in hiring new staff. In Camden, London, parents on the local authority panel worked with staff to developed a guide on 'Good Help for Families Manifesto'. The impact of any of these advisory panels has not been evaluated and should be as they proliferate.

### *The role of parent leadership*

Most child welfare parent advocacy programmes and organisations are parent-influenced in which non-impacted people are gatekeepers to the levers of power and decision making. Parent activist programmes tend to be parent-led and are more militant and adversarial such as JMAC for Families, *Rise Magazine*, and California Families Rise in the United States, PFAN in England and Indigenous organisations in Australia, Canada and the United States.

We believe that programmes and organisations that promote parent participation should be parent-led in partnership with allies. First, parents know best what they and their families need. They have experienced the system's harms and are best suited to address the changes needed. Second, power in the community is needed to change systems. The best way to build community power is by the mobilisation and leadership of people affected by the system. And third, organisations are needed to change child welfare systems. The most powerful organisation is one that is built on the strengths of all members of the community including parents with lived experience and people with learned experience and other skills.

### Creating a parent advocacy or activism programme

Parents and their allies often do not know how to begin to create a parent advocacy or parent activism programme. They have few financial resources, limited training capacity and parents have difficult lives filled with poverty, racism, domestic violence, homelessness and other trauma. Although many social workers have been strong supporters of parent advocacy, others have resisted parent participation. Social workers have been fearful that parents will tell them what to do, second guess their decisions, violate clients' confidentiality or reexperience their own trauma. Many approaches have been developed to overcome social workers' resistance including well defined job descriptions; testimony from case workers who were resistant to parent participation and changed their minds; research documenting the efficacy of parent advocacy; and direct contact between social workers and trained parent advocates.

Many resources are available to help start a parent advocacy or activism programme; these include *Rise Magazine* (2024), PFAN (2024), IPAN's Toolkit for Transformation (IPAN, 2024), International Review of Parent Advocacy in Child Welfare (Tobis et al, 2020), and BPNN (2024). Talking to each other, parents among themselves and parents with their allies, is the best way to begin.

### A strategy for change: a broad-based coalition to build power

A big tent is needed to create child welfare systems that nurture children and families. A wide range of political perspectives can contribute to systems changing. The coalition should include people on the left and the right when their interests coincide to support families. That big tent should include people who want to reform, transform, or abolish the current child welfare system.

Parents and their allies can work together while other parents will want to work without allies. Some people will want to work within or with government while others will want to work outside of government, pushing it to change.

All of these perspectives and alliances are needed to create a movement that will have the power to push governments to meet the needs of children and families. Unless pushed, governments will only do what is convenient which most often is not all that families need or deserve.

Parent activism in child welfare has begun to build community power. That activism is still only having influence in small ways in only a few jurisdictions in several high-income countries, but that movement has begun. The responsibility of parents and their allies is to add to that movement.

**References**

Ahuriri-Driscoll, A., Blake, D., Potter, H., McBreen, K. and Mikaere, A. (2023) 'A "forgotten" whakapapa: historical narratives of Māori and closed adoption', *Kōtuitui: New Zealand Journal of Social Sciences Online*, 18(2): 135–52.

Arsham, M. (2024) Email to the author, 26 October.

ATD 4th World (2024) Parent participation in child welfare, webinar, London, 6 June. Available from: https://atd-uk.org/2024/06/14/a-seminar-to-celebrate-progress-in-parent-advocacy/; https://www.atd-fourthworld.org/what-we-do/

Augsberger, A. and Collins, M.E. (2022) 'Family engagement in child welfare system-level change: a review of current models', *Family in Society: The Journal of Contemporary Social Services*, 4(4): 7.

Australian Institute of Health and Welfare (2002) 'Child protection Australia 2000-2001'. Available from: https://www.aihw.gov.au/getmedia/36588ac6-cf09-464b-a6ae-116872bceaa6/cpa00-01.pdf?v=20230605171040&inline=true

Be Strong Families (2024) Parent Café. Available from: https://www.bestrongfamilies.org

Bobo, K., Kendall, J. and Max, S. (2001) Organizing for Social Change: Midwest Academy Manual for Activists, Seven Locks Press.

BPNN (2024) Birth Parents National Network. Available from: https://ctfalliance.org/partnering-with-parents/bpnn/

Briggs, L. (2021) 'Twentieth century black and native activism against the child taking system: lessons for the present', *Columbia Journal of Race and Law*, 11(3): 611–38.

Bromwich, J.E. and Newman, A. (2024) 'Child abuse investigators traumatize families, lawsuit charges', *New York Times*, 20 February. Available from: https://www.nytimes.com/2024/02/20/nyregion/acs-nyc-family-trauma-lawsuit.html

Brown, J. and Dasgupta, S. (2024) 'Abolitionist child protection', *The Lancet*, 404(10458): 1096–7, 21 September.

California Labor Federation (2023) Axioms & Lessons for Organizers, Fred Ross Sr. and Fred Ross Jr. California Labor Federation.

Casey Family Programs (2021) 'How Do Parent Partner Programs Instil Hope and Support Prevention and Reunification: Appendix A: Snapshot of Research on Parent Partner Programs. Updated January 2021. Casey Family Programs.

Castellano, V. (2021) 'Walking a fine line: the struggle for parent advocacy in the NYC child welfare system', *City & Society*, 33(3): 518–41.

CBC News (2001) Alberta Natives Occupy Blue Quills School. Available from: https://www.cbc.ca/history/EPISCONTENTSE1EP16CH2PA3LE.html

Children and Young Persons Amendment Act (2022 No. 67). New South Wales, Section 106A Admissibility of certain other evidence [20], p 9. Available from: https://legislation.nsw.gov.au/view/pdf/asmade/act-2022-67

Cloud, E. (undated) List of grassroots organizations. Movement for Family Power.

Cocks, J., Johnston, L., Vega, J. and Thorpe, R. (2024) 'Parent and family peer advocacy in child welfare', in E. Fernandez, P. Welbourne, B. Lee and J.L.C. Ma (eds) *Routledge Handbook of Child and Family Social Work Research: Knowledge-Building, Application, and Impact*, Taylor & Francis.

Commission des droits de la personne et des droits de la jeunesse (2009) Myths and Realities: Indigenous Peoples in Canada. 2nd edn. Québec: Bibliothèque nationale du Québec. Available from: https://cdn-contenu.quebec.ca/cdn-contenu/adm/min/conseil-executif/publications-adm/srpni/administratives/documents/fr/mythes-realites-autochtones.pdf

Cox, J. (2025) Email to the author, 6 May.

CWOP (2008) A Parent Leadership Training Curriculum, CWOP, p 3.

Davis, M. (2019) Family is Culture: Independent Review of Aboriginal Out of Aboriginal Children in OOHC NSW, Report 2019. Available from: https://dcj.nsw.gov.au/documents/children-and-families/family-is-culture/family-is-culture-review-report.pdf

Devine, R., Benson, K., Fitz-Symonds, S., Westlake, D., Campbell, K. and Diaz, C. (2023) 'Peer parental advocacy: a narrative review of the literature', *Journal of Children's Services*, 18(3-4): 244–60. Available from: https://www.emerald.com/jcs/article-abstract/18/3-4/244/195254/Peer-parental-advocacy-a-narrative-review-of-the?redirectedFrom=fulltext

Diaz, C., Westlake, D. and Evans, L. (2021) *What is the perceived impact of Peer Parental Advocacy on child protection practice? A pilot evaluation.* CASCADE: Cardiff University.

Dogan, A. (no date) *Building on success: Parent partners in Contra Costa County*. Available from: http://mackcenter.berkeley.edu/sites/default/files/building_on_success_parent_partners_in_contra_costa_county.pdf

Ensign, K. (1990) Foster Care Summary: 1991, U.S. Department of Health and Human Services. Available from: https://aspe.hhs.gov/reports/foster-care-summary-1991-0

Fight CPS (2024) *Fight CPS and know your rights*. Available from: https://www.facebook.com/groups/1907532709464832/

FIN Australia (2024) *Family inclusion national network, Australia*. Available from: https://familyinclusionnetwork.com.au/

FISH (2022) *Family inclusion strategies in the Hunter, Listening Campaign*, October. Available from: https://drive.google.com/file/d/1AonLgbKZdQSDlhZdiHg1DrB1ucMW_o0r/view

Fisher, T. (2024) 'Parent Advocacy Slide Presentation, at the Telford Local Authority', UK, 4 June.

Fitt, K., Maylea, C., Costello, S., Kuyini, B. and Thomas, S. (2023) 'Independent non-legal advocacy in the child protection context: a descriptive review of the literature', *Child Abuse & Neglect*, 143. Available from: https://www.sciencedirect.com/science/article/pii/S0145213423002661

Global Women's Strike (2024) *Give us back our children*. Available from: https://globalwomenstrike.net/give-us-back-our-children/

Gordon, L. (1988) *Heroes of Their Own Lives: The Politics and History of Family Violence, Boston 1880–1960*, Viking.

Hands Off Our Tamariki (2024) (New Zealand) Available from: https://www.facebook.com/p/Hands-Off-Our-Tamariki-100066651048876/

Haskins, V. and Jacobs, M. (2002) *Stolen Generations and Vanishing Indians: The Removal of Indigenous Children as a Weapon of War in the United States and Australia*, 1870–1940. University of Nebraska. Available from: https://digitalcommons.unl.edu/cgi/viewcontent.cgi?article=1009&context=historyfacpub

Hélie, S., Trocmé, S., Collin-Vézina, D., Esposito, T., Morin, S. and Saint-Girons, M. (2022) *First Nations Component of the Quebec incidence study on the situations investigated by child protective services in 2019*. QIS-FN report.

Huebner, R.A., Willauer, T., Brock, A. and Coleman, Y. (2010) *START Family Mentors: Changing the Workplace and Community Culture and Achieving Results*. Available from: https://www.researchgate.net/publication/313242283_START_family_mentors_Changing_the_workplace_and_community_culture_and_achieving_results

Huebner, R.A., Young, N.K., Hall, M.T., Posze, L. and Willauer, T. (2017) 'Serving families with child maltreatment and substance use disorders: a decade of learning', *Journal of Family Social Work*, 20(4): 288–305.

IPAN (2024) Toolkit for Transformation. Available from: https://toolkit.parentadvocacy.net

Jacobs, M. (2016) 'Entangled histories: The Mormon Church and indigenous child removal from 1850 to 2000', *Journal of Morman History*, 42(2): 27–60. Available from: https://colab.ws/articles/10.5406 per cent2Fjmormhist.42.2.0027

Jacobs, M. (2020) 'Indigenous child removal and trans-imperial indigenous women's activism across settler colonial nations in the late twentieth century', in K.L. Hoganson and J. Sexton (eds) *Crossing Empires: Taking U.S. History into Trans-imperial Terrain*. Duke University Press, pp 281–302.

JMAC for Families (2024) HEAL. Available from: https://jmacforfamilies.org/heal

Legally Stolen Children (2024) Available from: https://legallystolenchildren.com/

Levitt, Z., Parsshina-Kottas, Y., Romero, S. and Wallace, T. (2023) 'A "War Against the Children"', *New York Times*, 25 September, p A16.

Lewis-Brooke, S., Bell, L., Herring, R., Lehane, L., O'Farrell-Pearce, S., Quinn, K. et al. (2017) 'Mothers apart: an action research project based on partnership between a local authority and a university in London', *Revista de Asistenta Sociala*, (3): 5–15.

Lewkowicz, D., Tayebjee, Z. and Isobel, S. (2024) Evaluation of the Pregnancy Family Conferencing Parent Supporters Pilot Project 2019–2023. Australia: Sydney Local Health District and the Dept. of Communities and Justice.

Loland, M. (2024) Interview with the author, 3 September.

Mack, M. (2021) 'The white supremacy hydra: how the family first prevention services act reifies pathology, control and punishment in the family regulation system', *Columbia Journal of Race and Law*, 11(3): 767.

Mad Angels Army (2024) (California). Available from: https://www.facebook.com/MadAngelsArmy/

Malone, C. (2024) Letter to the author, 23 October.

McAlister, J. (2022) Independent Review of Children's Social Care. UK: Department of Education. Available from: https://www.gov.uk/government/publications/independent-review-of-childrens-social-care-final-report

McGowan, M. (2022) 'People think it's all in the past: push to reform system taking Aboriginal kids from families', *The Guardian*, 13 March. Available from: https://www.theguardian.com/australia-news/2022/mar/14/people-think-its-all-in-the-past-push-to-reform-system-taking-aboriginal-kids-from-families

Milner, J. (2018) Reshaping Child Welfare in the United States, memorandum Log No. ACYF-CB-IM-18-05 from U.S. Department of Health and Human Services, Administration for Children and Families, Administration on Children, Youth, and Families, Children's Bureau. Available from: https://acf.gov/sites/default/files/documents/cb/im1805.pdf

Monkman, L. (2019) 'Grandmothers walk in protest against child welfare system, proposed federal legislation', *CBC News*, 10 May. Available from: https://www.cbc.ca/news/indigenous/winnipeg-grandmothers-walk-child-family-services-1.5130276

Movement for Family Power (2024) *What we do*. Available from: https://www.movementforfamilypower.org/what-we-do

NCCPR (2024) *National Coalition for Child Protection Reform*. Available from: www.NCCPR.org

Nicholson v Scoppetta (2004) New York City Court of Appeals. NY Slip Op 07617 [3NY3d 357], 26 October.

PAN (2024) *Parent Advocacy Network*. Available from: https://www.bestrongfamilies.org/pan-wales

Pecora, P. (2024a) Email to the author, 6 February.

Pecora, P. (2024b) Email to the author, 6 February.

PFAN (2022) *Parent, Families and Allies Network*. Available from: https://www.pfan.uk/the-way-forward

Phillips, N. (2025) 'Government responds to Children and Families Truth Commission Question in Parliament', *Voice of the Child Podcasts*, Researching Reform, 22 January. Available from: https://researchingreform.net/2025/01/22/government-responds-to-children-and-families-truth-commission-question-in-parliament/

PLAN (2024) *Parent Legislative Action Network*. Available from: https://jmacforfamilies.org/plancoalition

Poggio, M. (2025) 'NY court puts a limit on child welfare agency surveillance', *Law360*, 6 February. Available from: https://www.law360.com/appellate/articles/2294277/ny-court-puts-a-limit-on-child-welfare-agency-surveillance-

Rauber, D. (2010) 'From the Courthouse to the Statehouse: Parents as Partners in Child Welfare'. Available from: https://www.americanbar.org/content/dam/aba/publications/center_on_children_and_the_law/parentrepresentation/from_courthouse_to_statehouse.authcheckdam.pdf

Richardson, A. (2024) 'Civil suits by parents against family policing agencies', *Harvard Law Review*, 1 May. Available from: https://harvardlawreview.org/blog/2024/05/civil-suits-by-parents-against-family-policing-agencies/

*Rise Magazine* (2016) 'Wait, There's a Whole Story Here – How Rise's writing group is helping an agency listen to parents', Interview with Jeff Dannhauser, President and CEO of Graham Windham, 13 September. Available from: https://www.risemagazine.org/2016/09/graham-jess-2016/

*Rise Magazine* (2024) Available from: https://www.risemagazine.org

*Rise Magazine* (2020) 'New York reforming NY State Central Registry will provide justice and relief to families', 16 April. Available from: https://www.risemagazine.org/2020/04/scr-reforms/

*Rise Magazine* and TakeRoot Justice (2021) *An Unavoidable System: The Harms of Family Policing and Parents' Vision for Investing in Community Care.* Available from: https://takerootjustice.org/wp-content/uploads/2021/09/AnUnavoidableSystem.pdf

Rise Staff (2022) 'Centering parent leadership in the movement to abolish family policing', *Columbia Journal of Race and Law*, 12(1). Available from: https://doi.org/10.52214/cjrl.v12i1.9921

Roberts, D. (2022) *Torn Apart*. Basic Books.

Ross, N., Cocks, J., Foote, W. and Davies, K. (2023) 'Just Work as a Team: Reconstructing Family Inclusion from Parent, Carer and Practitioner Perspectives', Centre for Law and Social Justice, January. Available from: https://www.newcastle.edu.au/research/centre/law-and-social-justice/research/family-inclusion-report-2023

Saar-Heiman, Y., Damman, J.L., Lalayants, M. and Gupta, A. (2024) 'Parent peer advocacy, mentoring, and support in child protection: A scoping review of programs and services', *Psychosocial Intervention*. Available from: https://journals.copmadrid.org/pi/art/pi2024a5

Scottish Government (2024) Children's Social Work Statistics 2022–23, Chart 3. Available from: https://www.gov.scot/publications/childrens-social-work-statistics-2022-23-looked-after-children/documents/

Selivanoff, S. (2024) Email to the author, 4 November.

Shine Lawyers (2024) *First Nations Child Removal Class Action.* Available from: https://www.shine.com.au/service/class-actions/first-nations-child-removal-class-action

Slettebo, T. (2013) 'Partnership with parents of children in care: a study of collective user participation in child protection services', *British Journal of Social Work*, 23(3): 579–95.

Southwark Council (2024) Parent to Parent Peer Advocacy. Available from: https://www.southwark.gov.uk/childcare-and-parenting/parent-to-parent-peer-advocacy?chapter=3

Swan, D. (2024) 'I worked in child protection for 13 years. Aboriginal families know what's best for our children', *The Guardian*, 12 November. Available from: https://www.theguardian.com/australia-news/2024/nov/13/i-worked-in-child-protection-for-13-years-aboriginal-families-know-whats-best-for-our-children

Tobis, D. (2013) *From Pariahs to Partners: How Parents and their Allies Changed New York City's Child Welfare System*. Oxford University Press.

Tobis, D. (2019) 'Parents organizing a grassroots movement to reform child welfare', in *The Routledge Handbook of Critical Social Work*. Routledge, pp 278–88.

Tobis, D. (2024a) *Parent Activism in High Income Countries*. Available from: https://www.davidtobis.com

Tobis, D. (2024b) Methodology for Parent Activism Research. Available from: https://www.davidtobis.com

Tobis, D. (2024c) Participation by the author in two Parent Cafes with parents and social workers, one in Swansea, 20 June and one in Anglesey, 25 June, Wales.

Tobis, D. (2024d) Site visit by the author to the Kasper Dandelion Parent Advocacy Programme, in their office in Helsinki, 31 May.

Tobis, D. (2024e) Site visit by the author to the Telford Local Authority, 4 June.

Tobis, D., Bilson, A. and Katugampala, I. (2020) International Review of Parent Advocacy in Child Welfare: Strengthening Children's Care and Protection Through Parent Participation. Better Care Network and IPAN. Available from: https://betternetwork.org/sites/default/files/2020-10/BCN_Parent_Advocacy_In_Child_Welfare.pdf

Trescher, S. and Summers, A. (2020) Outcome Evaluation Report for Washington State's Parents for Parents Program, Center for Courts, Capacity Building Center, 13 January.

UNCRC (2021) United Nations Committee on the Rights of the Child 2021 Day of General Discussion, Children's Rights and Alternative Care, Outcome Report. Available from: https://www.ohchr.org/sites/default/files/2022-06/13Jun2022-DGD-Outcome-report-and-Recommendations.pdf

United Nations Guidelines for the Alternative Care of Children (2009) UN General Assembly (64th session): resolution adopted by the General Assembly. Available from: https://digitallibrary.un.org/record/673583?ln=en&v=pdf

University of Sydney (2019) After the Apology: Larissa Behrendt. Available from: https://www.sydney.edu.au/engage/events-sponsorships/sydney-ideas/2019/after-the-apology-larissa-behrendt.html

Washington State Department of Children, Youth & Families (2024) Practice Improvement: HB-1227. Available from: https: //dcyf.wa.gov/practice/practice-improvement/HB-1227

Whitworth, J. (2024) Interview with the author, 9 December.

Wisconsin Department of Children and Families (2024) Slide presentation, Parent Advocate Panel, Wisconsin Department of Children and Families, Connecting the Dots, Annual Child Welfare conference, 24 September.

Zoongizi Ode Inc. (2024) (formerly Fearless R2W Inc.). Available from: https://zoongiziode.ca

# 8

# Models of parental advocacy in child and family social work

*Shane Powell, Clive Diaz, Tim Fisher, Kar Man Au and Jourdelle Bennett*

## Introduction

Parental advocacy has emerged as a significant approach within child and family social work, supporting parents to navigate complex child welfare systems and engage meaningfully in decision-making processes. Research consistently documents the need for robust advocacy support, highlighting how parents experience child protection systems as challenging, stigmatising and disempowering (Smithson and Gibson, 2017; Diaz, 2020). Studies reveal that parents often feel judged and marginalised in their interactions with child protection professionals, thereby limiting their ability to express perspectives and participate in decisions about their children (Corby et al, 1996; Gibson, 2015; Muench et al, 2017). Parental advocates work to address such challenges by providing guidance, emotional support and practical assistance to help parents navigate system complexities and communicate effectively with professionals (Tobis et al, 2020).

This chapter examines models of parental advocacy in child and family social work through several key lenses. Beginning with fundamental concepts and terminology, it situates advocacy within contemporary child protection practice before exploring its theoretical underpinnings. The chapter's core presents empirical evidence from a mixed-methods study of a peer parental advocacy (PPA) service in an English local authority, analysing how this model influenced parent–social worker engagement, power dynamics and family outcomes through data from interviews and focus groups with parents, advocates and professionals. Critical ethical challenges are examined, particularly balancing parental rights with child safeguarding, confidentiality, boundaries and advocates' well-being.

## Definitions and significance
### Defining parental advocacy

Within the scope of child and family social work, parental advocacy refers to the provision of support, advice and representation to help parents navigate the child protection system and ensure that their rights and perspectives are upheld. Tobis et al (2020) define parental advocacy as 'a form of peer advocacy where parents who themselves have had experience of the child welfare system help other parents involved to navigate it. In addition, they also help to develop strategies to change the system' (p 20).

Tobis et al (2020) further delineate three principal forms of parental advocacy:

1. Case advocacy, which focuses on increasing parent participation in decisions regarding their own case and involvement with child protection. This may involve advocates being present during key decision points, assisting with case planning and supporting parents in ongoing decisions about their child's care.
2. Programme advocacy, where trained parent advocates work within social service agencies to assist parents struggling to safely raise their children or achieve reunification.
3. Policy advocacy, which encompasses parents' participation in advisory boards, conferences, academia, grassroots organising and political action to drive reform in policies, legislation and resources for family support.

At its core, parental advocacy is underpinned by a recognition of the power imbalances inherent within child protection practice that can disadvantage and disenfranchise parents. By having an advocate in their corner to provide guidance, model positive communication and amplify their voice, the goal is to promote parents' self-determination and meaningful participation in decision-making processes (Berrick et al, 2011).

Key components of parental advocacy include information sharing about the workings of the child welfare system, emotional support to help parents manage the stress and trauma of child protection involvement, practical assistance such as helping parents access their rights and entitlements, and representation in meetings to ensure that parental perspectives are heard (Lalayants, 2013; Tobis et al, 2020).

Parental advocacy in child welfare systems encompasses several distinct models, primarily categorised as peer, professional and legal advocacy (Powell et al, 2024). Peer advocacy, the most prevalent form identified in the literature, involves parents with lived experience of the child welfare system supporting others currently navigating it (Devine et al, 2023; Powell et al, 2024). These advocates leverage their personal experiences to provide empathetic support, practical guidance and system navigation assistance.

Professional advocacy, while less common, involves trained professionals without necessarily having personal experience in child welfare systems (Powell et al, 2024). These advocates typically possess expertise in child welfare policies and practices, offering support and representation in various child protection processes. Legal advocacy, the least represented in the literature reviewed by Powell et al (2024), involves legal professionals representing parents in child protection proceedings. This form of advocacy focuses on protecting parental rights within the legal framework of child welfare systems. Powell et al (2024) also identified hybrid models that integrate elements of peer, professional and legal advocacy, aiming to provide comprehensive support by combining the strengths of each approach.

The literature highlights the benefits of peer advocacy, given the power of shared experiences in developing trust and providing relevant support (Devine et al, 2023). As summarised by Ivec (2013): 'Peer support is highly effective when trying to engage people who may resist or refuse the help of professionals. Less stigma, less distance socially and the absence of a power differential exist when someone has a shared human experience and story' (p 35).

Peer advocates can serve as compassionate helpers while also engaging in social action to drive systemic change. While each model of advocacy offers unique benefits, the prevalence of peer advocacy in the literature underscores its potential to bridge gaps between families and child welfare systems. However, the relative efficacy of different advocacy types, and how they might be optimally combined, remains an area requiring further research and evaluation.

*Significance in social work practice*

The significance of parental advocacy in child and family social work is multifaceted, though centres on its capacity to empower parents within child protection processes. Research identifies complex power dynamics between parents and professionals as a major barrier to engagement, with the threat of child removal and feelings of judgement inhibiting parents' participation (Muench et al, 2017; Smithson and Gibson, 2017). Advocates help bridge this gap by providing supportive presence and translating system complexities, thereby creating conditions for honest communication. As Tobis et al (2020, p 21) note, this approach 'allows a more complete picture of a family's circumstances to emerge and can lead to better decision making.' Similarly, Berrick et al's (2011, p 185) study found advocacy provided parents with 'genuine encouragement in their capacity to change and hope that their family might be reunited.'

Enhanced parental participation through advocacy correlates with improved outcomes. Featherstone et al (2011) documented increased service engagement and better relationships between parents and social workers, while studies indicate higher reunification rates for families receiving advocacy support (Berrick et al, 2011; Lalayants, 2013). Beyond individual impact, advocacy drives systemic change by spotlighting oppressive practices and reframing interventions around participation and family empowerment (Tobis, 2013). Grassroots advocacy groups, particularly in the USA, have successfully reformed punitive policies and pioneered community-based approaches (Tobis et al, 2020).

Advocacy initiatives also catalyse shifts in professional attitudes and organisational cultures. Lalayants' (2013) research found that parent advocates in child safety conferences promoted more collaborative decision-making and encouraged workers' critical reflection on power dynamics. However, implementation challenges persist within risk-averse, time-pressured statutory settings (Featherstone et al, 2011). Some practitioners may view advocates as threatening their professional judgement, while resource constraints hinder sustainable service provision. Realising advocacy's transformative potential requires engaging with theoretical frameworks and evidence-based practice to authentically empower parents and drive reform.

## Theoretical frameworks

The development of parent advocacy in child welfare emerged from recognising the need to address power imbalances between parents and child welfare professionals, with various theoretical frameworks informing its evolution. An early milestone, New Zealand's 1989 Children, Young Persons and Their Families Act, introduced Family Group Conferences (FGCs) based on traditional Māori practices. These conferences brought together extended family networks to make decisions about children's care, representing a systemic shift toward family-led problem-solving (Tobis, 2020).

Building on this model, a significant reform movement emerged in New York City during the 1990s, led by parents with child welfare experience alongside professional allies including social workers, lawyers and administrators. This movement employed both top-down and bottom-up strategies to increase parental influence in child welfare decisions at case, programme and policy levels (Tobis, 2013). The impact was substantial, contributing to a dramatic reduction in children in out-of-home care from 50,000 in 1992 to fewer than 8,000 by 2020 (Tobis, 2020).

The New York City movement evolved through four distinct phases (Tobis, 2019): initial protest (1994–2001), where parents organised outside the system; collaboration (2002–12), marked by increased parent advocate employment within agencies; institutionalisation (2012–14), with advocates gaining influential positions; and a current phase characterised by both progress and renewed challenges in family engagement. Throughout these stages, the movement drew upon empowerment theory, strengths-based approaches and critical theories, emphasising both parental capabilities and the need to address structural inequalities affecting marginalised communities (Tobis, 2013).

Parent advocacy initiatives developed across the United States through multiple pathways and influences, with distinct regional approaches responding to local contexts and needs (Tobis, 2020). Rather than representing a simple expansion of the New York City model, these diverse programmes emerged through various collaborations between parents, professionals and policy makers, each with unique characteristics and emphases. Evidence of improved outcomes and cost savings through reduced care placements contributed to their growth and sustainability in different jurisdictions (Birth Parent National Network, 2017). The approach has now gained traction internationally, with programmes emerging in the United Kingdom, Ireland, Australia, Finland, Norway and Canada. The Birth Parent National Network alone documented 60 advocacy groups in the USA by 2017, while international research identified over a hundred programmes globally (Birth Parent National Network, 2017; Tobis, 2020).

Parent voices have increasingly been incorporated into child welfare policy discussions, although their influence varies and operates alongside numerous other stakeholders. While parent advocates contributed perspectives to the development of the 2018 Family First Prevention Services Act in the USA, this legislation resulted from complex policy negotiations involving multiple constituencies, including professionals, researchers and policy makers (Children's Bureau, 2018; Chapin Hall, 2023). Parent advocacy work generally focuses on strengthening families, preventing unnecessary child removals and promoting reform at case, programme and policy levels (Tobis, 2020, 2019).

Parent advocacy programmes in child welfare are grounded in a diverse range of theoretical frameworks, often incorporating multiple perspectives to guide their design, delivery and intended outcomes (Tobis, 2013; Saar-Heiman et al, 2024). A comprehensive review of 24 programmes by Saar-Heiman et al (2024) identified three primary categories of theoretical underpinnings: empowerment theory and strengths-based approaches; mutual aid ideas and social network theories; and critical theories. Additionally, several programmes drew upon other frameworks such as system change, social support and family inclusion (Williamson and Gray, 2011; Lalayants, 2012a; Leake et al, 2012).

## Empowerment theory and strengths-based approaches

Empowerment theory and strengths-based approaches were the most prevalent theoretical frameworks identified in the literature, underpinning

15 of the 24 programmes reviewed by Saar-Heiman et al (2024). These humanistic perspectives emphasise individuals' capacity for self-determination, the development of personal agency and the enhancement of self-efficacy (Cohen and Canan, 2006; Berrick et al, 2011; Leake et al, 2012). Programmes grounded in these theories focus on creating opportunities for parents to build upon their strengths, express their needs and concerns, and gain control over their lives (Saar-Heiman et al, 2024).

Empowerment theory posits that individuals obtain dominion over their lives through a process of increasing awareness, developing skills and mobilising resources (Zimmerman, 2000). In the context of parent advocacy, this encompasses supporting parents to navigate the complexities of the child welfare system, assert their rights and actively participate in decision-making processes that affect their families (Cohen and Canan, 2006; Lalayants, 2012b, 2015). For example, the Iowa Parent Partners programme, which aims to increase reunification rates and reduce repeat maltreatment, is grounded in empowerment theory (Midwest Child Welfare Implementation Center [MCWIC], 2014; Chambers et al, 2019). By providing information, emotional support and practical assistance, parent advocates help to bridge power imbalances between parents and child welfare professionals, thereby empowering parents to have a stronger voice in their cases (Leake et al, 2012; Tobis, 2013).

Strengths-based approaches shift the focus from deficits to the inherent capabilities and resources of individuals and families (Saleebey, 2009). Parent advocacy programmes adopting this perspective recognise the resilience and expertise of parents who have experienced the child welfare system, viewing them as valuable partners in the process of change (Berrick et al, 2011; Leake et al, 2012). The Contra Costa Parent Partners Program, which aims to increase reunification rates and reduce time to reunification, is informed by empowerment theory, social support and a strengths-based approach (Berrick et al, 2011) By harnessing parents' strengths and supporting their self-determination, these programmes aim to promote positive outcomes for families and challenge the stigma and disempowerment often associated with child welfare involvement (Saar-Heiman et al, 2024).

## Mutual aid ideas and social network theories

Nine of the programmes reviewed by Saar-Heiman et al (2024) were informed by mutual aid ideas and social network theories. In contrast to the more individualistic focus of empowerment and strengths-based approaches, these frameworks emphasise the relational aspects of parents' lives and the importance of formal and informal support networks (Cameron and Birnie-Lefcovitch, 2000; Soffer-Elnekave et al, 2020).

Mutual aid refers to the reciprocal process of giving and receiving support within a group, based on shared experiences and a sense of solidarity

(Steinberg, 2010). Parent advocacy programmes grounded in mutual aid principles create spaces for parents to come together, share their stories and learn from one another (Leake et al, 2012; Lalayants et al, 2015). The Child Welfare Organizing Project (CWOP) in New York City, which aims to promote meaningful parent involvement and system transformation, is guided by principles of radical social work, political advocacy, empowerment, lived experience and mutual support (Lalayants, 2012a, 2012b, 2014, 2015, 2021; Lalayants et al, 2015; Castellano, 2021). Through peer support and collective action, parents can challenge feelings of isolation and stigma, build a sense of community and develop strategies for navigating the child welfare system (Soffer-Elnekave et al, 2020; Cameron, 2002).

Parents Anonymous represents another prominent example of mutual aid in parent support, operating as a universal service with a focus on parents involved with child protection. This programme is guided by principles of mutual aid, strengths-based practice and trauma-informed care, creating non-judgemental environments where parents can share experiences and develop supportive networks (Polinsky et al, 2010, 2011; Ainsworth, 2019; Burnson et al, 2021). Through structured but parent-led group sessions, participants build resilience, enhance parenting skills and develop social connections that extend beyond formal services.

Social network theories highlight the way individuals are embedded in webs of relationships that shape their experiences, resources and opportunities (Borgatti et al, 2009). Parent advocacy programmes informed by these theories recognise the significance of parents' social connections and work to strengthen both informal and formal support networks (Cameron and Birnie-Lefcovitch, 2000; Soffer-Elnekave et al, 2020). The Minnesota One-Stop for Communities Parent Mentor Programme, which aims to support successful parent navigation of the child welfare system and promote child and family well-being, is guided by principles of mutual aid, community responsibility, indigenous social work and culturally responsive practice (Soffer-Elnekave et al, 2020). By fostering a sense of belonging and enhancing parents' social capital, these programs aim to mitigate the stress and isolation often experienced by families involved with the child welfare system (Cameron, 2002; Lalayants et al, 2015).

## Critical theories

A smaller number of programmes (5) in the Saar-Heiman et al (2024) review were underpinned by critical theories, which focus on the social structures that generate and perpetuate inequality within child welfare systems. These frameworks, including radical social work and anti-oppressive practice, aim to underscore the ways in which child welfare policies and practices can have a disproportionate impact on marginalised communities, particularly families living in poverty and those from ethnic minority backgrounds (Bywaters et al, 2016; Bilson, 2019).

Parent advocacy programmes informed by critical theories prioritise system-level change and advocacy, seeking to challenge the structural inequities that contribute to families' involvement with child welfare services (Tobis, 2013). These programmes often engage in grassroots organising, policy advocacy and efforts to amplify parents' voices in decision-making processes at the organisational and systemic levels (Saar-Heiman et al, 2024). The Child Welfare Organising Project (CWOP) in New York City, mentioned earlier, is one such programme that functions on the operating assumption that the child protection system is structurally racist and predominantly harms Black, Asian and minority ethnic communities and families living in poverty (Castellano, 2021).

Critical approaches to parent advocacy emphasise the importance of building alliances between parents and professionals to work towards transformative change (Tobis, 2013). By recognising the expertise of parents with lived experience and collaborating to address systemic issues, these programmes aim to shift power dynamics and promote more equitable and just child welfare practices (Saar-Heiman et al, 2024). Ultimately, parent advocacy programmes grounded in critical theories seek to disrupt the status quo and advocate for fundamental reforms to child welfare systems that aim to better support families and communities (Tobis, 2013; Bilson, 2019).

## Other theoretical frameworks

In addition to the three main categories of theoretical frameworks identified by Saar-Heiman et al (2024), several specific approaches have distinctive emphases in parent advocacy implementation. System change theory focuses on transforming child welfare structures by engaging parents as reform partners (Williamson and Gray, 2011). Social support theory emphasises comprehensive assistance to help parents navigate child welfare challenges (Cohen and Wills, 1985; Berrick et al, 2011). Family inclusion theory promotes collaborative partnerships that recognise family expertise in decision-making (Tobis, 2013; Ainsworth and Berger, 2014).

## Rights-based approaches to parental advocacy

Beyond the theoretical frameworks previously discussed, rights-based approaches have emerged as significant in reshaping parental advocacy. Professor Anna Gupta has made substantial contributions in developing rights-based approaches that challenge dominant risk-focused paradigms in child protection. With colleagues Brid Featherstone, Kate Morris and

Sue White, she developed the Social Model of Child Protection, which reframes child welfare concerns within broader social and economic contexts while advocating for practices that recognise parents' rights and strengths (Featherstone et al, 2018).

Building on this work, Gupta and Yuval Saar-Heiman developed the Poverty-Aware Paradigm for Child Protection (PAPCP), which explicitly rejects neoliberal approaches that blame individual parents and instead addresses structural inequalities while supporting parents' rights (Saar-Heiman and Gupta, 2024). This paradigm recognises how socio-economic conditions fundamentally shape family circumstances and parenting capacity, challenging individualistic explanations of child maltreatment.

Recent literature shows a shift from promoting basic parental participation to supporting parental activism as a pathway to transformative system change. Saar-Heiman and Gupta (2024) distinguish between participation and activism, with the latter involving challenging power structures and developing community agency. This distinction highlights the evolution from viewing parents as service recipients to recognising them as potential catalysts for systemic reform.

## Power theory in parental advocacy

Power theory provides essential conceptual tools for understanding the dynamics of parental advocacy in child welfare. Several key concepts from power theory are particularly relevant:

1. *Power-with versus Power-over:* This distinction, drawn from feminist theory, differentiates between collaborative approaches that share power with parents versus oppressive approaches that exercise power over them. Parental advocacy seeks to promote 'Power-with' dynamics that recognise parents' expertise and agency.
2. *Critical consciousness:* Drawing on Freire's work, this concept involves developing understanding among parents about how structural factors like poverty and inequality influence how families are treated within child welfare systems. Advocacy programmes often aim to foster this awareness as a foundation for collective action.
3. *Experiential expertise:* This concept recognises the unique knowledge that parents with first-hand experience bring to child welfare contexts. It challenges professional dominance by validating lived experience as a legitimate form of knowledge.
4. *Transformative participation:* This approach moves beyond basic case participation toward challenging and changing power relations within child welfare systems. It seeks not only to improve individual cases but to reform the underlying structures that maintain inequity.

Research reveals how power imbalances manifest in child welfare systems that are often 'legalistic and adversarial' with a 'focus on individualized notions of risk and parental pathology with little attention to social harms' (Featherstone et al, 2018). Parents frequently experience these systems as 'stigmatising, inhumane, and harmful' (Bilson et al, 2022). Parental advocacy models seek to address these dynamics by redistributing power and amplifying parents' voices in decision-making processes.

## Empirical evidence: a case study of peer parental advocacy

Building on the theoretical frameworks discussed in the previous section, this section now turns to empirical evidence regarding the implementation and impact of parental advocacy in child protection practice. The section presents findings from a mixed-methods evaluation of a PPA service in an English local authority, as detailed in Diaz et al's (2023) project report, 'The perceived impact of PPA on child protection practice'. (By examining the experiences and perspectives of parents, advocates and child protection professionals involved with the service, valuable insights can be gained from the mechanisms by which advocacy influences parental engagement, power dynamics and – ultimately – outcomes for children and families.

## The Camden model: a pioneer in peer parental advocacy

The Camden model of PPA represents one of the most influential developments in this field in the UK context. Tim Fisher established the Camden Family Advisory Board (FAB) in 2014, beginning with informal coffee mornings for parents with experience of child protection services. This initiative evolved when Fisher co-designed a training programme called 'Empowering Families' and later co-ordinated the groundbreaking 'Camden Conversations' process – a family-led inquiry into child protection practices that directly led to establishing the first formal PPA programme in the UK (Diaz et al, 2023).

The model operates on several core principles: valuing lived experience as expertise, explicitly addressing power imbalances, and working across three levels of advocacy (case, programme and policy). Research by Diaz et al (2023) identified four key mechanisms enabling effective PPA:

1. *Engagement:* Creating connections through shared experiences.
2. *Communication:* Making complex processes understandable.
3. *Trust:* Building relationships often difficult to establish with professionals.
4. *Support:* Providing emotional and practical assistance throughout the process.

Kar Man Au, who joined the FAB as one of its original four members, has been instrumental in developing and implementing the Camden model. Au brings a unique perspective as both a parent with lived experience of the child protection system and a researcher, having co-authored academic work on lived experience perspectives and contributed to studies evaluating the Camden model's effectiveness.

## Relational activism as a theoretical foundation

The Camden model is theoretically grounded in the concept of 'relational activism', developed by Fisher and his colleague Becca Dove, which makes 'change happen through personal and informal relationships' (Dove and Fisher, 2019). This approach builds upon foundations first proposed by O'Shaughnessy and Kennedy in 2010, who identified relationship building as a form of activism operating within conventional social change campaigns.

Three key values define relational activism:

1. *Be curious and connect:* Resisting polarisation by maintaining curiosity about others.
2. *Show up with vulnerability:* Acknowledging that meaningful change requires emotional honesty.
3. *Act together:* Focusing on collective action where each person contributes their unique strengths.

This theoretical framework provides the foundation for the Camden model, where relationship-building becomes the locus for social change within child protection systems. It offers an alternative to traditional, professionally-dominated approaches by emphasising authentic connection and partnership. In practice, this means that peer parental advocates work through relationships rather than adversarial advocacy, creating spaces where both parents and professionals can engage differently.

## Study context and methodology

The PPA service evaluated in this study was established in the London Borough of Camden in 2019. Camden is an inner-London authority with a diverse population and mixed levels of deprivation, with approximately 31 per cent of children living in low-income families (Diaz et al, 2023). The advocacy service was developed in partnership with the London Family Group Conference (FGC) Learning Partnership, which created an Open College Network (OCN) accredited qualification in parent advocacy. Parents with lived experience of the child protection system completed this training, which included 72 hours of formal instruction across 12 sessions, written assignments and reflective work to become peer parental advocates.

The evaluation aimed to understand the perceived impact of the PPA service on child protection practice in Camden by addressing the following research questions:

1. What are the key ingredients of the PPA service in Camden?
2. What are parents' and professionals' experiences of the PPA service?
3. What potential impacts (both positive and negative changes) do parents and professionals who work with the PPA service identify?
4. Is it feasible to carry out an experimental or quasi-experimental evaluation in the future and, if so, what would the key considerations for designing such a study be?

To answer these questions, a mixed-methods, realist evaluation design was employed. Realist evaluation seeks to understand not merely whether an intervention works, but what works, for whom, and under what circumstances – by examining the interplay between context, mechanisms, and outcomes (Pawson and Tilley, 1997). Data collection occurred over an 8-month period from November 2021 to June 2022 and involved multiple methods:

1. Semi-structured interviews with 21 participants (7 parents, 6 peer parental advocates [PPAs], 4 social workers, 3 service managers, and 1 child protection chair). Participants were purposively sampled to ensure representation of different stakeholder perspectives. Interviews lasted between 45–90 minutes, were audio-recorded and fully transcribed.
2. Two focus groups with a total of 12 participants (5 parents, 4 PPAs, and 3 managers), designed to explore collective experiences and check preliminary findings. Each focus group lasted approximately 2 hours.
3. Structured observations of 1 online PPA meeting and 5 child protection conferences where PPAs were present, using an observation schedule to document interactions and practices.
4. Five stakeholder sessions with service designers, managers, and advocates to develop and refine the programme theory through an iterative process.

Ethical approval was granted by Cardiff University's School of Social Sciences Research Ethics Committee. All participants provided informed consent and were offered opportunities to review their interview transcripts.

Thematic analysis of the qualitative data was conducted using Braun and Clarke's (2006) six-stage approach: familiarisation with the data, initial coding, searching for themes, reviewing themes, defining and naming themes, and producing the report. Initial coding was conducted by two researchers independently, with regular meetings to compare and refine the coding framework. An initial programme theory was developed and then iteratively refined based on the empirical findings to produce a final logic model of the key contextual factors, intervention components, mechanisms and outcomes underpinning effective PPA in Camden. NVivo 12 software was used to organise and manage the data analysis process.

## Key findings

The evaluation highlighted a range of key themes regarding the implementation and impact of the PPA service:

*Navigating the complexity of the child protection system*

Both parents and professionals emphasised the complexity of the child protection system, with overlapping roles, unfamiliar terminology and 'information overload' creating an intimidating and often overwhelming experience for families. Many parents reported feeling judged, disempowered and confused, leading to feelings of anger and distress. In this context, PPAs were perceived to play a crucial role in providing practical and emotional support. As Parent 2 explained: 'The advocate that I have ... has been brilliant. It's just basically someone that understands the system and understands the whole process, court and social services element itself'.

PPAs assisted parents in making sense of child protection processes and expectations, explaining complex terminology in accessible language. Professionals recognised the unique value of this support coming from someone with lived experience, as captured in this social worker's reflection: 'I think a very well-trained advocate with lived experience of child protection processes themselves can be very, very helpful in those contexts ... they could feel very held, emotionally held, by that' (Social Worker 1).

*Rebalancing power relations*

A central theme was the power imbalance between parents and professionals, which could inhibit parents' meaningful engagement in child protection processes. Parents described feeling 'so small' in the face of the authority held by social workers and others in the system (PPA 1).

PPAs were seen to play an important role in equalising these power dynamics, as articulated by this service manager: '... in terms of sort of equalising power, which, you know, is a big part of advocacy, then someone who really has been there and done it, you know, is perhaps able to do that to the greatest extent' (Service Manager 2).

By providing independent support and 'bridging the gap' between families and professionals, PPAs empowered parents to find their voice and communicate more effectively in an otherwise daunting and disempowering context. PPAs helped to build parents' confidence in expressing their wishes and participating actively in decision-making.

However, some professionals noted the challenges this rebalancing of power could create, with enhanced parental participation generating additional work in an already pressured system. As one service manager explained:

> We want our parents to hold as much power as they can within the process, but when you do that, it gives us a huge challenge as the authority, because somebody who was disempowered is suddenly much more powerful ... the processes that we go through only add to ... the workload rather than reduce the workload. (Service Manager 1)

This tension between empowering parents and managing increased workloads highlights the complex dynamics at play in implementing PPA support. While the benefits for families are clear, the systemic challenges cannot be ignored. Striking a balance between parental empowerment and efficient service delivery remains a key consideration for policy makers and practitioners alike.

## *Building trust between parents and professionals*

Parental distrust and fear of child protection services was another key issue highlighted. Many parents, especially those with prior experiences of child removal, reported feeling hostile or resistant to social work involvement. PPAs played a vital role in shifting these dynamics by acting as an intermediary and 'bridging the gap' between families and professionals. As one service manager put it: 'if somebody is not trusting you ... it can only be a good thing to bring somebody else on board who has more experience of this process, and who can help hopefully build that relationship between the two sides' (Service Manager 1).

Over time, PPA involvement helped to challenge parents' negative perceptions of the child protection system and build a more constructive working relationship. Parents reflected on how their views had shifted:

> It has changed. Because I know that they're just there to do their job and to likesafeguard the children and that. (Parent 1).

> They're not there just to take your children away ... their aim is to [help] children to be safe, but they'll work with you to make sure that you can give a safe environment to the children. (Parent 2)

This shift enabled parents to engage more openly and collaboratively with interventions, improving information sharing and joint working to support children's safety and well-being.

## Effective support and supervision for PPAs

The importance of providing regular, attuned support and supervision for PPAs themselves was also emphasised. While PPAs' lived experience was vital to their ability to connect with and assist parents, it could also make them more vulnerable to emotional triggers or difficulties with boundaries. Having access to tailored training relevant to local needs and issues was important, as explained by this PPA:

> I think the support you need is based on the clients that the local authority has. Like, Camden has a lot of, like mental health, and, like, domestic violence: very specific type of dramas they deal with, you know? So having that kind of familiarity with those is ... would allow you to better support that family. (PPA 1)

Beyond formal training, opportunities for regular individual and group-based supervision, check-ins, and debriefing were vital to promote PPAs' own well-being and enable them to maintain appropriate boundaries. As one PPA put it:

> I need to be aware of the boundary, which I think is crucial ... I am providing the information and support for them but not trying to sort out their problem. I can voice for them but not make the decision for them ... I should always remain neutral in my position. (PPA 6)

The findings from this research underscore the critical role of high-calibre advocacy in fostering meaningful parental involvement and achieving favourable results. A crucial element in maintaining this quality appears to be the provision of appropriate oversight. Consequently, these testimonials highlight the necessity of robust supervision, comprehensive training, and continuous support for peer advocates who leverage their personal experiences to assist others.

## Peer versus professional advocacy

A final cross-cutting theme was the debate around the relative merits of peer and professional advocacy models. Some stakeholders expressed reservations about whether PPAs would have sufficient specialist knowledge to assist parents with particularly complex needs or legal issues, compared to professional advocates with extensive training and experience.

However, many participants highlighted the unique benefits of peer advocacy, which enabled a more authentic and empathetic connection with parents based on shared experiences and understanding. As one parent powerfully articulated:

> I think for me there's something very powerful about lived experience and knowing that someone has been there and for a parent, say, going into a child protection conference to be supported by someone else who has in the past themselves been through a child protection conference brings a very unique sort of support and equalisation of power. (Parent 6)

While professional advocates may be viewed as 'just another professional in the room', PPAs could more effectively build trust, convey empathy, and reduce the sense of isolation and shame experienced by parents within the child protection system. Participants emphasised the importance of PPAs being able to draw on their own experiences to connect with parents, while also maintaining appropriate boundaries and professionalism.

## Analysis and discussion

The findings from this mixed-methods evaluation illuminate how theoretical frameworks manifest in practical advocacy. Mapping the empirical data onto the initial programme theory enabled identification of four key mechanisms underpinning effective peer advocacy:

1. Active PPA engagement with parents demonstrates empowerment theory in action, as advocates' lived experiences enable authentic connections and tailored support. This embodies Zimmerman's (2000) conception of empowerment as increasing awareness and developing skills through shared understanding. PPAs help humanise the process and reduce powerlessness by engaging proactively throughout parents' child protection involvement (Diaz et al, 2023).
2. Facilitating effective communication in child protection conferences operationalises critical theory's focus on addressing power imbalances (Bilson, 2019). PPAs achieve this by providing accessible information about processes, supporting parents to articulate views, and advocating on their behalf when needed (Diaz et al, 2023). This practical application of critical perspectives highlights the challenges of redistributing power within established hierarchies, as some professionals perceived PPA involvement as threatening to institutional authority.
3. Building trust between parents and child protection workers reflects mutual aid principles outlined by Steinberg (2010), with PPAs serving

as intermediaries who demonstrate empathy and encourage engagement. Many parents enter the system with fear or hostility, but consistent with social network theory (Borgatti et al, 2009), PPAs help forge constructive relationships by bridging divides between families and professionals (Diaz et al, 2023).
4. Increasing parents' decision-making power exemplifies strengths-based approaches (Saleebey, 2009) by recognising and elevating parental expertise. PPAs facilitate collaborative approaches that promote sustainable progress by amplifying parents' voices in contexts where they typically feel excluded (Diaz et al, 2023).

While lived experience is vital for peer advocacy, it increases support needs around boundaries and emotional processing, reflecting Lalayants' (2021) emphasis on preventing secondary trauma through comprehensive training.

The debate between peer and professional models illuminates theoretical tensions between experiential and professional knowledge. Most stakeholders valued PPAs' unique role, consistent with mutual aid approaches emphasizing shared experience (Soffer-Elnekave et al, 2020). However, concerns about complex cases requiring specialist knowledge suggest benefits in combining approaches, with PPAs providing daily support while accessing professional guidance when needed.

Camden's PPA model integrates multiple theoretical frameworks. The emphasis on building parents' agency and confidence demonstrates empowerment theory, while advocacy addressing power imbalances reflects critical perspectives. The treatment of lived experience as an asset embodies strengths-based principles (Saleebey, 2009), and the partnership ethos aligns with family inclusion frameworks (Ainsworth and Berger, 2014). Although systemic advocacy was not primary, PPAs' insights contribute to improving processes over time, consistent with critical theory's focus on institutional change.

However, the evaluation reveals barriers to realising theoretical aspirations in practice. Organisational norms, risk-averse attitudes, resource constraints, and power differentials pose challenges to reform (Diaz et al, 2023). Fully embedding PPA services requires sustained commitment to shifting mindsets and developing receptive environments, as predicted by critical theorists examining institutional resistance to change.

This case study demonstrates how theoretical frameworks can guide effective advocacy implementation. The findings support broader evidence about advocacy's benefits for engagement and decision-making, while highlighting practical challenges in operationalising theoretical principles. Although further research is needed to quantify outcomes, there are strong grounds for developing PPA as part of a more participatory approach to child protection (Devine et al, 2023).

## Ethical considerations and challenges

Parental advocacy holds significant promise for humanising child protection systems and amplifying the voices of marginalised parents. However, its implementation also raises complex ethical issues that warrant careful consideration. This section explores four key domains of ethical challenge: balancing parental rights and child welfare; confidentiality and information sharing; power dynamics in advocacy relationships; and resource allocation and sustainability.

### Balancing parental rights and child welfare

A fundamental tension exists between upholding the rights of parents to care for their children and the state's duty to safeguard children's safety and wellbeing when maltreatment concerns arise. Parental advocates must navigate this delicate balance, working to promote parents' perspectives and self-determination while prioritising the best interests of the child (Collings et al, 2018; Powell et al, 2024). There may be instances where an advocate feels a parent's wishes conflict with a child's welfare, necessitating difficult judgements about when and how to intervene.

As noted by Douglas and Walsh (2009), 'advocacy for parents does carry some risk that their interests may displace the interests of their child' (p 215). Advocates must remain vigilant that empowering parents does not come at the expense of children's safety. Maintaining child-centricity is vital to ensure advocacy empowers rather than endangers children. Clear protocols for reporting safety concerns and seeking supervisor guidance can help advocates manage these dilemmas (Tobis et al, 2020). Robust training, supervision and case review processes are essential to equip advocates with the skills and support to uphold children's rights within an advocacy framework (Fitz-Symonds et al, 2023; Powell et al, 2024).

Furthermore, as highlighted in Powell et al's (2024) scoping review, the proliferation of peer advocacy models raises questions about how shared lived experiences may influence perspectives on risk and safety. While experiential wisdom is a strength, it is crucial that peer advocates receive adequate training and ongoing support to maintain objectivity and prioritise child welfare (Powell et al, 2024). Regular reflective supervision and clear decision-making protocols can help peer advocates navigate complex situations where their own experiences may colour judgements.

### Confidentiality and information sharing

Respecting client confidentiality is a core tenet of advocacy relationships built on trust. However, the high stakes of child protection work may justify some limits to confidentiality to prevent imminent harm. Advocates must be transparent with parents about the boundaries of confidentiality and their duties to share information related to child safety (Fitz-Symonds et al, 2023; Powell et al, 2024). As Tarleton (2013, p 684) emphasises, specialist advocates 'need to be clear that their advocacy relationship with the parent is bounded by their responsibility to safeguard the child.'

Agreeing on processes for seeking consent to share information and explaining the rationale can make disclosure feel less of a betrayal. Within advocacy organisations, maintaining secure record keeping and privacy protocols is also vital. At a systemic level, developing information-sharing agreements between independent advocacy services and statutory agencies can enable advocates to access key details to provide effective support while safeguarding sensitive data (Featherstone et al, 2011). Regular refresher training on confidentiality and its limits is important to ensure advocates maintain ethical practice in dynamic case situations (Haworth et al, 2022; Powell et al, 2024).

Powell et al (2024) also highlight the need for clear guidelines around information sharing between peer advocates and professionals. While open communication is important for coordinated support, it is vital that peer advocates do not feel pressured to divulge private details shared by parents in confidence. Explicit confidentiality policies and consent procedures can help maintain trust and role clarity.

*Power dynamics in advocacy relationships*

Though parental advocacy aims to rebalance power between the state and families, the advocacy relationship itself is not immune to power imbalances. Parents may feel reliant on advocates or hesitant to challenge them for fear of losing support (Tobis et al, 2020). Inequities can be especially stark when advocates differ from parents in socioeconomic status, race, gender or other identities (Collings et al, 2018; Powell et al, 2024).

Advocates must be reflexive about their own power and take steps to minimise its misuse, such as regularly seeking feedback, respecting self-determination and being clear about role boundaries. Supervision plays a crucial role in interrogating power dynamics and promoting anti-oppressive practice (Fitz-Symonds et al, 2023). As Damman (2018, p 109) found, 'Recognising power differentials between system professionals and the parents they serve is critical to supporting meaningful involvement rather than replicating oppressive dynamics'.

Peer advocacy models may be less susceptible to stark power differentials than professional approaches, but both require ongoing attention to empowerment principles. Powell et al (2024) note that even within peer relationships, advocates with more child welfare experience may be perceived as having greater expertise or authority. Transparent discussions about power, positionality and boundaries should be integrated into peer advocate training and supervision.

Ultimately, quality advocacy requires a partnership approach in which parents are respected as experts on their own lives (Lalayants et al, 2021). Amplifying parent leadership in advocacy programme design, evaluation and governance can further mitigate power imbalances (Tobis et al, 2020). As evidenced in Powell et al's (2024) review, initiatives that centre parent voice and leadership, such as the Child Welfare Organizing Project, show promise in reforming paternalistic systems.

## *Resource allocation and sustainability*

Parental advocacy programmes frequently operate with precarious funding and stretched capacities, reflecting child welfare systems' chronic under-resourcing of family support in favour of investigation (Featherstone et al, 2018). These resource constraints limit programmes' ability to serve all eligible families, maintain appropriate service intensity, and support advocates' professional development (Walsh et al, 2019; Powell et al, 2024). Short-term funding cycles further undermine sustainable planning and raise justice concerns about advocacy access (Diaz et al, 2023). As Fitt et al (2023, p 6) observe, 'Lack of resources to meet demand is a key ethical consideration, potentially disadvantaging some families based on luck and timing rather than need'.

Programmes have developed various strategies to optimise limited resources, including careful triage, caseload monitoring, and ring-fenced funding (Lalayants, 2013). Cost-benefit analyses demonstrating advocacy's impact on reducing care entries and expediting reunification can strengthen investment arguments (Bohannan et al, 2016). However, transparent prioritisation criteria remain essential for equitable service allocation, given persistent resource constraints (Powell et al, 2024).

Addressing these challenges requires broader commitment to early support and family preservation. This might include sustained campaigning for adequate funding (Douglas and Walsh, 2009) and evaluation to build the economic case for advocacy investment (Powell et al, 2024). Meanwhile, protecting advocate wellbeing through caseload management, peer support, and reflective practice remains crucial for sustainable service delivery (Fitz-Symonds et al, 2023).

While not a panacea, parental advocacy represents a valuable tool for promoting inclusive practice when properly resourced and implemented. Success requires both practical measures, such as clear organisational policies and training, and broader societal commitment to addressing structural inequities underlying marginalised communities' disproportionate child protection involvement (Featherstone et al, 2018).

## Future directions for research and practice

Parental advocacy in child protection has gained increasing attention in recent years, yet as evidenced by this chapter's exploration of the current landscape, significant gaps remain in our understanding of effective implementation and impact. This section outlines key areas for further research and provides practical guidance for practitioners seeking to integrate advocacy into their work.

### Gaps in current research

While existing studies have begun to illuminate the potential of parental advocacy, the evidence base remains limited in several important ways. First, most research to date has been conducted in the United States, with a handful of studies from other countries such as the United Kingdom, Australia and Canada (Powell et al, 2024). International research is needed to understand how advocacy models translate across diverse systems and contexts.

Second, the preponderance of qualitative and observational studies means that causal links between advocacy and outcomes are difficult to establish. As Diaz et al (2023) note, robust research using comparison groups and measuring child protection outcomes is vital to substantiate perceived benefits and causally link advocacy approaches to decision impacts. Well-designed experimental and quasi-experimental studies are essential to build a more conclusive evidence base.

Third, the focus of most research on individual case advocacy means that our understanding of programme and policy advocacy appear underdeveloped. Studies that rigorously evaluate system-level reforms and parents' participation in organisational governance and policy development are crucial to realising the full transformative potential of parental advocacy (Tobis et al, 2020).

Finally, the perspectives of children and young people are notably absent from much of the current literature. Incorporating their voices and experiences is vital to ensure advocacy upholds children's rights and best interests. Participatory research methods that engage children and youth as co-researchers could yield valuable insights (Evans et al, 2024).

### Potential areas for future study

Building on these identified gaps, critical research priorities emerge. Longitudinal research examining families' trajectories could illuminate advocacy's enduring impact on placement stability and child well-being, while economic analyses would strengthen the case for sustainable investment (Bohannan et al, 2016). Understanding the comparative efficacy of peer and professional advocacy models remains crucial for matching approaches to family needs (Collings et al, 2018). Additionally, research must examine advocacy's intersection with other family support interventions and its potential for addressing systemic inequities, particularly in amplifying marginalised voices (Damman, 2018). Implementation research is also vital, investigating how organisational culture, leadership, and resources influence advocacy's integration within resistant bureaucracies (Fitz-Symonds et al, 2023).

## Practical guidance for practitioners

Effective integration of advocacy into child protection practice requires strategic implementation. Research suggests key approaches for promoting sustainable advocacy services within existing systems.

Successful implementation requires raising awareness through multiple entry points while emphasising independence and non-stigmatising approaches (Tobis et al, 2020). This awareness-building must be accompanied by cultivation of partnership-based organisational culture, supported by strong leadership commitment and champions for change (Fitz-Symonds et al, 2023). Equitable access demands robust referral pathways, with particular attention to marginalised groups, using demographic data to monitor and address disparities (Damman, 2018). Equally important is fostering positive relationships between advocates and child protection staff, through joint training and clear role delineation, positioning advocacy as a resource rather than threat (Lalayants, 2017). Investment in comprehensive training and supervision for advocates, particularly supporting those with lived experience, provides the foundation for sustainable practice (Haworth et al, 2022).

Best practices for supporting families centre on including parents' perspectives through active listening, empathy, and creating space for them to articulate their goals and concerns (Berrick et al, 2011). Information about child protection processes and rights must be conveyed in accessible language, supported by written resources families can reference (Featherstone and Fraser, 2012). Practical barriers to participation require attention through provision of transportation, childcare, and interpreter services where needed (Leake et al, 2012). Careful pacing of interactions, with time allowed for processing information, helps prevent overwhelming parents during stressful proceedings (Tobis et al, 2020). Building social capital through connections to community resources and peer networks strengthens family support systems (Lalayants et al, 2015).

Key resources support implementation efforts. The International Review of Parent Advocacy in Child Welfare provides comprehensive guidance for programme development (Tobis et al, 2020), while *Rise Magazine* offers practical toolkits developed by parents (Rise, 2022). The Detroit Center for Family Advocacy evaluation findings detail lessons from multidisciplinary approaches (University of Michigan Law School [UMLS], 2013), and the Best Interests of the Child Assessment framework helps structure parent participation in decision-making (Lennox et al, 2022). Successful implementation requires shifting from adversarial approaches to genuine partnership, recognising parents as experts in their own lives.

## Conclusion

This chapter has examined parental advocacy in child and family social work, synthesising current research, theoretical foundations, implementation challenges, and future directions. Throughout, parents' voices have emerged as fundamental to creating humane child protection systems.

The diverse landscape of peer, professional, and hybrid advocacy models offers multiple pathways for elevating parents' voices, though predominantly US-based evidence highlights the need for international research (Powell et al, 2024). Studies consistently demonstrate advocacy's positive impact on engagement, communication, and outcomes (Tobis et al, 2020; Lalayants et al, 2021). By addressing power imbalances and providing practical support, advocates enable meaningful participation for marginalised parents (Collings et al, 2018; Fitz-Symonds et al, 2023).

However, realising advocacy's transformative potential requires confronting systemic barriers, including stigma, adversarial cultures and resource constraints (Damman, 2018; Featherstone et al, 2018). Success demands sustained effort to reshape institutional mindsets and embed advocacy through robust training, supervision, and collaboration (Haworth et al, 2022; Fitz-Symonds et al, 2023). Further research through longitudinal studies, economic analyses and participatory methodologies is essential (Bohannan et al, 2016; Evans et al, 2024).

The evidence makes a compelling case for parental advocacy's role in humanising child protection. Though not a panacea, advocacy represents a vital step toward compassionate, participatory practice. When parents are genuinely heard, opportunities for meaningful change emerge. Investing in advocacy signals commitment to reform.

## References

Ainsworth, A. (2019) *Effectively Preventing and Treating Child Abuse and Neglect by Strengthening Families: Evaluation Brief 2016–2019*. California State University.

Ainsworth, F. and Berger, J. (2014) 'Family inclusive child protection practice: the history of the family inclusion network and beyond', *Children Australia*, 39(2): 60–4. doi: 10.1017/cha.2014.1

Berrick, J.D., Cohen, E. and Anthony, E. (2011) 'Partnering with parents: promising approaches to improve reunification outcomes for children in foster care', *Journal of Family Strengths*, 11(1): Article 14.

Berrick, J.D., Young, E.W., Cohen, E. and Anthony, E. (2011) 'I am the face of success': peer mentors in child welfare', *Child & Family Social Work*, 16(2): 179–91. doi: 10.1111/j.1365-2206.2010.00730.x

Bilson, A. (2019) 'The government's adoption drive isn't achieving its aims', *Community Care*. Available from: http://bilson.org.uk/wp_new/wp-content/uploads/2018/06/community-care-update.pdf

Bilson, A., Featherstone, B., Morris, K. and White, S. (2022) 'Humane child protection systems: a framework for reform', *British Journal of Social Work*, 52(7): 3897–914.

Birth Parent National Network (2017) *Parent Partnership Compendium of Organizations*. National Alliance Children's Trust and Prevention Funds.

Bohannan, T., Gonzalez, C. and Summers, A. (2016) 'Assessing the relationship between a peer-mentoring program and case outcomes in dependency court', *Journal of Public Child Welfare*, 10(2):176–96. doi: 10.1080/15548732.2016.1155523

Borgatti, S.P., Mehra, A., Brass, D.J. and Labianca, G. (2009) 'Network analysis in the social sciences', *Science*, 323(5916): 892–95.

Braun, V. and Clarke, V. (2006) 'Using thematic analysis in psychology', *Qualitative Research in Psychology*, 3(2): 77–101. doi: 10.1191/1478088706qp063oa

Burnson, C., Covington, S., Arvizo, B., Qiao, J. and Harris, E. (2021) 'The impact of Parents Anonymous on child safety and permanency', *Children and Youth Services Review*, 124: 105973.

Bywaters, P., Brady, G., Sparks, T. and Bos, E. (2016) 'Inequalities in child welfare intervention rates: the intersection of deprivation and identity', *Child & Family Social Work*, 21(4): 452–63.

Cameron, G. (2002) 'Motivation to join and benefits from participation in parent mutual aid organizations', *Child Welfare*, 81(1): 33–57.

Cameron, G. and Birnie-Lefcovitch, S. (2000) 'Parent mutual aid organizations in child welfare demonstration project: a report of outcomes', *Children and Youth Services Review*, 22(6): 421–40.

Castellano, V. (2021) 'Walking a fine line: the struggle for parent advocacy in the NYC child welfare system', *City & Society*, 33(3): 518–41.

Chambers, J.M., Lint, S., Thompson, M.G., Carlson, M.W. and Graef, M.I. (2019) 'Outcomes of the Iowa Parent Partner program evaluation: stability of reunification and re-entry into foster care', *Children and Youth Services Review*, 104: Article 104353. doi: 10.1016/j.childyouth.2019.05.030

Chapin Hall at the University of Chicago (2023) *Home Visiting in the Family First Context*. Chapin Hall Policy Brief. Available from: https://www.chapinhall.org/wp-content/uploads/FFPSA-HV-Brief.pdf

Children's Bureau (2018) *Program Instruction ACYF-CB-PI-18-09*. U.S. Department of Health and Human Services. Available from: https://www.grandfamilies.org/Portals/0/Documents/FFPSA/FFPSA%20Guide.pdf

Cohen, E. and Canan, L. (2006) 'Closer to home: parent mentors in child welfare', *Child Welfare*, 85(5): 867–84.

Cohen, S. and Wills, T.A. (1985) 'Stress, social support, and the buffering hypothesis', *Psychological Bulletin*, 98(2): 310–57.

Collings, S., Spencer, M., Dew, A. and Dowse, L. (2018) ' " She was there if I needed to talk or to try and get my point across": specialist advocacy for parents with intellectual disability in the Australian child protection system', *Australian Journal of Human Rights*, 24(2): 162–81. doi: 10.1080/1323238X.2018.1478595

Corby, B., Millar, M. and Young, L. (1996) 'Parental participation in child protection work: rethinking the rhetoric', *The British Journal of Social Work*, 26(4):475–92. doi: 10.1093/oxfordjournals.bjsw.a011120

Damman, J.L. (2018) *Birth parent involvement at a system level in child welfare: Exploring the perspectives of birth parents in parent partner programs*. Doctoral dissertation. University of Kansas. Available from: https://kuscholarworks.ku.edu/handle/1808/27615

Devine, R., Benson, K., Fitz-Symonds, S., Westlake, D., Campbell, K. and Diaz, C. (2023) 'Peer parental advocacy: a narrative review of the literature', *Journal of Children's Services*, 18(3/4): 244–60.

Diaz, C. (2020) *Decision Making in Child and Family Social Work: Perspectives on Participation*. Policy Press.

Diaz, C., Fitz-Symonds, S., Evans, L., Westlake, D., Devine, R., Mauri, D. et al. (2023) *The Perceived Impact of Peer Parental Advocacy on Child Protection Practice: A Mixed-Methods Evaluation. What Works for Early Intervention and Children's Social Care*. Available from: https://orca.cardiff.ac.uk/id/eprint/156171/

Douglas, H. and Walsh, T. (2009) 'Mothers and the child protection system', *International Journal of Law, Policy and the Family*, 23(2): 211–29.

Dove, B. and Fisher, T. (2019) Becoming unstuck with relational activism. *Stanford Social Innovation Review*. Available from: https://ssir.org/articles/entry/becoming_unstuck_with_relational_activism

Evans, L., Fitz-Symonds, S., Long, F., Roberts, L., Diaz, C. and Powell, S. (2024) ' "They seem to listen more now I have an advocate": a study into the implementation of parental advocacy in Wales', *Journal of Children's Services*, 19(2): 89–104. Available from: https://doi.org/10.1108/JCS-05-2023-0027

Featherstone, B. and Fraser, C. (2012) '"I'm just a mother. I'm nothing special, they're all professionals": parental advocacy as an aid to parental engagement', *Child & Family Social Work*, 17(2): 244–53. doi: 10.1111/j.1365-2206.2012.00839.x

Featherstone, B., Fraser, C., Ashley, C. and Ledward, P. (2011) 'Advocacy for parents and carers involved with children's services: making a difference to working in partnership?', *Child & Family Social Work*, 16(3): 266–75. doi: 10.1111/j.1365-2206.2010.00738.x

Featherstone, B., Gupta, A., Morris, K. and White, S. (2018) *Protecting Children: A Social Model*. Policy Press.

Fitt, K., Maylea, C., Costello, S., Kuyini, B. and Thomas, S. (2023) 'Independent non-legal advocacy in the child protection context: a descriptive review of the literature', *Child Abuse & Neglect*, 143: 106285. doi: 10.1016/j.chiabu.2023.106285

Fitz-Symonds, S., Evans, L., Tobis, D., Westlake, D. and Diaz, C. (2023) 'Mechanisms for support: a realist evaluation of peer parental advocacy in England', *British Journal of Social Work*, 54(1): 341–62. doi: 10.1093/bjsw/bcad200

Gibson, M. (2015) 'Shame and guilt in child protection social work: new interpretations and opportunities for practice', *Child & Family Social Work*, 20(3): 333–43. doi: 10.1111/cfs.12081

Haworth, S., Bilson, A., Drayak, T., Mayes, T. and Saar-Heiman, Y. (2022) 'Parental partnership, advocacy and engagement: the way forward', *Social Sciences*, 11(8): 353. Available from: doi: 10.3390/socsci11080353

Ivec, M. (2013) *A Necessary Engagement: An International Review of Parent and Family Engagement in Child Protection*. Anglicare Tasmania.

Lalayants, M. (2012a) Child Welfare Organizing Project: Community connections. Program evaluation. Final Report. CWOP, Silberman School of Social Work & National Resource Center for Permanency and Family Connections.

Lalayants, M. (2012b) 'Parent engagement in child safety conferences: the role of parent representatives', *Child Welfare*, 91(6): 9–42. Available from: https://www.jstor.org/stable/48623366

Lalayants, M. (2013) 'Parent representation model in child safety conferences', *Child Welfare*, 92(5): 107–36. Available from: https://www.jstor.org/stable/48623494

Lalayants, M. (2014) 'Parent representation model in child safety conferences', *Child Welfare*, 92(5): 107–36. Available from: https://www.jstor.org/stable/48623494

Lalayants, M. (2015) 'Partnership between child protective services and parent representatives', *Child & Family Social Work*, 22(S1): 40–50. Available from: https://onlinelibrary.wiley.com/doi/10.1111/cfs.12217

Lalayants, M. (2017) 'Partnership between child protective services and parent representatives', *Child & Family Social Work*, 22: 40–50. doi: 10.1111/cfs.12217

Lalayants, M. (2021) 'Secondary traumatic stress among parent advocates in child welfare', *Journal of Family Social Work*, 24(5): 341–62. doi: 10.1080/10522158.2021.2003921

Lalayants, M., Baier, M., Benedict, A. and Mera, D. (2015) 'Peer support groups for child welfare-involved families', *Journal of Family Social Work*, 18(5): 305–26. doi: 10.1080/10522158.2015.1026015

Leake, R., Longworth-Reed, L., Williams, N. and Potter, C. (2012) 'Exploring the benefits of a parent partner mentoring program in child welfare', *Journal of Family Strengths*, 12(1): Article 6.

Lennox, C., Jordan, A., O'Donnell, M. and Seymour, A. (2022) 'The Best Interests of the Child Assessment Tool'. Available from: https://www.griffith.edu.au/__data/assets/pdf_file/0020/1429310/Best-Interests-of-the-Child-Assessment-Tool.pdf

Midwest Child Welfare Implementation Center (MCWIC) (2014) Iowa Parent Partner Program. Iowa Department of Health and Human Services. Available from: https://hhs.iowa.gov/programs/CPS/parent-partners

Muench, K., Diaz, C. and Wright, R. (2017) 'Children and parent participation in child protection conferences: a study in one English local authority', *Child Care in Practice*, 23(1): 49–63. doi: 10.1080/13575279.2015.1126227

O'Shaughnessy, S. and Kennedy, E.H. (2010) 'Relational activism: reimagining women's environmental work as cultural change', *Canadian Journal of Sociology*, 35(4): 551–72. doi: 10.29173/cjs7507

Pawson, R. and Tilley, N. (1997) *Realistic Evaluation*. SAGE Publications.

Polinsky, M.L., Pion-Berlin, L., Long, T. and Wolf, A.M. (2011) 'Parents Anonymous® outcome evaluation: promising findings for child maltreatment reduction', *Journal of Juvenile Justice*, 1(1): 33–47.

Polinsky, M.L., Pion-Berlin, L., Williams, S., Long, T. and Wolf, A.M. (2010) 'Preventing child abuse and neglect: a national evaluation of Parents Anonymous groups', *Child Welfare*, 89(6): 43–62.

Powell, S., Fitz-Symonds, S., Wilkins, D., Westlake, D., Long, F., Evans, L. et al (2024) '*Understanding How and Under what Circumstances Parental Advocates Support Parents to Participate in Decision-Making: A Scoping Review*', *Child Care in Practice*. doi: 10.1080/13575279.2024.2354823

Rise Magazine (2022) Rise resources. Available from: https://www.risemagazine.org/resources/

Saar-Heiman, Y. and Gupta, A. (2024) 'Beyond participation: parent activism in child protection as a path to transformative change', *Children and Youth Services Review*, 157: 107443. doi: 10.1016/j.childyouth.2024.107443

Saar-Heiman, Y., Damman, J.L., Lalayants, M. and Gupta, A. (2024) 'Parent peer advocacy, mentoring, and support in child protection: a scoping review of programs and services', *Psychosocial Intervention*, 33(2): 73–88. doi: 10.5093/pi2024a5

Saleebey, D. (2009) *The Strengths Perspective in Social Work Practice*. 5th edn: Pearson Education.

Smithson, R. and Gibson, M. (2017) 'Less than human: a qualitative study into the experience of parents involved in the child protection system', *Child & Family Social Work*, 22(2): 565–74. Available from: doi: 10.1111/cfs.12270

Soffer-Elnekave, R., Haight, W. and Jader, B. (2020) 'Parent mentoring relationships as a vehicle for reducing racial disparities: experiences of child welfare-involved parents, mentors and professionals', *Children and Youth Services Review*, 109: 104682.

Steinberg, D.M. (2010) 'Mutual aid: a contribution to best-practice social work', *Social Work with Groups*, 33(1): 53–68. doi: 10.1080/01609510903316389

Tarleton, B. (2013) 'Expanding the engagement model: the role of the specialist advocate in supporting parents with learning disabilities in child protection proceedings', *Journal of Public Child Welfare*, 7(5): 675–90. doi: 10.1080/15548732.2013.845643

Tobis, D. (2013) *From Pariahs to Partners: How Parents and Their Allies Changed New York City's Child Welfare System*. Oxford University Press.

Tobis, D. (2019) 'Parents organizing a grassroots movement to reform child welfare', in *The Routledge Handbook of Critical Social Work*. Routledge.

Tobis, D., Bilson, A. and Katugampala, I. (2020) *International Review of Parent Advocacy in Child Welfare: Strengthening Children's Care and Protection through Parent Participation*. Better Care Network and IPAN. Available from: https://bettercarenetwork.org/sites/default/files/2020-10/BCN_Parent_Advocacy_In_Child_Welfare.pdf

University of Michigan Law School (UMLS) (2013) *Detroit Center for Family Advocacy Pilot Evaluation Report, 7/2009-6/2012*. Available from: https://legislature.maine.gov/doc/8785

Walsh, J., Rudman, H. and Burton, R. (2019) *Evaluation: New Beginnings Greater Manchester Pilot Project*. University of Sheffield.

Williamson, E. and Gray, A. (2011) 'New roles for families in child welfare: strategies for expanding family involvement beyond the case level', *Children and Youth Services Review*, 33(7): 1212–16. doi: 10.1016/j.childyouth.2011.02.013

Zimmerman, M.A. (2000) 'Empowerment theory: psychological, organizational, and community levels of analysis', in J. Rappaport and E. Seidman (eds) *Handbook of Community Psychology*, Springer, pp 43–63.

# 9

# Advocacy for children in care

*Sammi Fitz-Symonds and Lorna Stabler*

## Introduction

In the complex landscape of child welfare, where decisions made by adults have a profound impact on the lives of vulnerable children and young people, the role of advocacy is crucial. This chapter explores the critical importance of advocacy for children in care, highlighting its transformative potential in promoting participatory practices, safeguarding rights and enhancing well-being. As we explore this vital aspect of child protection, this chapter will discuss how advocacy empowers the often-unheard voices of children in care and advocate for their meaningful involvement in decisions that shape their lives.

Advocacy, in the context of children in care, is more than a service: it is a fundamental shift in how we perceive and interact with children within the care system. It is the process of supporting and enabling children and young people to express their views, participate in decision-making processes and have those views taken seriously (Boylan and Dalrymple, 2011). As Dalrymple (2005) aptly notes, advocacy is about 'speaking up for children and young people, and empowering them to make sure their rights are respected and their views and wishes are heard at all times'. This definition underscores the dual role of advocacy: to amplify the child's voice and to empower them to self-advocate. Others emphasise that the role of advocacy is supporting children to express dissatisfaction with the service and make complaints (Boylan and Ing, 2005), to navigate statutory processes (Oliver and Dalrymple, 2008) and to facilitate clearer communication and understanding of complex decisions for children (Boylan and Dalrymple, 2009).

Advocacy is intrinsically linked to participatory practices in child protection. Traditional child welfare approaches have often been criticised for being adult-centric, with professionals making decisions 'for' rather than 'with' children (Thomas and Percy-Smith, 2010). Advocacy challenges this paradigm, promoting what Hart (1992) terms 'genuine participation' – whereby children are informed, consulted and collaborate in decision-making. This shift towards participatory practices aligns with the growing recognition of children as active agents rather than passive recipients of care (James and Prout, 2015). In the area of child protection, where decisions can have life-altering consequences, participatory practices facilitated by advocacy are particularly crucial. They lead to more informed decisions because children often have insights into their situations that adults may overlook (Cashmore, 2002). Furthermore, when children feel their views are respected, they are more likely to engage with support services and adhere to care plans, enhancing the effectiveness of interventions (Bell, 2002). As Kennan et al (2018) argue, 'participation is not just a right, but also a pragmatic necessity for effective child protection.'

For children in care, who often experience feelings of powerlessness and loss of control (Munro, 2001), advocacy is a vital mechanism to realise their rights. It ensures that their perspectives, experiences and aspirations are not just heard but actively considered in care planning, placement decisions, education and health matters. Moreover, advocacy contributes significantly to children's well-being. Research by Stein (2009) reveals that children who have a say in decisions about their lives experience improved self-esteem, a stronger sense of identity and better mental health outcomes. In contrast, the lack of participation can lead to feelings of alienation, disengagement from services, and poorer long-term outcomes (McLeod, 2007). Advocacy, therefore, is not a luxury but a necessity for the holistic development and well-being of children in care.

This chapter provides a comprehensive exploration of advocacy for children in care. We begin by examining the legal and policy landscape that mandates and shapes advocacy services, from international conventions to national legislation and local authority responsibilities. This section underscores the statutory duty to provide advocacy and the pivotal role of independent advocates. Next, we discuss the nature of advocacy practices through an empirical study conducted in an English local authority. This research illustrates the effectiveness of advocacy in amplifying children's voices in decision-making processes, the challenges faced, and the perspectives of both children and professionals. The findings offer valuable insights for enhancing participatory approaches in social work.

This chapter then explores the ethical considerations and challenges inherent in advocacy work. Issues of confidentiality, power imbalances and the tension between a child's wishes and their best interests are critically examined. We also confront practical barriers to accessing advocacy, particularly for marginalised groups. Looking to the future, we explore emerging directions for advocacy research and practice. From harnessing digital technologies to exploring different advocacy models, this section outlines a vision for a more comprehensive, accessible and child-centred advocacy framework.

## Legal and policy framework for advocacy

The provision of advocacy services for children in care is not simply a gesture but a fundamental right enshrined in international conventions and national legislation. This section explores the legal and policy framework that underpins advocacy for children in care, emphasising the role of international treaties, national laws, government policies and the responsibilities of independent advocates. Understanding this framework is crucial for practitioners, policy makers and researchers to appreciate the significance of advocacy and to ensure that looked-after children's rights are respected and their voices heard.

## International conventions

The cornerstone of children's rights globally is the United Nations Convention on the Rights of the Child (UNCRC), adopted in 1989 and ratified by all UN member states except the United States (UN General Assembly, 1989). The UNCRC recognises children as rights holders and establishes universal standards for their protection, development and participation. Several articles in the UNCRC are particularly relevant to advocacy for children in care. These include the following:

- Article 12: The right to express views freely in all matters affecting the child, with due weight given to these views according to the child's age and maturity.
- Article 13: The right to freedom of expression, including the freedom to seek, receive, and impart information.
- Article 20: Special protection and assistance for children deprived of their family environment.

These articles collectively establish a child's right to participate in decisions that affect them, a principle that lies at the heart of advocacy (Lundy, 2007). The UN Committee on the Rights of the Child (UNCRC) (2009) has emphasised that Article 12 applies to all aspects of alternative care, including placement decisions, care plans and review processes. This international framework places a legal obligation on states to ensure that children in care have access to advocacy services that enable their meaningful participation.

## National legislation in the UK

In England, the rights of children in care are primarily governed by the Children Act 1989 and the Children and Families Act 2014. These Acts enshrine the principles of the UNCRC in domestic law and establish specific provisions for advocacy. The Children Act 1989 mandates that local authorities provide advocacy services to children in need, including those in care, to promote their welfare and facilitate their participation in decisions affecting their lives.

The Children Act 1989 introduced the concept of 'looked-after children' and placed a duty on local authorities to safeguard and promote their welfare (Section 22). It is also mandated that children's wishes and feelings be ascertained and given due consideration in decisions about their care (Section 20[6]). This legal requirement forms the basis for advocacy services because it necessitates mechanisms for children to express their views (Dickens et al, 2015).

The Children and Families Act 2014 further strengthened advocacy provisions, particularly for children with special educational needs and disabilities (SEND). Section 19 of the Act requires local authorities to have regard to the views, wishes and feelings of children and their parents in decisions relating to SEND. This is crucial because many children in care have SEND and may face additional barriers to participation (Department for Education, 2018).

## Government policies and guidelines

Beyond legislation, various government policies and guidelines have shaped the provision of advocacy services. The Department for Education's 'National Standards for the Provision of Children's Advocacy Services' (Bell, 2002) set out key principles for advocacy, including independence, accessibility and child-centredness. These standards, although not statutory, have been influential in defining good practice.

More recently, the 'Working Together to Safeguard Children' guidance (Department for Education, 2018) has emphasised the importance of ascertaining the wishes and feelings of children in child protection processes. It states that children should be actively involved in planning processes and decision-making, and that advocacy services should be made available where necessary.

For children in care, the 'Children Act 1989 guidance and regulations Volume 2: care planning, placement and case review' (Department for Education, 2021) is particularly relevant. It stipulates that children must be informed about their entitlement to advocacy and how to access these services. This guidance also emphasises that advocacy should be available at all stages of the care process, from initial placement decisions to leaving care.

## Roles and responsibilities of independent advocates

Independent advocates play a crucial role in realising children's rights to participation. Their primary responsibility is to empower children to express their views and to ensure that these views are heard and considered by decision-makers (Oliver et al, 2006).

Key responsibilities include the following:

1. Representing the child's views: advocates must accurately represent the child's views, even if they conflict with the advocate's personal opinions or the views of professionals.
2. Providing information: advocates must ensure that children understand their rights, the decision being made and the potential implications.
3. Challenging decisions: if a child's views are not given due weight, advocates may challenge decisions through formal complaints procedures or legal routes.
4. Maintaining confidentiality: advocates must respect children's privacy, only sharing information with the child's consent, except where there are safeguarding concerns.
5. Promoting participation: advocates should support children to participate directly in meetings and decisions wherever possible, rather than simply speaking on their behalf.

The independence of advocates is crucial. As Thomas and others (2016) argue, advocacy is most effective when advocates are perceived as separate from social work and care systems. This independence allows children to trust that advocates will prioritise their views and interests, even when these conflict with professional opinions or resource constraints.

## *Statutory requirements for local authorities*

Local authorities have statutory duties to provide or commission advocacy services. The Children Act 1989 (Section 26A, as amended) requires local authorities to make arrangements for advocacy services for looked-after children, children in need and care-leavers who wish to make representations (including complaints) about their care. This duty extends to providing information about advocacy services and how to access them.

Additionally, the Adoption and Children Act 2002 (Section 119) extended the right to advocacy to children subject to care proceedings. This ensures that children's voices are heard in court decisions that profoundly affect their lives.

The statutory framework also recognises that some groups of children may face additional barriers to accessing advocacy. For example, the Children and Young Persons Act 2008 (Section 11) requires local authorities to have particular regard to the advocacy needs of disabled children and young people leaving care. This recognition of diverse needs is crucial for ensuring equity in access to advocacy (Franklin and Knight, 2011).

Despite these legal requirements, research suggests that the provision of advocacy services remains inconsistent across local authorities (Brady, 2011).

Factors such as budget constraints, lack of awareness among professionals and inadequate referral processes can hinder children's access to advocacy. This highlights the need for ongoing monitoring and enforcement of statutory duties.

Overall, the legal and policy framework for advocacy in England is robust, grounded in international human rights conventions and national legislation. This framework recognises advocacy as a key mechanism for realising children's rights to participation, particularly for vulnerable groups such as children in care. It places clear duties on local authorities and defines the crucial role of independent advocates. However, the translation of this framework into consistent, high-quality practice remains a challenge.

## Empirical research: advocacy in practice

This section highlights some of the key findings of a research study conducted within a local authority in England (Fitz-Symonds et al, 2024) that explored the role of advocacy in promoting participation among care-experienced children and young people. The study focused on understanding how advocacy services empower young people in care, facilitate decision-making and contribute to more child-centred practices within the child protection system. The research findings provide valuable insights into the effectiveness of advocacy in social work practice and its impact on both the children and professionals involved.

### *Overview of the research study*

The study was conducted within an in-house advocacy service operating in a large local authority. The study used a realist-informed methodology to explore the key mechanisms, outcomes and contextual factors that shape the effectiveness of advocacy services. The research sought to answer the following questions:

- How do those who deliver, refer into and receive advocacy services in the local authority perceive the impact of these services?
- What contexts and mechanisms enable or hinder positive outcomes for care-experienced children and young people in advocacy?
- How does the advocacy service facilitate children's meaningful participation in decision-making about their lives?
- What lessons can be drawn from this service to inform the wider delivery of advocacy for care-experienced children and young people?

The research was conducted in three phases, utilising a mixed-methods approach that included interviews, focus groups and collaborative workshops. Participants included advocates, care-experienced young people, operational staff, senior practitioners and experienced advocacy academics. The researchers employed a Context-Mechanism-Outcome framework to identify how advocacy interventions functioned in specific contexts to produce certain outcomes. This framework was used to refine an initial programme theory of how advocacy services lead to positive change.

## Key findings on the effectiveness of advocacy services

The findings of the study revealed several important insights into the effectiveness of advocacy services for children in care. Overall, the research found that advocacy plays a crucial role in amplifying the voices of children and young people, helping them participate meaningfully in decision-making processes that affect their lives. However, the effectiveness of advocacy is influenced by various contextual factors such as the structure of the service, the relationships between advocates and professionals, and the individual needs of young people.

## Impact on young people's participation in decision-making

One of the key aims of advocacy is to enhance the participation of children and young people in decisions about their care. This study found that young people's participation occurred at varying levels, often shaped by their age, personal circumstances and previous experiences with decision-making. For example, older children were more likely to express their views confidently, while younger children required more encouragement and scaffolding to engage in the process.

In some cases, the advocacy service was able to facilitate significant participation in decision-making. One example involved a young person who was able to choose the date of their move to a new placement, illustrating how advocacy can empower children to take control of important decisions. This aligns with research that highlights the importance of participatory practices in fostering a sense of ownership and control among children in care (Kennan et al, 2018).

Despite these successes, the study also revealed that participation was not always fully child-led. In some instances, decision-making processes remained adult-centric, with young people perceiving that adults were still largely in control. This reflects broader critiques of child protection systems, which have historically been criticised for being overly adult-dominated (Thomas and Percy-Smith, 2010).

## Young people's perceptions of advocacy support

Children and young people in the study expressed positive views about the support they received from advocates. Many highlighted the importance of having someone who listened to them, respected their views and helped them navigate complex processes such as care-planning meetings, complaints procedures and educational decisions. One of the most valued aspects of advocacy support was the sense of having an independent adult on their side. Young people described advocates as being distinct from social workers and other professionals because they were solely focused on representing their views, even when those views conflicted with what other adults thought was best. This is consistent with existing literature that emphasises the role of advocacy in giving children a voice and ensuring that their views are taken seriously in care planning and decision-making (Boylan and Dalrymple, 2011).

However, some young people also expressed confusion about the role of advocates, particularly regarding the temporary, issue-based nature of advocacy. For example, there was an expectation among some young people that advocates would provide ongoing support across all areas of their lives, rather than focusing on specific issues. This highlights the need for clearer communication about the scope and limits of advocacy services, a point also raised in previous research on advocacy (Oliver et al, 2006).

*Professional perspectives on advocacy*

Professionals involved in the study, including advocates, social workers and senior managers, generally viewed advocacy as a valuable tool for supporting children's participation in decision-making. Advocates, in particular, emphasised the importance of building trusting relationships with young people, maintaining independence from the local authority and being clear about the limits of their role. However, professionals also identified several challenges in delivering effective advocacy. One key issue was the perception of advocacy as being somewhat limited in its ability to challenge systemic issues. While individual advocates could support children in resolving specific problems, there was less capacity to address broader structural inequalities within the care system, such as resource constraints and power imbalances between professionals and young people. This is a common challenge in advocacy work, as noted by Boylan and Braye (2006), who argue that advocacy often remains constrained by the structures of the child protection system it operates within.

The findings of this study contribute to a growing body of literature that highlights the importance of advocacy in promoting participatory, child-centred approaches to social work. Advocacy is increasingly recognised as a key mechanism for ensuring that children's voices are heard and respected, particularly in contexts where they may otherwise be marginalised or overlooked (Dalrymple, 2005). One of the key contributions of this study is its focus on the lived experiences of children and young people who receive advocacy support. The findings underscore the importance of flexible, responsive advocacy services that can adapt to the diverse needs of care-experienced young people. This is consistent with the broader literature on children's participation, which emphasises the need for participation to be tailored to the individual circumstances and preferences of each child (Cashmore, 2002).

However, the study also highlights some of the limitations of current advocacy practices. While advocacy can empower children to participate in decision-making at the individual level, it remains constrained by systemic barriers such as limited resources, high caseloads and a lack of awareness about advocacy services among professionals. This echoes findings from previous research, which has shown that advocacy services are often inconsistently delivered and under-resourced (Pona and Hounsell, 2012).

## How does advocacy contribute to a more participatory and child-centred approach?

Advocacy contributes to a more participatory and child-centred approach in social work by shifting the focus from adult-led decision-making to a model that actively involves children and young people in shaping their own lives. As highlighted by the study, advocates play a crucial role in facilitating power-sharing between children and professionals, ensuring that children's views are not only heard but also acted upon. This aligns with Hart's (1992) model of 'genuine participation', whereby children are collaborators in decision-making rather than passive recipients of adult decisions. Moreover, advocacy supports the realisation of children's rights as enshrined in the UNCRC (UN General Assembly, 1989), particularly Article 12, which guarantees children the right to express their views in all matters affecting them. By advocating for children's rights, advocacy services help to create a more equitable and inclusive social work system that respects the autonomy and agency of young people.

## What are the barriers to effective advocacy and how can they be addressed?

The study identified several barriers to effective advocacy that need to be addressed to improve the delivery of advocacy services for children in care. These barriers include:

- Resource constraints: high caseloads and limited funding for advocacy services can reduce the quality and availability of support for young people. Advocates in the study reported feeling stretched by their workloads, which limited their ability to provide consistent, personalised support to all young people.

- Lack of understanding: both young people and professionals sometimes lacked a clear understanding of the role and purpose of advocacy. This could lead to confusion or unrealistic expectations about what advocacy services could achieve. Better communication and outreach are needed to ensure that children, social workers and other professionals fully understand the benefits and limitations of advocacy.
- Systemic power imbalances: despite the efforts of advocates to empower young people, the child protection system remains largely adult-dominated. Structural barriers, such as hierarchical decision-making processes and the prioritisation of professional opinions over children's views, can limit the impact of advocacy. Addressing these power imbalances requires a cultural shift within the child protection system to value and prioritise children's voices in all aspects of care planning and decision-making.

To address these barriers, advocacy services should be adequately resourced, with manageable caseloads and consistent funding. Additionally, awareness campaigns should be implemented to ensure that young people, families and professionals are informed about the availability and benefits of advocacy services. Finally, advocacy services should be integrated into wider efforts to reform the child protection system, ensuring that children's participation is not seen as a tokenistic exercise but as a fundamental right that informs all aspects of social work practice.

### *How can advocacy move beyond individual casework to address systemic issues?*

While the individual benefits of advocacy are well-documented, there is a growing recognition of the need for advocacy services to address systemic issues that affect children in care. Advocacy can and should extend beyond individual casework to address broader issues such as resource allocation, policy gaps and structural inequalities within the child welfare system.

Advocacy services can play a key role in systemic change by identifying patterns and trends from individual cases and using this information to inform policy and practice at the organizational level. For example, insights gained from advocacy work can highlight systemic failures in providing adequate educational support or exposing issues related to placement stability. This data can then be used to advocate for broader reforms within the care system, such as improved funding for educational services or changes to placement protocols.

Collective advocacy, where groups of care-experienced young people come together to raise concerns and push for systemic change, is one way to extend advocacy beyond individual casework. This approach can be particularly effective in addressing recurring issues that affect large numbers of children in care, such as the availability of mental health services or the consistency of placement stability (Brady, 2011).

## *What is the impact of austerity on advocacy services?*

The ability of advocacy services to support children in care is often constrained by the availability of resources. Austerity measures and budget cuts to local authorities have had a significant impact on the provision of advocacy services, leading to reduced capacity and limited access for young people who need support. Research indicates that advocacy services are often unevenly distributed across local authorities, with some areas experiencing significant gaps in provision due to financial constraints (Children's Commissioner, 2019).

Resource constraints can also lead to high caseloads for advocates, limiting the amount of time they can dedicate to each young person. This can result in less personalised support and reduced effectiveness in advocating for children's needs. Moreover, austerity measures have forced many advocacy services to rely on short-term funding arrangements, making it difficult to plan for long-term support and systemic change.

To mitigate the effects of resource constraints, advocacy services need to explore alternative funding models, such as partnerships with charitable organisations or community-driven advocacy initiatives. Additionally, there is a need for stronger statutory support for advocacy services, ensuring that all children in care have access to the support they need, regardless of budgetary pressures.

## Ethical considerations and challenges

Advocacy for children in care involves navigating a complex landscape of ethical considerations and challenges. Advocates must operate with the highest regard for children's rights and welfare, ensuring that their voices are heard while safeguarding their interests. This section explores five key ethical concerns: confidentiality and information sharing, power imbalances between children and professionals, balancing the child's wishes with their best interests, ensuring the independence of advocates and addressing challenges in accessing advocacy services.

### *Confidentiality and information sharing*

Confidentiality is a cornerstone of ethical advocacy practice, particularly in child welfare where sensitive personal information is often shared. Advocates must establish a relationship of trust with children by reassuring them that the information they disclose will remain private, unless there is a safeguarding concern. Confidentiality allows children to express their views and feelings openly, without fear that this information will be used against them or shared with professionals without their consent. However, managing confidentiality can be challenging in the child welfare system, which involves multiple professionals – social workers, educators, healthcare providers – who may need access to certain information in order to make informed decisions. Advocates must navigate this balance carefully, ensuring that they do not inadvertently breach a child's trust while still complying with legal and ethical obligations regarding information sharing. For instance, if a child discloses information that suggests they are at risk of harm, advocates are legally and ethically required to share this information with the relevant authorities.

The advocacy role requires transparency from the outset, explaining to children the limits of confidentiality. Advocates should be clear about the circumstances under which they would have to share information, such as when a child's safety is at risk (Thomas et al, 2016). This ensures that children understand the process and are not blindsided if an advocate needs to break confidentiality in the interests of safeguarding. The tension between confidentiality and information sharing is highlighted in the literature. Franklin and Knight (2011) emphasise that confidentiality is essential to establishing trust in advocacy relationships but must be handled with care to avoid undermining the advocate's role. Advocates must develop strong communication skills to explain these complexities to children in an age-appropriate way, ensuring that they remain engaged in the advocacy process.

### Power imbalances between children and professionals

One of the central ethical challenges in advocacy for children in care is addressing the inherent power imbalances between children and professionals. Children in care are often in vulnerable positions, with limited agency in decisions that significantly affect their lives. They may feel powerless when interacting with social workers, foster carers and other adults who have authority over them. Advocates are tasked with mitigating these power imbalances by ensuring that children's voices are amplified in decision-making processes. This involves not only giving children the opportunity to express their views but also helping them understand their rights and the implications of decisions being made about their care. As Boylan and Dalrymple (2011) note, advocacy is about empowering children to take control of their own narratives, thereby shifting the power dynamic in their favour.

However, power imbalances are not easily dismantled. Professionals often hold the ultimate decision-making authority and children may feel that their views, even when voiced, do not carry enough weight. Research by McLeod (2007) suggests that many young people in care feel that their participation in decision-making is tokenistic, with adults ultimately making the decisions for them.

Advocates must work within these constraints to ensure that children's views are taken seriously, even if they are not the final decision-makers. This requires a careful balance of supporting the child's voice while navigating the complex dynamics of child protection systems that are often adult-centric (Thomas and Percy-Smith, 2010). Advocates must also be aware of their own positions of power and ensure that they do not replicate the same power imbalances that they are trying to challenge.

### Balancing the child's wishes with their best interests

One of the most difficult ethical dilemmas in advocacy arises when a child's expressed wishes conflict with what professionals or caregivers believe to be in their best interests. Advocates are responsible for representing the child's voice, even if it contradicts the views of other professionals involved in their care. However, they must also consider the potential consequences of supporting a child's wishes that may not align with their long-term well-being. For example, a child may express a strong desire to return to a family environment that professionals have deemed unsafe. In such cases, advocates must carefully navigate these tensions, supporting the child in expressing their views while also working to ensure that the child understands the reasoning behind the professionals' decisions (Oliver et al, 2006). The advocate's role is to ensure that the child's voice is heard, but not necessarily to argue for decisions that may place the child at risk.

Dalrymple (2005) highlights the need for advocates to be clear about their dual responsibility: representing the child's views and ensuring that these views are considered within the broader framework of the child's welfare. Advocates must be transparent with the child about their role and the limitations of their influence, particularly in situations where the child's wishes may not be fully realised. The principle of 'best interests' is a fundamental component of child welfare practice, but it can be at odds with advocacy, which prioritises the child's right to participation and expression. The UNCRC (UN General Assembly, 1989) enshrines both the child's right to have their views heard (Article 12) and the need to prioritise their best interests (Article 3). Advocacy sits at the intersection of these rights, requiring a nuanced approach that considers both the child's autonomy and their safety.

### Ensuring independence of advocates

The independence of advocates is a critical ethical consideration because it underpins their ability to represent the child's voice without undue influence from other professionals or systems. Independent advocacy is essential for ensuring that children feel safe in expressing their views, knowing that the advocate is solely focused on their interests. As Boylan and Braye (2006) argue, ensuring the independence of advocates is crucial for building trust with children and enabling meaningful participation.

However, ensuring independence can be challenging, particularly when advocacy services are provided by organisations that are closely linked to the local authority or child welfare system. Research by Oliver et al (2006) found that children are more likely to trust advocates whom they perceive as independent from the professionals involved in their care. This highlights the importance of advocates maintaining a clear boundary between their role and that of social workers, foster carers and other authorities.

The perception of independence is just as important as actual independence. Children may be wary of advocates who work within the same system as the professionals they are advocating against, even if the advocate's role is technically independent. This challenge may be particularly pronounced when services are in-house, whereby advocates are employed by the same local authority that provides care for the child.

Advocacy services must be structured in ways that protect and promote the independence of advocates. This includes clear communication to children about the advocate's role, boundaries and the distinction between advocacy and other services they may receive. Regular training and supervision can also help advocates maintain their independence and avoid conflicts of interest.

### Challenges for children in accessing advocacy services

Access to advocacy services is another significant ethical concern because not all children in care have equal opportunities to engage with an advocate. Geographic, linguistic and cultural barriers can make it difficult for some children to access advocacy, particularly those living in rural areas or belonging to marginalised communities. Children in rural areas may face additional challenges in accessing advocacy services due to the limited availability of local resources. Travel distances, lack of transportation and scarce funding for rural services can all contribute to disparities in advocacy provision. This creates an ethical concern around equity of access – children in urban centres may have greater access to advocacy, while those in remote areas are left without the same support.

Language barriers also pose a significant challenge to accessing advocacy services, particularly for children from migrant or refugee backgrounds who may not speak English as their first language. It is important that advocates and advocacy services ensure that these children have access to translation and interpreting services and that their rights are upheld, even if communication requires additional resources and time (Pona and Hounsell,

2012). Advocacy services must be proactive in addressing these barriers by ensuring that they are inclusive and accessible to all children, regardless of their location or language.

Another access issue relates to awareness of advocacy services. Research suggests that many children in care are unaware of their right to an advocate, or how to access one. This is particularly true for children with disabilities or those who are in more vulnerable positions, such as unaccompanied asylum-seeking children (Franklin and Knight, 2011). Ensuring that advocacy services are widely promoted and that all children understand how to engage with an advocate is an ethical imperative for the sector.

The ethical considerations and challenges involved in advocacy for children in care are numerous and complex. Advocates must navigate issues of confidentiality, power imbalances and conflicting interests, all while ensuring that their independence is maintained. Access to advocacy services must also be addressed to ensure that all children, regardless of their circumstances, can benefit from this vital support. Advocacy plays a crucial role in safeguarding children's rights and ensuring their participation in decisions that affect their lives. However, addressing the ethical challenges inherent in this work requires careful consideration and a commitment to child-centred practice. Ensuring that children feel heard, respected and supported in their advocacy journeys is essential for fostering trust and achieving better outcomes in the care system.

## Future directions for research and practice

As advocacy for children in care continues to evolve, there is a growing need to expand the evidence base and refine advocacy services to ensure that they are both effective and equitable. Several key areas for future research and practice include the need for longitudinal studies; the exploration of group and collective advocacy; integrating digital technologies; improving training for advocates working with diverse groups; and developing policy recommendations for a more comprehensive advocacy framework. This section explores these priorities while discussing how technology and the voices of children and young people can shape the future of advocacy services.

### *Need for longitudinal studies on the long-term impact of advocacy*

Current research on advocacy services primarily focuses on short-term outcomes, such as improved participation in decision-making and immediate changes in care arrangements (Diaz, 2020). However, there is a pressing need for longitudinal studies that examine the long-term impact of advocacy on the lives of care-experienced young people. These studies could track young people as they transition from care to independence, assessing how advocacy influences their educational attainment, employment, mental health, relationships, and overall life satisfaction.

Longitudinal research could also provide valuable insights into whether the benefits of advocacy are sustained over time. For example, do young people who received advocacy support continue to feel empowered in navigating complex systems, such as higher education or healthcare, once they leave care? Such studies would be instrumental in understanding how advocacy contributes to building resilience and fostering positive life outcomes in the long term. Additionally, longitudinal research could help identify any gaps in the current advocacy system that may only become apparent as young people grow older and face new challenges.

### Exploring group and collective advocacy approaches

While individual advocacy remains critical, there is growing recognition of the need to explore group and collective advocacy models, which empower young people to advocate not only for themselves but also for their peers. Collective advocacy, such as youth councils, advisory boards, or peer-led groups, provides an avenue for young people to engage in systemic change by addressing shared concerns and pushing for reforms in the care system.

Collective advocacy can amplify the voices of care-experienced children and young people, allowing them to address broader systemic issues such as resource allocation, service delivery, and policy gaps. This approach also fosters a sense of solidarity and mutual support among young people, as they come together to identify common problems and collaborate on solutions (Boylan and Dalrymple, 2011). The report on advocacy services in Birmingham highlighted how advocacy campaigns driven by young people themselves – based on trends identified through individual advocacy cases – have led to tangible changes in local authority practices (Fitz-Symonds et al, 2024). Such examples demonstrate the potential of collective advocacy to influence broader reforms. Moving forward, there is a need to formalise and expand these approaches, ensuring that collective advocacy is integrated into existing service models.

### Training and support for advocates working with diverse groups

Advocates play a critical role in ensuring that the voices of care-experienced young people are heard. However, working with diverse groups of young people – such as those from ethnic minority backgrounds, LGBTQ+ youth, or those with disabilities – requires specialised knowledge and skills. To be effective, advocates must be trained in cultural competence, trauma-informed care and the specific needs of marginalised groups.

The report emphasised that advocates need to be flexible and adaptable in their approaches, tailoring their support to the individual needs and preferences of the young people they work with (Fitz-Symonds et al, 2024). Training should therefore focus on helping advocates develop a nuanced understanding of the unique challenges faced by different groups of young people in care. This includes awareness of language barriers, cultural differences, and the distinct experiences of young people with disabilities or mental health issues.

Moreover, advocates themselves should reflect the diversity of the young people they serve. Recruiting advocates from a wide range of backgrounds, including care-experienced individuals, can enhance the credibility and relatability of advocacy services. Lived experience can be a valuable asset in advocacy, as it allows advocates to better understand and empathise with the young people they support (Thomas et al, 2016). However, there is no set list of attributes needed by advocates.

*Policy recommendations for a more comprehensive advocacy framework*

To ensure that advocacy services are effective and equitable, there is a need for stronger policy support and a more comprehensive advocacy framework. Current advocacy provision in England is uneven, with services varying significantly across local authorities in terms of availability, quality, and access (Children's Commissioner, 2019). A national framework for advocacy services could help standardise provision, ensuring that all children in care have access to high-quality advocacy, regardless of where they live.

Policy recommendations should also focus on ensuring sustainable funding for advocacy services. Austerity measures and budget cuts have severely impacted the capacity of advocacy services, leading to high caseloads and limited access for many young people. Local authorities must be required to allocate sufficient resources to advocacy services, and statutory guidance should mandate that all care-experienced children and young people are informed of their right to an advocate.

In addition to addressing funding issues, policy changes should promote the integration of advocacy into all aspects of the care system. Advocacy should not be viewed as a separate service but as an integral part of the decision-making process for children in care. This would ensure that young people's voices are consistently heard and considered in all care planning, reviews and transitions (Oliver et al, 2006).

## How can the voices of children and young people shape the future of advocacy services?

At the heart of any future developments in advocacy services must be the voices of the children and young people who use them. Advocacy services should be co-designed with care-experienced young people, ensuring that their perspectives shape the services they receive. This can be achieved through the establishment of youth advisory boards, participation groups, and regular feedback mechanisms that allow young people to share their experiences and offer suggestions for improvement (Kennan et al, 2018).

By actively involving young people in the design and delivery of advocacy services, providers can ensure that these services are responsive to their needs and priorities. Children and young people are the experts on their own lives, and their insights are invaluable in creating advocacy services that are effective, accessible, and child-centred.

## Conclusion

This chapter has explored the critical role of advocacy in promoting the rights and participation of care-experienced children and young people, shedding light on its impact on both individual outcomes and broader systemic challenges. By focusing on case studies, empirical research, ethical considerations, and future directions for research and practice, this chapter has underscored the value of advocacy in fostering a more child-centered and participatory approach within the child welfare system.

One of the key takeaways from this chapter is that advocacy plays a vital role in empowering children in care, ensuring that their voices are not only heard but acted upon. As illustrated in the case studies, advocacy services help children articulate their views and concerns in critical areas such as care planning, education, health and placement transitions. This leads to improved outcomes, such as securing appropriate educational support, minimizing disruptions during placement changes, and fostering a sense of control over their lives. Advocacy helps to level the playing field for children in care, who often experience power imbalances in their interactions with professionals and systems that have significant control over their futures.

The chapter also highlighted the importance of balancing children's wishes with their best interests, a central ethical challenge in advocacy. Advocates are tasked with representing the child's voice, even when it may conflict with professional judgments about what is best for the child. This requires a careful and nuanced approach, ensuring that the child's perspectives are taken into account while safeguarding their wellbeing. This balance is crucial in maintaining the integrity of advocacy and ensuring that it remains a tool for both empowerment and protection.

A recurrent theme throughout the chapter is the need for independence in advocacy. Independence is fundamental to ensuring that children trust advocates to represent their views impartially, without influence from the professionals or systems that govern their care. The importance of maintaining this independence, particularly in in-house advocacy services where advocates may be seen as too closely aligned with local authorities, cannot be overstated. Children are more likely to engage with advocacy services and share their thoughts, opinions, wishes and feelings if they believe that advocates are working solely in their interest, free from external pressures.

However, the chapter also identified several challenges that limit the effectiveness of advocacy services. Access to advocacy remains uneven, with significant disparities based on geographic location, language barriers, and the availability of resources. Children in rural areas, those from minority ethnic backgrounds, and those with disabilities or communication needs often face additional obstacles in accessing advocacy support. Addressing these barriers is crucial for ensuring that all care-experienced children have equal access to the benefits of advocacy, regardless of their circumstances.

Resource constraints are another significant challenge. Austerity measures and budget cuts have reduced the capacity of advocacy services, leading to high caseloads and limited availability of advocates. This has a direct impact on the quality and reach of advocacy services, leaving many children without the support they need. The chapter emphasised the need for sustained and adequate funding for advocacy services, alongside stronger statutory guidance to ensure that every child in care is made aware of their right to an advocate.

Looking ahead, the chapter discussed future directions for research and practice that are essential for enhancing the effectiveness of advocacy services. There is a pressing need for longitudinal studies that examine the long-term impact of advocacy on care-experienced young people. Understanding how advocacy shapes their outcomes as they transition into adulthood – whether in terms of education, employment, mental health, or relationships – is key to refining and improving advocacy services over time.

In addition, the chapter highlighted the potential of group and collective advocacy approaches. While individual advocacy remains critical, collective advocacy offers a powerful way for young people to come together to address systemic issues within the care system. Youth-led campaigns, participation groups, and advisory boards allow care-experienced children to advocate for broader reforms that affect not just themselves but their peers. This shift from individual to collective advocacy could play a crucial role in driving systemic change in the child welfare system.

The integration of digital technologies into advocacy services was also identified as a promising future direction. The COVID-19 pandemic demonstrated the potential of digital tools to enhance access to advocacy, particularly for children in rural areas or those who prefer virtual communication. Technology can make advocacy more accessible and responsive, but it must be adopted thoughtfully, ensuring that it complements rather than replaces traditional in-person support. Digital platforms, apps, and online resources can expand the reach of advocacy, but they must be designed to be inclusive and accessible to all young people.

Finally, the chapter stressed the importance of involving care-experienced children and young people in shaping the future of advocacy services. Their insights, experiences, and perspectives are invaluable in creating advocacy models that are truly responsive to their needs. Co-designing services with young people ensures that advocacy remains relevant, effective, and grounded in the realities of those it seeks to support.

In conclusion, advocacy is a powerful tool for promoting the rights, participation, and welfare of care-experienced children and young people. However, to maximise its impact, advocacy services must address current challenges, including barriers to access, resource limitations, and the need for greater independence and inclusivity. By focusing on these areas and continuing to develop the evidence base through research, advocacy can become an even more effective mechanism for empowering young people and ensuring that their voices shape the decisions that affect their lives.

## References

Bell, M. (2002) 'Promoting children's rights through the use of relationship', *Child & Family Social Work*, 7(1): 1–11.

Boylan, J. and Braye, S. (2006) 'Paid, professionalised and proceduralised: can legal and policy frameworks for child advocacy give voice to children and young people?', *Journal of Social Welfare and Family Law*, 28(3–4): 233–48.

Boylan, J. and Dalrymple, J. (2009) *Understanding Advocacy for Children and Young People*. McGraw-Hill Education (UK).

Boylan, J. and Dalrymple, J. (2011) *Effective Advocacy in Social Work*. Sage.

Boylan, J. and Ing, P. (2005) '"Seen but not heard" – young people's experience of advocacy', *International Journal of Social Welfare*, 14(1): 2–12.

Brady, L. (2011) 'Developments in practice: using independent advocacy services to promote the rights of looked after children', *Adoption & Fostering*, 35(4): 78–87. Available from: https://doi.org/10.1177/030857591103500411

Cashmore, J. (2002) 'Promoting the participation of children and young people in care', *Child Abuse & Neglect*, 26(8): 837–47.

Children's Commissioner (2019) *Advocacy for Children: A Snapshot*. Children's Commissioner for England.

Dalrymple, J. (2005) 'Constructions of child and youth advocacy: emerging issues in advocacy practice', *Children & Society*, 19(1): 3–15.

Department for Education (2018) *Working together to safeguard children: A guide to inter-agency working to safeguard and promote the welfare of children*. Department for Education.

Department for Education (2021) *The Children Act 1989 guidance and regulations: Volume 2: Care planning, placement and case review*. Department for Education. Available from: https://assets.publishing.service.gov.uk/media/60e6fb43d3bf7f56896127e5/The_Children_Act_1989_guidance_and_regulations_Volume_2_care_planning__placement_and_case_review.pdf?

Diaz, C. (2020) *Decision Making in Child and Family Social Work: Perspectives on Participation*. Policy Press.

Dickens, J., Schofield, G., Beckett, C., Philip, G. and Young, J. (2015) *Care Planning and the Role of the Independent Reviewing Officer: Findings from Research*. Centre for Research on Children and Families, University of East Anglia.

Fitz-Symonds, S., Stabler, L. and Diaz, C. (2024) *Understanding how Advocacy Services Support Care-Experienced Young People to Participate in Decision-Making*. What Works for Children's Social Care. Available from: https://foundations.org.uk/our-work/publications/understanding-how-advocacy-services-support-care-experienced-young-people-to-participate-in-decision-making/

Franklin, A. and Knight, A. (2011) *Someone on Our Side: Advocacy for Disabled Children and Young People*. The Children's Society.

Hart, R.A. (1992) *Children's Participation: From Tokenism to Citizenship*. UNICEF Innocenti Essays.

James, A. and Prout, A. (eds) (2015) *Constructing and Reconstructing Childhood: Contemporary Issues in the Sociological Study of Childhood*. Routledge.

Kennan, D., Brady, B. and Forkan, C. (2018) 'Supporting children's participation in decision making: systematic literature review exploring the effectiveness of participatory processes', *The British Journal of Social Work*, 48(7): 1985–2002.

Lundy, L. (2007) '"Voice" is not enough: conceptualising Article 12 of the United Nations Convention on the Rights of the Child', *British Educational Research Journal*, 33(6): 927–42. Available from: https://doi.org/10.1080/01411920701657033

McLeod, A. (2007) 'Whose agenda? Issues of power and relationship when listening to looked-after young people', *Child & Family Social Work*, 12(3): 278–86.

Munro, E. (2001) 'Empowering looked-after children', *Child & Family Social Work*, 6(2): 129–37.

Oliver, C.M. and Dalrymple, J. (2008) *Developing Advocacy for Children and Young People*: Current Issues in Research, Policy and Practice.

Oliver, C., Knight, A. and Candappa, M. (2006) *Advocacy for Looked After Children and Children in Need: Achievements and Challenges*. Thomas Coram Research Unit, Institute of Education, University of London.

Pona, I. and Hounsell, D. (2012) *The Value of Independent Advocacy for Looked After Children and Young People*. The Children's Society. Available from: https://fostercareresources.wordpress.com/wp-content/uploads/2014/12/the-value-of-advocacy_final.pdf

Stein, M. (2009) *Quality Matters in Children's Services: Messages from Research*. Jessica Kingsley Publishers.

Thomas, N. and Percy-Smith, B. (2010) *A Handbook of Children and Young People's Participation: Perspectives from Theory and Practice*. Routledge.

Thomas, N., Crowley, A., Moxon, D., Ridley, J., Street, C. and Joshi, P. (2016) 'Independent advocacy for children and young people: developing an outcomes framework', *Children & Society*, 30(2): 94–106. Available from: https://doi.org/10.1111/chso.12132

UN Committee on the Rights of the Child (2009) General Comment No. 12: The right of the child to be heard, CRC/C/GC/12. United Nations.

UN General Assembly (1989) Convention on the Rights of the Child, United Nations, Treaty Series, vol. 1577: United Nations.

# PART III

# Rights and innovation

# 10

# Children in Care Councils

*Clive Diaz, Sammi Fitz-Symonds and Elen Newton*

## Introduction

The past two decades have seen an increasing acknowledgement of the rights of children and young people to participate meaningfully in decision-making about their care. The introduction of Children in Care Councils (CiCCs), under the 'care matters' reforms in England, challenged local authorities to find meaningful ways and processes that would give young people in care the opportunity to contribute their views to the planning and provision of services (Thomas and Percy-Smith, 2011). The purpose of CiCCs is 'to ensure that every child has the opportunity to air their views' and so that children and young people 'should be able to put their experiences of the care system directly to those responsible for corporate parenting' (Department of Education and Skills 2007, p 21).

The global COVID-19 pandemic necessitated the introduction of various measures such as lockdowns and social distancing to mitigate the spread of the virus. This led to many local authorities adapting how they worked with children in their care. At the heart of social work practice is the need to build meaningful relationships with children and physically engaging with a child in person is key to this. With restrictions on socialising in person imposed, this became a major challenge for social workers.

## Background

Before the COVID-19 pandemic, CiCCs were held in-person. When the first lockdown was implemented in March 2020, local authorities were forced to consider how they could continue to provide children in care with an opportunity to meaningfully participate in decision-making at a strategic and individual level while minimising the spread of the virus. Convening CiCC meetings online rather than in person challenged traditional assumptions around how participation and decision-making at both the individual and collective level can occur effectively.

Several qualitative studies have been carried out to assess the impact of lockdowns and COVID-19 restrictions on care-experienced young people as well as those who care for or support them and the services they provide (Cook and Zschomler, 2020; Roberts et al, 2021; Dadswell and O'Brien, 2022; Munro et al, 2022). The requirement to socially distance meant that social workers and the children and young people they supported needed to stay connected via alternative means. When in-person contact became a health concern, social services departments were required to adapt their practice almost immediately. In particular, 'virtual home visits' using online platforms such as WhatsApp and Zoom videoconferencing were adopted by child protection social workers in England during the first few months of the pandemic (Cook and Zschomler, 2020; Ferguson et al, 2021). Throughout the post-pandemic recovery period, many services have continued to engage with service-users via online platforms and hybrid models of working are increasingly common. So far, there has been limited research on how this new way of working has an impact on how young people, parents and family members feel that their voices are heard, and the extent to which their views are taken into account in decision-making forums.

Research into CiCCs is currently limited with a lack of literature exploring how they work in different local authorities, how they support young people, how they influence policy and practice, and how children and young people feel about participating in them. This is surprising, given their statutory role in shaping how corporate parenting should be carried out. By exploring and foregrounding the views of CiCC members, this study seeks to rectify this gap in research. It provides an important platform for care-experienced young people to express their thoughts and perceptions of participation in CiCCs during lockdown, and during our study they were able to provide very detailed accounts as part of this research. Despite ongoing research in the UK exploring how vulnerable young people can be safeguarded and families supported (Ferguson et al, 2020), and the experiences of care-experienced individuals in lockdown in general (Roberts et al, 2021), this study is the first to explore in depth the views of care-experienced young people about the impact of lockdown on CiCCs and the effect on their ability to make their voices heard. Given that digital platforms have become an increasingly common tool for engagement in social work practice following the lockdown periods, it is important that research continues to explore the lessons that can be learned and how services can be adapted in the future to increase meaningful participation for children and families.

This study considered what has been the impact for CiCCs of the move to online and/or socially distanced meetings, and how this has had an impact on their members. We also considered whether CiCCs have a voice in local authorities' strategic decision-making regarding children in care and whether this has changed since COVID-19. Finally, we looked at the impact of COVID-19 and the lockdown on the mental health of children in care and how CICCs have supported young people with mental health difficulties.

## Methodology

The study adopted a qualitative mixed-methods approach, grounded in a social pedagogical framework, to explore the operation and experiences of CiCCs. A key aim was to understand how care-experienced young people and participation workers navigated changing participation practices during this period. The research was developed in collaboration with three local authorities in the north-east of England. The project used a multi-layered design involving several methods.

A survey was distributed to participation professionals working with CiCCs across 12 local authorities in the north-east. The survey explored how CiCCs were operating during COVID-19, including frequency and format of meetings, engagement levels and adaptations made. These findings informed the selection of the final three local authorities.

Three focused conversations were held online with CiCC members from the selected local authorities. These sessions followed the ORID (Objective, Reflective, Interpretive, Decisional) model developed by the Canadian Institute of Cultural Affairs. This method allowed participants to move from surface-level observations to deeper reflection and decision-making about their experiences. For example, one exercise used during these conversations involved young people collectively creating a visual representation of their CiCC journey during COVID-19. Artist-facilitated workshops were also conducted with CiCC members using online platforms. These sessions used art-making (for example, colour-based emotional timelines and visual storytelling) as a vehicle for reflecting on and expressing pandemic-era experiences.

Finally, interviews were held online with five participation professionals from the three local authorities. These conversations explored:

- the perceived impact of CiCCs on strategic and operational decision-making;
- challenges and innovations introduced during the pandemic; and
- reflections on engagement, inclusion and youth voice.

## Findings

There were four significant findings from the analysis of the survey, focus groups, interviews and focused conversations.

*1. The shift to socially distanced and online meetings had both positive and negative consequences on the role CiCCs had in supporting young people's mental well-being and membership*

Prior to lockdowns commencing in March 2020, CiCCs' staff met in person and engaged in a range of activities. The frequency of these meetings varied between local authorities, although most were either fortnightly or weekly. Although policy was a focus of these meetings, they also involved day trips and other social activities, with a focus on enjoyment and building relationships between members. The young people highlighted that, following lockdown measures, they missed meeting fellow care-experienced people face-to-face and engaging in activities as part of their roles within the CiCC. One young person spoke about the loss of social opportunities with other care-experienced young people: 'The people here understand what we've been through but our friends outside of this don't know what it's like 'cos they haven't experienced it'.

The social element of CiCC was often perceived as the most important factor for young people, providing opportunities to empathise, mutually recognise and help others in similar circumstances. One creative workshop participant described their CiCC as 'a little lighthouse in the storm' – a phrase that emerged during the visual mapping exercise and was echoed by others. For many, the meetings provided continuity amid uncertainty and felt like 'something was still happening'.

Young people were not solely motivated by self-interest: they also wanted to support each other. The researchers initially assumed that 'having a voice' would be most important, but the data collected suggested that the young people were more invested in the social rather than the agentic benefits of the group. This suggests that either (a) the groups' activities had a strong social element, even if the primary aim was focused on influencing policy, indicating an oblique benefit of the group; or (b) that opportunities to socialise in groups outside the CiCC were lacking. Socialisation and 'having a voice' are not mutually exclusive, although this places some pressure on CiCCs to fulfil multiple needs. While the CiCC leads were focused on supporting the young people to have their 'voices' heard, they recognised that mental well-being and social interaction could at times be more important, not least during a pandemic.

In general, young people were negative about moving CiCC meetings online. Most who took part in this study stated that they experienced Zoom fatigue because much of their school/college work was also online. As one young person explained:

> I've got really bad mental health right. Let's just say I don't like doing it online at all, it's just boring, I'm not going to lie, because you cannot do activities like in person ... Like literally, I just fall asleep looking at the screen ... so like for me, when I was doing virtual for college all day, I would fall asleep during some of the lessons. (Young person)

Many of the care-experienced young people who took part in the study talked about how the pandemic and lockdown had had a negative impact on their mental health and emotional well-being. Common feelings included 'living in the unknown', a 'roller-coaster' of emotions and the idea of a 'return to normal'. The detrimental impact of increased social isolation due to COVID-19 restrictions has been highlighted in other studies (Roberts et al, 2020, Roberts et al, 2021).

We have data about how the young people were feeling during lockdown, as well as what they perceived to be the major factors affecting the well-being of all children in care. Nationally, the loss of social contact due to school closures, as well as increased risk of domestic abuse and loss of a 'safe space', have contributed to a decline in mental well-being generally. Feelings of loneliness and anxiety were increased during lockdown for children in care, especially care leavers (National Youth Advocacy Service [NYAS], 2020).

When the meetings went online, one lead commented:

> They weren't together as a group and I think that's one of our biggest things during COVID, for that social interaction to support young people who are isolated. So it was massive for them and to be fair, the feedback that I got from the young people all the time was like: when can we meet back up? I think that was probably the biggest thing for the young people during this time ... but that was the feedback that I got, which is why we worked so hard to bring them back face to face in a social distanced way. (CiCC lead)

The CiCC leads believed that the group needed to serve the young people as best as possible, even if this meant that the activity did not always focus on influencing policy making. During the pandemic, the need for social interaction may well have outweighed the need to communicate with and inform Children's Services senior managers. One lead commented: 'Our online stuff was kind of tilted a little bit more towards being sociable and having a bit of fun and staying in touch' (CiCC lead).

The dual impact of fun and agency was a potent mix: a dual objective of having influence but also meeting as a group of young people in care and enjoying each other's company was a key part of some of the more effective CICCs. Positive relationships with staff and other young people in care were also highlighted. One young person even noted that they felt that they had 'made friends with the staff'. Another young person specifically noted that while they had re-evaluated their friendships during lockdown, their (2–3 month) involvement in their local authority CiCC had been helpful because they were among other care-experienced young people:

> Because no one that I know, like, my age, are in care. And then when I came here [to the CiCC], I met quite a few other people who had

gone through the same stuff as me, so I can sort of relate to them. And it's actually really nice. (Young person)

The role and importance of friends in young people's lives had been previously overlooked by some practitioners and only emerged when they co-produced reports with CiCC members.

One CiCC lead explains:

Friendship was massive in the early stages of lockdown. The young people presented a report called 'Circle of Trust'... In their circle of trust was friends. Right in the middle. And that wasn't on the circle of trust by the practitioners. So they campaigned for that to be talked about more in reviews. Talk to our social workers about your friends. Do you see them? How often do you see them? Does your foster carer support and promote that? You know, so that was a big massive thing. The concept of how important that was to care-experienced young people. (CiCC lead)

Creative sessions revealed that friendship was not merely a social bonus of CiCCs, but central to their function. In one activity, young people created a 'Circle of Trust' diagram to illustrate who they relied on most during the pandemic. Friends from their CiCC appeared at the very centre of these circles – often in place of or alongside family and professionals. This visual exercise challenged practitioners' assumptions, with one CiCC lead noting that staff had not initially included peers in their own versions of the diagram. For many young people, the CiCC became a key source of emotional connection, filling social gaps created by disrupted peer networks during lockdown.

While online meetings were considered less favourable by all the participants, they were not without value. Some of the young people noted that the routine of meetings, having a platform to share their voice and having regular contact with other care-experienced young people helped with coping with boredom during lockdown and improving confidence. The following comments illustrate some of the young people's personal experiences:

[CiCC] was the only thing that was normal that was going on in my life. I wasn't allowed to attend school; it was all remote. They weren't asking for any work to be sent to them so I literally had nothing to do. (Young person)

[CiCC] was the only thing that was normal and getting the extra things to do, like making cards for the key workers that were going in and doing the drawings on the front of the cards and stuff ... I think doing all that was just normal. Something normal to keep us all going. (Young person)

The CiCC lead helped me get involved with an agency within Children's Services a lot more and it's helped with my ... confidence and anxiety. (Young person)

There were also some specific examples of resilience in the face of challenges, such as in the following statement made by a young person:

Seeing how strong you actually are, 'cos if someone had told me I'm going to be in a global pandemic for a year, I wouldn't have thought I was fine; I would have thought I'd have been going mad. But we all survived. We all made it through. (Young person)

CiCCs are currently attended by only a small proportion of all the young people in care, so recruiting new members is important. The pandemic had an adverse impact on the ability of CiCCs to recruit new members, with the fact that many were now being conducted online being a significant barrier. For some, meeting virtually was considered more anxiety-inducing than doing so in person. One CiCC lead commented:

When we bring new people into the group, we'll do a home visit and then we'll bring them along and I think we'd struggled with the idea of bringing people into a virtual space where they don't know anybody and they may have only met myself or one of my team once and we just thought that wasn't ... It didn't feel safe and it didn't feel comfortable. (CiCC lead)

Another CiCC lead made a similar comment: 'Because we weren't recruiting; nobody wanted to ... Well, they seemed to not want to join, so we decided that we would kind of put a freeze on, you know, recruiting, just because it was difficult carrying out the virtual meetings.'

## 2. A lack of consistency in how local authorities supported CiCCs during the pandemic had an impact on how CiCCs influenced policy and decision-making at a strategic and operational level

When it came to facilitating CiCC meetings, there were clear differences in how each local authority responded during the first lockdown: three reported ceasing all sessions; two met 'less frequently', two continued to 'meet as normal' and one met 'more frequently'. One local authority noted issues with the age of young people involved in CiCCs as a barrier to continuation: 'Unfortunately, our younger group has not really run during COVID as we struggled to keep young people virtually' (CiCC lead).

Those who continued to facilitate CiCC meetings did so virtually during this time, using platforms such as Microsoft Teams, Zoom and Google virtual meets. After the first lockdown, five participants identified the continued use of these methods of facilitating their CiCC meetings during this time. Furthermore, the three local authorities whose sessions had stopped took up using the virtual platforms just mentioned. One professional stated that they attempted 'to continue sessions via digital platforms but not as regularly as once a week' and another shared that numbers of participants 'built up gradually' when taken online.

Moreover, four of the professionals surveyed gave examples of adapted additional forms of communicating that they were providing to their CiCCs during the lockdown period: phone, email, IQPost me, WhatsApp, Facebook and creating a newsletter.

In one local authority, the CiCC meetings had returned to being held in person (in line with the National Youth Agency guidance) in the summer of 2020, and remained in person during the second and third lockdowns in England in late 2020 and early 2021, but this had necessitated moving to a different building with larger rooms to allow for social distancing measures.

Corporate Parenting Panels (CPPs), consisting of local counsellors and senior managers, was a key channel through which CiCCs could influence policy before the pandemic. Indeed, one of the principle reasons for CiCC's inception was to feed back into and assist with the steering of policy that would have an impact on the children in care. Our research found concerning results regarding the continued interface between these two forums during the pandemic. Most worryingly, one CiCC had ceased involvement with the CPP completely:

> Pre-COVID, we ran regular corporate parenting meetings, where our young people, our Children in Care Councils had a regular slot; they had good relationships with them. But that all stopped during COVID; they didn't even go online, so obviously the impact on them key strategic decisions was probably nil. (CiCC lead)

In another local authority, the continued relationship between the CiCC and the CPP is now under review. One forum, however, was able to adapt the meetings to an online format, which was felt to provide young people with opportunity to still have an influence:

> We sharply moved to an engagement process; what I would call mini Corporate Parenting Panel meetings, made up of senior managers and

the CPP chair and vice-chair, which provided a platform for young people to engage in, share ideas and opinions of senior management and then that could be filtered back down, which resulted in quite a lot ... of change during COVID. (CiCC lead)

In most of the local authorities that participated in this study, however, links between the CiCC and the CPP seemed to be reduced since the first lockdown in March 2020. This was concerning because a key purpose of a CiCC is to have an impact on decision-making at a strategic level.

### 3. CiCCs provide significant support for ongoing training and resource outputs within local authorities

At an operational level, much of the positive work carried out before the pandemic by the CiCCs did appear to continue. Their influence could be seen, for example, in campaigns around language and the improvement of review meetings. Training for police officers and social workers offered by some CiCCs had positive feedback and appeared to have an impact on practice by professionals. The language campaign seemed to be particularly powerful in terms of impact. One CiCC lead elaborated as follows:

So that training is amazing and that's all ran by young people. So we took that virtually. We weren't sure how that would work ... The young people embraced it and were really good. The feedback was really powerful ... and the young people developed that and have tweaked the training session a couple of times during lockdown. I think, if I've got my numbers right, during that lockdown period, I think they supported 28 future foster carers with that training and that seems to be the most popular training led by the young people because the evaluations suggest that. (CiCC lead)

The young people also enjoyed the interviewing and training of police officers and social workers As one of them commented: 'Yeah, I enjoyed the training. And speaking with like, potential foster carers and social workers, that was like the first time I've done that, like COVID-19 was the first time I've had the chance to do that and that was fun.'

The language campaign emerged from conversations around stigma and from the back of a national campaign, 'Language that Cares', led by The Adolescent in Children's Trust (TACT). It emerged naturally and independently in different CiCCs from conversations between the young people and managers. This more organic change is likely to have a greater impact on multiple levels than tweaking individual policies within limited parameters. These types of changes have a direct impact on young people's well-being and are expected to be more far-reaching, as one explained: 'Yeah, like we've changed "contact" to "family time" and that, so now all social workers in [the LA] use the language that we've come up with, so like "family time" and like, placements are called "homes", 'cos it's our home, not a placement.'

Ongoing contact with senior managers, awareness of who key people were and having regular informal, face-to-face contact had a positive impact on the young people. Many commented on the sense of importance they felt in being able to communicate directly with senior managers, and they did not feel intimidated by this. The move to online platforms was seen as an opportunity to reach more people and one young person noted that the digital format meant that senior managers were less able to pull out at the last minute because they were conducting all their meetings from home: 'I think it's allowed us all to meet up with like, higher-end people, 'cos they can't back out and be like: "oh, I can't get to [the LA]" and stuff like that. 'Cos it's like virtual; they can just hop on a computer.'

At other times, CiCC meetings were held in the same building and managers would drop in ad hoc. One CiCC lead commented:

> Children's social care are all based in this building, so ... Our Director of Children's Social Care comes to pretty much every meeting. Even if he can't stay, he'll always pop in to like, talk to the young people, just see how they're doing and then go off. They all know him. And other managers ... And the building we're in, obviously having directors and managers and things, things get actioned a lot quicker. Because they're there and they can hear it. Do you know what I mean? So they hear it first hand from young people. (CiCC lead)

This worked both ways: staff felt they could approach young people on the CiCCs to get feedback on ideas or information about specific initiatives or issues. There was a sense that the two-way engagement was sometimes more important than the one-way idea of children influencing strategic decisions. Opportunities to speak with staff within Children's Services and across other services were framed by CiCC leads as 'networking', which the young people broadly agreed was 'a good thing'. For some, this was considered helpful for their future careers.

The training that some CiCCs had carried out for police and social workers had clearly worked well and seemingly had an impact on practice by professionals. One lead explains:

> The young people went 'I think we should develop training to our police. Last Thursday, they facilitated a pilot session with 12 senior police officers, linked to the safeguarding team aligned to some practitioners on the beat. And that was extremely powerful and that

was led by young people aged between 10 and 20. That was on relationships, safety, communication ... I mean, it was quite diverse. You had like, a 12-year-old talking about the ... the connection he'd had with police because of his family. Let's say that. As a result of that, on and off, they'd been to his house, been in, been out, you know ...? He's aligned that to trauma. And then we had a 20-year-old who has a lot of knowledge around CSE. (CiCC lead)

Involving young people in social work professionals' interviews has become policy in some local authorities, a particularly positive development. One young person explains: 'Yeah, now every social worker that goes for an interview or, I think it's every professional that works with children and young people have to have a young person's interview.'

Future training is also planned for corporate parent panel members. One CiCC lead explained: 'So our young people are going to deliver some training to the corporate parents around what corporate parenting should be like and what they sort of want from our corporate parents but that's another thing that we're just working on at the moment.'

These findings demonstrate the important work that the CiCCs are doing at an operational level. Crucially, their activities give a voice to young people in several ways through involvement with other Children's Services groups; creative activities that feed back on particular aspects of the service; enabling direct contact with senior managers; co-creation of informational or training documents, or campaigns around, for example, language or training. Most of the young people who took part in this study felt 'heard' through their work with CiCCs. However, it is important to recognise that young people who choose to become CiCC members are likely to be those with confident personalities and therefore more likely than others to make their voices heard.

## *4. CiCCs can be good at employing structures attuned to young people's needs and perspectives*

CiCCs work particularly well when their staff listen to and consider children's needs and views of how they want the council to run. As one lead noted:

> The biggest thing is just them having somewhere to go where they feel comfortable voicing their opinions. Obviously, they'll always have that option of speaking to social workers and IRO's ... But 'cos I'm not a social worker, it's more of an independent voice. For them to come and kind of speak to us. Erm, and for us to support them. (CiCC lead)

The CiCC activities give a voice to young people in several ways: through involvement with other Children's Services groups; creative activities that feed back on particular aspects of the service; enabling direct contact with senior managers; and co-creation of informational or training documents, or campaigns around, for example, language or training. One young person noted:

> We talk all the time. We always have a voice. We talk too much, really. Some people might not want our opinions and we just give them. Like, erm, if we are unhappy with something, they're going to know about it ... at the end of the day, it's making a difference for us; we need our voices to be heard and we're not scared of getting our voices heard. (Young person)

While the young people recognised the importance of having a say in strategic policy relating to their service, they also recognised the diversity of each other's needs and the necessity of ensuring others' voices are heard. There was a general understanding that CiCCs should not be the only place for care-experienced young people to be able to voice their opinions.

## Reflections and implications

This research not only highlighted the challenges faced by CiCCs during the COVID-19 pandemic but also offered valuable insight into how creative, relationship-based practices can strengthen participation under pressure. The reflections shared by young people and participation workers alike suggest that CiCCs are more than consultative mechanisms – they are social ecosystems that support emotional well-being, build peer solidarity and provide continuity in times of disruption.

The findings reinforce the idea that how participation happens matters just as much as whether it happens at all. The most impactful moments described by young people were not always about influencing strategy but about feeling seen, heard and connected. This calls for a broader framing of participation – not only as input into policy but also as a process of belonging and mutual recognition.

Creative methods such as visual metaphors, artistic expression and facilitated conversations offered safe and accessible routes into reflection, especially for those who may have struggled with traditional discussion formats. These approaches revealed insights that might have been missed in more formal settings and they underscored the importance of trust, emotional safety and continuity of relationships in participation work.

For local authorities, the implications are clear: meaningful participation requires consistent investment – not only in terms of time and resources, but also in building the kinds of relationships and structures that enable young people to participate on their own terms. The pandemic has made visible both the fragility and the resilience of participatory systems. As services move forward, it is crucial to retain and build on the practices that kept young people engaged, supported and connected during one of the most challenging periods in recent memory.

## Conclusions

This study explored the views and perspectives of 'experts by experience', children and young people in care as well as the views of participation leads who work alongside children in care who attend CiCCs. The involvement of participation leads, who have corporate parenting responsibilities, was aimed at ensuring that we understood the agency perspectives of how COVID-19 and the lockdown had had an impact on CiCCs as well as opportunities to contrast and compare with accounts provided by care-experienced young people.

There were key differences between CiCCs in terms of how they adapted to COVID-19 and the lockdown. For example, one local authority found a large enough building/room space to meet in person while socially distancing, while most of the others met online. Meeting online was generally unpopular for both young people and staff, mainly due to 'Zoom fatigue' and some concerns about privacy. However, they all understood the reasons for moving online and identified advantages around reducing travel and accessing senior managers. In one local authority, the CiCCs' representation on the CPP had stopped happening – for then at least. Conversely, in some local authorities, online meetings made it easier to reach a wider audience and have more regular contact with senior managers. The lack of consistency on multiple levels between how CiCCs worked across this area of England was noteworthy. We also found that there was a great deal of variation in terms of impact that CiCCs had on strategic decision-making. A key issue was access to senior managers and, in some cases, this reduced during COVID-19. In some local authorities, meeting online reduced opportunities to have ad-hoc meetings with senior managers.

In relation to well-being, the lockdown experience was likened to a roller-coaster with emotional ups and downs. Some young people spoke about how friendships and animals helped them manage these emotions. Friendship and contact with animals were cited as being especially helpful. We found evidence of remarkable resilience from some of the children who took part in this study.

CiCC meetings were important opportunities for staying in touch with friends, especially other care-experienced young people. CiCC leads recognised that well-being and mental health needs might be heightened during lockdown and steered group activities towards this. A prominent theme here was the social element of the CiCC. Our findings suggest that, when the first lockdown started in March 2020, the young people were more invested in social benefits than having a voice over strategic decision-making. Socialisation and 'having a voice' are not mutually exclusive, although they do place some pressure on CiCCs to fulfil multiple needs.

CiCCs thatwere identified in the survey as doing more interesting and better-quality work enjoyed good relationships with – and access to – senior managers, policy makers and other strategic decision-makers. We worked in more depth with those CiCCs because we were keen to highlight good practice. However, there were limited examples of high-level policy change. Critically, there were changes at implementation level: for example, young people were now involved in training professionals, including social workers and the police. This increasesd understanding of the needs of care-experienced children but also directly affected the types of encounters they would have.

**References**

Cook, L.L. and Zschomler, D. (2020) 'Virtual home visits during the COVID-19 pandemic: social workers' perspectives', *Practice*, 32(5): 401–8.

Dadswell, A. and O'Brien, N. (2022) 'Participatory research with care leavers to explore their support experiences during the COVID-19 pandemic', *The British Journal of Social Work*, 52(6): 3639–57.

Department of Education and Skills (2007) *Care matters: time for change.* 6937-DFES-Working with Parents. Available from: https://assets.publishing.service.gov.uk/media/5a7ecc6ded915d74e33f27b8/Care_Matters_-_Time_for_Change.pdf

Ferguson, H., Kelly, L. and Pink, S. (2020) *Research Briefing One: Child Protection, Social Distancing and Risks from COVID-19.* University of Birmingham.

Ferguson, H., Kelly, L. and Pink, S. (2021) 'Social work and child protection for a post-pandemic world: the re-making of practice during COVID-19 and its renewal beyond it', *Journal of Social Work Practice*, 36(1): 5–24.

Munro, E., Friel, S., Baker, C., Lynch, A., Walker, K., Williams, J. et al. (2022) *CCTC Final Report: Care Leavers' Transitions to Adulthood in the Context of COVID-19.* University of Bedfordshire.

National Youth Advocacy Service [NYAS] (2020) *New 'Young Lives in Lockdown' research shows increase in loneliness and anxiety among children in care and care leavers.* Available from: https://www.nyas.net/about-us/news/new-young-lives-in-lockdown-research-shows-increase-in-loneliness-and-anxiety-among-children-in-care-and-care-leavers

Roberts, L., Rees, A., Bayfield, H., Corliss, C., Diaz, C., Mannay, D. and Vaughan, R. (2020) Young people leaving care, practitioners and the coronavirus (COVID 19) pandemic: experiences, support, and lessons for the future. Project Report. CASCADE/Cardiff University.

Roberts, L., Mannay, D., Rees, A., Bayfield, H., Corliss, C., Diaz, C. et al. (2021) '"It's Been a Massive Struggle": Exploring the Experiences of Young People Leaving Care during COVID-19'. Available from: https://orca.cardiff.ac.uk/141485/1/Main%2Bdocument%2BACCEPTED%2B20%2BMay%2B2021.pdf

Thomas, N. and Percy-Smith, B. (2011) '"It's about changing services and building relationships": evaluating the development of Children in Care Councils', *Child & Family Social Work*, 17(4): 487–96.

# 11

# Digital participation and technology in social work

*Sammi Fitz-Symonds and Shane Powell*

## Introduction

Digital technologies are reshaping the landscape of child and family social work, offering new avenues for engagement, communication and service delivery. Yet, alongside these innovations, they present profound questions about power, access and participation. As digital platforms become embedded within practice, from virtual case conferences and online portals to predictive analytics and artificial intelligence (AI)-enabled tools, social workers must grapple with how these technologies shape and support or hinder the meaningful involvement of children, young people and families in decisions that affect their lives.

This chapter positions digital participation, defined as the use of digital tools and spaces to enable service users' voice, choice and influence, as a central concern for social work. We explore the extent to which digital technologies can uphold and expand or constrain participation, particularly for children and families who have historically been marginalised within social care systems. Drawing on the participation frameworks of Hart (1992), Shier (2001) and Lundy (2007), we critically analyse how digital tools and infrastructures may support more inclusive, rights-based approaches, or inadvertently reinforce tokenism and exclusion.

While the COVID-19 pandemic accelerated the adoption of digital platforms within social work (Mishna et al, 2012), it also amplified existing inequalities in digital access and literacy. For some, digital tools enabled new forms of flexibility and autonomy; for others, they created or deepened barriers to participation. As such, this chapter foregrounds questions of digital equity, ethical design and participatory governance, situating technology not as a neutral force but as a space where values, relationships and power dynamics are constantly negotiated.

Chapter 12 examines how digital platforms are used in social work communication, service delivery, data analytics and predictive technologies. Throughout, we ask: who is being heard, who is excluded, and who is shaping these systems? We argue that digital transformation must be approached not simply as a matter of efficiency or innovation, but as an opportunity and a challenge to deepen participatory practice in ways that reflect social work's core commitment to rights and relational engagement.

## Digital platforms and participation

*Digital spaces as participatory environments*

Digital platforms have become an integral feature of contemporary social work practice. These platforms, ranging from secure messaging systems and shared electronic records to video conferencing tools and online service portals, have transformed how professionals communicate and how services are delivered. They offer the potential to improve access, responsiveness and continuity in support, particularly for those facing barriers such as geography, disability or transport challenges (López-Pelaez and Marcuello-Servós, 2018; Baginsky et al, 2020).

Importantly, they also hold the potential to support more participatory relationships between practitioners and the people they support. For example, asynchronous communication through messaging platforms allows service users greater flexibility to reflect before responding, thereby potentially creating safer and more empowering forms of dialogue (Chan and Holosko, 2016). Similarly, mobile applications and online portals can give individuals more autonomy in managing their care, accessing self-help resources and contributing to their case records (Ramsey and Montgomery, 2014; Steiner, 2021).

However, the participatory potential of digital platforms is not automatic. The functionality of a system, whether or not it supports two-way interaction, allows users to view or update their information, or enables real-time discussion shapes the extent to which it supports meaningful involvement. For instance, a care-experienced young person granted access to their file gains transparency but not necessarily influence over decision-making. In this sense, digital tools can enable participation only to the degree that they are designed to do so.

*From access to influence*

While digital access is a necessary precondition, genuine participation requires going beyond technical inclusion to address questions of influence and power. Drawing on frameworks such as Lundy's (2007) model of participation, encompassing space, voice, audience and influence, we can interrogate whether digital environments create the conditions for children and families to express views and be meaningfully heard in matters affecting them. Similarly, Shier's (2001) model reminds us that participation must move from 'openings' to 'opportunities' and, ultimately, to 'obligations' if it is to be sustained and embedded in organisational practice.

Virtual case conferences and online meetings have, for example, increased the feasibility of involving a broader range of participants, including parents and young people (Mishna et al, 2012; Baginsky et al, 2020). Yet, presence in a digital meeting does not guarantee that an individual's voice is listened to, or indeed acted upon. Digital fatigue, power imbalances or unfamiliarity with the platform can all reduce the quality of engagement and discourage participation (Cook and Zschomler, 2020; Kong et al, 2022).

Evidence from child protection settings during the pandemic shows that virtual formats may unintentionally silence voices, especially those of children, if adequate supports are not in place (Baginsky and Manthorpe, 2021). These findings align with What Works research that calls for blended models of participation, whereby digital methods enhance rather than replace in-person interaction (Featherstone et al, 2014).

*Designing for equity and inclusion*

Digital systems that assume equal access and digital literacy risk further entrenching existing inequalities. As Helsper and Reisdorf (2017) argue, digital exclusion is deeply intertwined with social exclusion: those without access to technology, skills or support are often already marginalised. These challenges are especially pronounced among care leavers, disabled individuals and those living in poverty (Beaunoyer et al, 2020).

To be participatory, digital platforms must be designed not just for convenience but also for equity. This includes multilingual interfaces, compatibility with assistive technologies and user testing with those who will actually use the systems. Wherever possible, service users should be involved in the co-design of tools, helping to shape the features, language and interfaces that govern their digital interactions with social care services.

Some local authorities are beginning to model this approach. For example, Camden Council's Data Charter (Camden Council, 2023) was co-developed with residents and included the creation of communication materials in multiple languages and formats to ensure transparency and accountability in the use of AI and data (Equality and Human Rights Commission, 2023). This represents a promising example of participatory governance in digital service design.

Nevertheless, initiatives like these remain the exception rather than the norm. As digital transformation continues, it is vital that participation remains a central design principle, embedded not only in the tools themselves but also in the organisational cultures and professional practices that surround them.

## Theoretical models of digital participation

Understanding digital participation in social work requires a grounding in established frameworks of children's rights and participatory practice. While digital technologies offer novel tools for engagement, their ability to foster meaningful participation depends on how they are embedded within social work systems and relationships. Theories of participation provide a valuable lens for assessing not only whether digital tools are used but also whether they promote authentic, equitable and impactful involvement.

## Hart's Ladder of Participation

Hart's (1992) seminal 'Ladder of Participation' remains a foundational model for distinguishing between forms of participation that are genuinely empowering and those that are merely symbolic. Hart's model presents a hierarchy ranging from non-participation (manipulation, decoration and tokenism) to degrees of actual participation (assigned but informed, consulted and informed, adult-initiated with shared decisions, and child-initiated and directed).

In digital contexts, this framework raises important questions. A social care app that allows young people to report their views before a case conference might be considered 'consulted and informed' – but only if those views are acknowledged and used to inform decisions. Conversely, inviting a child to a virtual meeting without supporting them to understand the process or express their views meaningfully may amount to tokenism, particularly if the technology or power dynamics inhibit full engagement (Baginsky et al, 2020; Mishna et al, 2012).

Digital participation should not be conflated with digital access. A young person attending a meeting online or submitting feedback through an app is not necessarily experiencing participation as defined by Hart, unless their input is respected and influences the outcome. Thus, Hart's Ladder is a useful diagnostic tool for evaluating where digital practices fall on the spectrum between tokenism and empowerment.

## Shier's Pathways to Participation

Building on Hart's work, Shier (2001) proposed the 'Pathways to Participation' model, which focuses not only on levels of participation but also on the commitment of organisations to facilitate it. Shier outlines five levels of participation, each linked to three organisational stages: openings (willingness), opportunities (procedural mechanisms) and obligations (structural or legal commitment). These include listening to children, supporting them to express their views, taking their views into account, involving them in decision-making, and sharing power and responsibility.

This model is particularly relevant for digital practice. Many social work organisations may have the openings for digital engagement, such as video calls or surveys, but not the opportunities (for example, training, digital literacy support) or the obligations (for example, policy frameworks, accountability mechanisms) to ensure that service users' digital participation shapes practice meaningfully.

For example, an online portal that enables families to review their social care plans may seem participatory on the surface. But, if families cannot update information, leave comments or see how their feedback informs decision-making, then it remains a one-way process. Similarly, virtual consultations that are logged but not acted upon can become performative rather than transformative.

Shier's model urges us to ask not only 'Is participation possible?' but also 'What structural and cultural supports are in place to ensure that it is meaningful and sustained?' In digital contexts, this translates to considerations such as: Are young people supported to use platforms safely and confidently? Are their contributions acknowledged and followed up? Are systems designed with their input from the outset?

## *Lundy's model of participation*

Lundy's (2007) model further operationalises Article 12 of the UN Convention on the Rights of the Child (UNCRC) by proposing four interrelated elements necessary for meaningful participation: space, voice, audience and influence:

- Space refers to the provision of safe, inclusive opportunities for children to express their views.
- Voice relates to facilitating the expression of those views, ensuring that children are supported to articulate their perspectives.
- Audience means that the child's views must be listened to by those with the power to act.
- Influence implies that the child's views are not only heard but taken seriously and acted upon where appropriate.

This model is particularly powerful when applied to digital environments. A well-designed digital feedback tool may offer space and voice, but – without mechanisms to ensure audience and influence – it risks becoming a digital suggestion box with no meaningful outcome.

During the pandemic, virtual child protection conferences became commonplace (Baginsky and Manthorpe, 2021). While this enabled continuity of services, these also revealed how children's voice could be diluted when they struggled to engage meaningfully in unfamiliar digital formats. Issues such as poor internet connectivity, lack of digital confidence, or not having a quiet, private space to speak can all limit the quality of digital participation, highlighting the need for intentional design and adequate support (Ferguson et al, 2022; Pink et al, 2022).

Moreover, practitioners may lack the training or institutional mandate to ensure that children's input is not only listened to but meaningfully considered. Embedding audience and influence into digital practice therefore requires more than technological solutions – it also requires cultural and systemic change.

## Synthesising models for digital practice

Taken together, Hart, Shier and Lundy provide a robust conceptual toolkit for evaluating and improving digital participation in social work. These models push us to ask the following:

- Does the platform enable different forms of engagement (voice, feedback, co-decision-making)?
- Are there clear mechanisms through which input leads to action?
- Are marginalised voices actively included, or further excluded, by the design?
- Do digital systems align with social work values of empowerment, anti-oppression and rights?

These frameworks also help us to distinguish between *informational access* (reading one's records), *expressive access* (communicating views) and *relational participation* (being involved in shared decision-making). A chatbot that answers questions about entitlements may offer informational access, but – unless integrated with human-led relational processes – it cannot meet higher participatory thresholds.

The challenge for social work, then, is to ensure that the digital tools adopted, whether by local authorities, third-sector providers or national bodies, move beyond tokenistic consultation and instead foster sustained, equitable and relational participation.

# Case examples of participatory digital practice

While the use of digital platforms in social work continues to evolve, a number of UK local authorities and organisations have begun exploring more participatory applications of technology. These case examples illustrate how digital tools can be used not just to deliver services more efficiently but also to involve children, young people and families more meaningfully in decisions affecting their lives.

## Camden Council: co-designing data governance

Camden's co-produced Data Charter represents a rare example of participatory governance in digital infrastructure. Initially launched in

2021 and reviewed with residents in 2023, the charter was developed to increase transparency and build public trust in the borough's use of data and AI (Equality and Human Rights Commission, 2023). Residents were engaged in shaping the principles that would guide how their data was used and accessed, including the design of communication materials in multiple languages and formats.

Although this initiative focused on data governance rather than front line social work, it illustrates how co-production and participation can be embedded into digital strategy at a systemic level. Importantly, the project addressed audience and influence (Lundy, 2007), offering an example of how users can shape digital systems from the ground up. Such approaches demonstrate how digital participation can extend beyond feedback forms into shared ownership of policy and process.

### *Leeds City Council: integrating participation through stability*

Leeds has placed a strong emphasis on workforce development and relational practice, which has enabled more thoughtful integration of digital tools. Between 2013 and 2015, the proportion of social workers with over two years' experience rose from 52 per cent to over 80 per cent (*Community Care*, 2024). This continuity has supported the adoption of digital case management tools and communication systems in ways that reinforce, not replace, face-to-face engagement.

While Leeds' digital strategy has not explicitly branded itself as participatory, its broader Child-Friendly Leeds agenda aligns with a participatory ethos. Digital tools have been used to supplement direct work, including enabling children to record their views on tablets, access their own plans and communicate between reviews. These practices, when used alongside in-person meetings, reflect a blended approach that can enhance space and voice for children (Lundy, 2007), provided that those inputs are listened to and acted upon.

### *Swindon Council: artificial intelligence tools supporting inclusive practice*

In 2024, Swindon Council piloted an AI transcription tool known as 'Magic Notes', which records and summarises conversations during adult social care assessments. While primarily aimed at increasing efficiency, the tool was found to support participation for social workers with learning difficulties, visual impairments or for whom English was an additional language (*Community Care*, 2024).

Although Magic Notes is a practitioner-facing tool, its inclusive design and positive impact on workforce diversity has implications for participatory values. When practitioners themselves are better supported by technology, they may be more equipped to focus on relational aspects of their work. Moreover, tools that reduce administrative burden can free up time for deeper engagement with service users. However, as with all AI tools, transparency, accuracy and practitioner oversight are crucial to ensure that these benefits do not come at the cost of user trust or control.

Similarly, Microsoft's Copilot tool, which uses large language models to assist with real-time summarisation and task automation, is increasingly being integrated into social work contexts via Microsoft Teams. Like Magic Notes, Copilot aims to reduce administrative load by generating meeting summaries, action lists and document drafts. While promising in terms of efficiency, these tools raise important questions about data privacy, reliability and the implications of AI-mediated communication for professional judgement and service user participation.

Recent reporting suggests that the use of Magic Notes and similar AI transcription tools is expanding rapidly across local authorities in both England and Wales. Councils are trialling these tools not only to reduce administrative burden but also to explore their potential for improving documentation accuracy and workforce support (Koutsounia, 2024). While many of these trials remain outside formal research frameworks, the growing uptake signals a sector-wide interest in AI-enabled solutions. This makes the need for robust evaluation and ethical scrutiny even more urgent, particularly regarding how such tools affect relationships, data use and the participatory dimensions of practice.

### *Barking and Dagenham: automation and front line engagement*

Barking and Dagenham's deployment of the AutonoMe app for people with learning disabilities illustrates how automation and digital tools can support self-management and independence. AutonoMe, for instance, uses accessible video prompts and routines to help individuals develop life skills, offering service users greater agency over their daily lives (Local Government Association, 2021).

These technologies contribute to usage access (Van Dijk and Hacker, 2003) and can empower individuals to take more active roles in their care planning. However, such tools must be evaluated not only on their usability but on whether they enable users to set their own goals, influence support strategies and provide feedback on the services they receive.

### *Youth-led and co-produced platforms*

Outside local authorities, a number of youth-led initiatives and participatory design projects have begun to explore how digital platforms can be used to centre lived experience. While not yet widespread, examples include the following:

- Online youth forums that inform service design or local strategies (for example, via Zoom or social media).
- Co-produced websites and apps developed by care leavers and designed to share resources or advocate for change.
- Digital storytelling projects, where young people use video, podcasts or blogs to document their experiences and influence policy.

Such initiatives align closely with the higher rungs of Hart's Ladder (1992), particularly where young people initiate and lead the work. However, these practices often operate in the voluntary sector and are not always integrated into statutory services. For digital participation to become embedded, these models must be supported, resourced and adopted as part of everyday professional practice.

## Children's voices in digital life

While much of the discussion around digital participation in social work focuses on formal platforms, such as case portals, feedback tools and virtual meetings, this overlooks the fact that children and young people are already active participants in digital spaces. They use social media, messaging apps, gaming platforms and video-sharing services to express themselves, build communities and engage with the world around them. These informal, child-led forms of participation are not peripheral. Rather, they are central to how many young people experience agency, identity and connection.

For social work to truly embed digital participation, it must move beyond service-controlled tools and recognise the wider digital lives of children. This includes acknowledging both the opportunities and the risks that these platforms present and also understanding how young people are using them to advocate, organise and express their views on issues that affect them.

### *Informal participation as expression and advocacy*

Children's participation often takes place in spaces not designed for them but which they appropriate for their own purposes. Social media platforms like TikTok, Instagram and YouTube have become arenas for youth-led storytelling, activism, and peer support. Care-experienced young people, for instance, have used these platforms to share their journeys, challenge stigma and build solidarity. Hashtags, such as #CareExperienced and #FosterCareAwareness, have allowed young people to connect across geographical boundaries and speak directly to the public and policy makers.

These acts of participation may not be formally recognised by services, but they meet the core criteria of Lundy's (2007) model: they offer space, facilitate voice and reach wide audiences. In some cases, such informal expression has influenced mainstream narratives or even policy debates, with youth-generated content being cited in campaigns or inquiries. Yet, these forms of participation often sit outside the purview of professionals who may not be aware of, or feel unsure about, how to engage with such platforms.

## Opportunities for engagement and relational practice

Engaging with the digital lives of young people offers new opportunities for relational practice. Social workers who take an interest in how young people express themselves online can build trust, affirm identity and understand their perspectives in richer ways. For example, a young person who shares their art or videos online may be using these as a means of processing trauma, connecting with peers or advocating for change.

This is not to suggest that professionals should monitor or invade young people's digital spaces. Rather, it highlights the importance of creating safe, supported opportunities for young people to bring their digital experiences into conversations if they wish to. Encouraging reflection, curiosity and mutual learning around digital life can open new dimensions of participation within practice.

Moreover, digital engagement projects that begin with young people's interests, such as podcasting, gaming or social media storytelling, can offer inclusive, creative routes into participation. Such approaches have been used effectively by youth charities and participation workers, particularly with groups who may feel excluded from more formal processes.

## Bridging the gap between formal and informal participation

There remains a significant gap between the participatory energy of young people online and the often-procedural nature of digital participation within services. Formal platforms used by social care, such as digital review forms or council feedback tools, can feel sterile, inaccessible or disconnected from young people's real concerns and ways of communicating.

Bridging this gap requires co-production and creativity. Service providers might, for instance, collaborate with young people to create participatory content on social media platforms, or develop feedback tools that reflect young people's language, humour and digital culture. Digital youth councils or peer-led forums hosted on accessible platforms could offer a more engaging space for shaping services.

It also requires a shift in how participation is conceptualised. If participation is understood narrowly, as attendance at meetings or formal consultation, it will exclude the rich forms of digital expression already taking place. A broader, rights-based approach would value these existing contributions and explore how services can listen, learn and respond to them.

Incorporating children's broader digital lives into participatory frameworks is not a distraction from professional systems but, instead, a necessary rebalancing. By recognising that children are already participating online, often in sophisticated and courageous ways, social work can develop more responsive, respectful and effective digital practices. This involves not only building better tools but also building better relationships – ones that honour the digital voices young people are already raising.

## Digital exclusion and participation barriers

While digital technologies offer new opportunities for participation, they also risk entrenching existing inequalities if not designed and implemented with care. Digital exclusion is not simply about lacking a device or internet access: it is a complex, layered phenomenon influenced by structural disadvantage, digital literacy, language, accessibility and professional practice. Without deliberate effort to address these barriers, digital social work risks becoming a space where only the most privileged voices are heard.

### *Access*

Access to digital devices and the internet remains a significant challenge for many children and families. Although mobile phone ownership and broadband coverage have expanded in recent years, the quality, stability and cost of access vary greatly. According to the UK Parliament (2021) debate, it was estimated that 1.8 million children in the UK lacked access to a laptop or tablet during the COVID-19 lockdowns, making it difficult for them to engage with education, let alone digital services. Many households rely on pay-as-you-go data or shared devices, thereby limiting private, reliable access to digital platforms.

In social work contexts, these barriers can prevent service users from attending virtual meetings, accessing online records or participating in digital consultations. During the pandemic, some local authorities reported an increase in missed appointments or disengagement when services moved online, especially among families experiencing poverty or housing instability (Baginsky and Manthorpe, 2021). Simply offering digital platforms does not guarantee access – particularly for those already marginalised.

### *Digital literacy and confidence*

Even when access is available, digital participation depends on the confidence and skill to use the technology effectively. For some children and young people – particularly those with disabilities or limited literacy, or those new to the country – navigating digital systems can be intimidating or confusing.

Older adults, including kinship carers or parents with limited digital experience, may also struggle with interfaces that are not intuitive or user-friendly.

Helsper and Reisdorf (2017) argue that digital inequalities are relational: they reflect and reinforce pre-existing social inequalities. A parent with low literacy or a history of trauma may not only lack confidence in using a platform but may also fear surveillance or misinterpretation if they submit information digitally. Similarly, a child in care who has experienced placement instability may lack a consistent adult to support them in accessing online systems or expressing their views through digital means.

These issues highlight the importance of digital mediation – the role of practitioners, carers or peer supporters in helping users engage meaningfully with digital tools. Participation is unlikely to emerge in environments where digital use is unsupported, unconfident or intimidating.

## Language, accessibility and cultural inclusion

Language and communication are key to participation. If digital systems are available only in English, or rely on formal, technical language, they may exclude speakers of other languages or those with cognitive or communication differences. Despite legal obligations under the Equality Act 2010 and the Public Sector Equality Duty, many digital tools used in local government and social work settings remain inaccessible to disabled users or those with limited literacy.

Accessible design involves more than compliance checklists. It means developing platforms that are intuitive, multilingual, compatible with screen readers or alternative input devices, and culturally sensitive in content and imagery. In practice, however, few local authorities involve service users – especially disabled children or families with additional needs – in the co-design of digital systems (Kids, 2021).

Where accessibility is not built in from the outset, participation is not only limited but selectively so: it privileges those who already find systems easy to use and marginalises those who do not.

## The digital divide within the workforce

Barriers to digital participation also exist within the professional workforce. Some practitioners lack confidence in digital systems, receive insufficient training or operate in environments where IT infrastructure is outdated or unreliable. Research by Cook and Zschomler (2020) during the pandemic found that, while many social workers adapted well to digital practice, others struggled to balance new technologies with existing relational models.

This has implications for how participation is supported. A social worker unsure how to run a secure video meeting, or reluctant to use online forms, may default to more closed, professional-led modes of working. Even when platforms are available, digital participation is constrained if staff are not equipped or supported to use them in participatory ways.

This echoes Shier's (2001) emphasis on the need for organisational obligation, not just opportunity. Digital participation will remain inconsistent unless agencies build the systems, training and cultures that make it a routine and expected aspect of practice.

*Privacy, surveillance and trust*

Digital systems also raise significant questions about privacy, surveillance and data ethics. Many families express concern that what they share online may be misinterpreted, stored indefinitely or used to penalise rather than support them (Gillingham, 2019). For children in care, whose entire histories may be digitised across multiple systems, the stakes are particularly high.

Lundy's (2007) model reminds us that space and voice must be safe and trusted in order to be used. A child is unlikely to engage openly with a chatbot, video call or case file system if they fear judgement, exposure or negative consequences. Building trust in digital participation requires transparency about how data will be used, choice over how and when to engage, and the opportunity to correct or challenge digital records.

These concerns are compounded when AI or predictive analytics are used in decision-making. If parents or young people believe that an algorithm is making judgements about them based on incomplete or biased data, their willingness to participate meaningfully and honestly can be eroded (Eubanks, 2018). Digital inclusion is not just about access or design: it is also about cultivating a culture of digital ethics, transparency and shared governance. This includes recognising that data is never neutral, and that participation means enabling people to shape not just their own experiences but the systems that shape them.

*Intersectionality and cumulative disadvantage*

Finally, digital exclusion must be understood through an intersectional lens. Barriers to participation are rarely experienced in isolation. A care-experienced young person who is neurodivergent, living in temporary accommodation and has English as an additional language may face multiple, compounding exclusions that make digital participation all but impossible without proactive support.

In such cases, participation is not only about giving access to platforms but also about relational scaffolding: ensuring that digital tools are embedded in human relationships, advocacy and tailored support. Without this, digital practice may replicate the very inequalities social work seeks to address.

*Ethical considerations and the risk of tokenism*

While digital tools can offer new avenues for participation, their use also raises ethical tensions, particularly around voice, power and authenticity. Without careful attention to design, context and follow-through, digital participation can become tokenistic or even harmful. Participation is not simply a matter of inviting service users to engage: it requires structures and cultures that listen, respond and adapt, based on what people say.

Tokenism in digital participation often arises when tools are used to create the *appearance* of inclusion without transferring any real power or influence. For example, social care teams may roll out a new feedback app or parent portal but fail to embed a process for reviewing, acting on or responding to input. If a child provides their views before a meeting through an online form, but the professionals in the meeting never reference or incorporate that information, the process becomes hollow. Even worse, it can reinforce disillusionment.

This disconnect reflects the lower rungs of Hart's (1992) Ladder of Participation – particularly 'consultation' without follow-through or 'decoration', whereby participation is symbolic rather than substantive. The same risk exists with digital surveys, polls or consultation platforms that gather data for reports but do not feed back to participants or influence outcomes.

Lundy (2007) cautions that audience and influence are just as important as space and voice in participatory practice. In digital contexts, this means ensuring that platforms are not just expressive but also dialogical, enabling service users to see where their input goes and what impact it has. Otherwise, digital engagement may simply reproduce the top-down dynamics of analogue systems in a faster, more automated way.

*Speed and scale versus depth and meaning*

A further ethical challenge in digital practice is the trade-off between speed and depth. Digital tools allow for rapid consultation with large numbers of users, which can be appealing to stretched services seeking quick feedback. However, the risk is that participation becomes shallow, prioritising volume over nuance and data over dialogue.

For example, a chatbot might gather hundreds of interactions from young people using children's services, but – if those interactions are restricted to predetermined multiple-choice questions – they may not surface complexity or emotion. In addition, responses may be aggregated in ways that flatten diverse experiences into neat metrics – what Eubanks (2018) terms 'automating inequality'. In such cases, data can appear more democratic than it is.

Social work is fundamentally relational. While digital tools can supplement and strengthen relationships, they cannot replace the reflective, trust-based processes that genuine participation often requires (Ferguson et al, 2022). Ethical digital practice must therefore balance the convenience of technology with the time, empathy and responsiveness that participation demands.

## Informed consent and control over data

A recurring ethical concern is the question of consent, particularly when participation involves entering data into systems that are opaque, persistent and potentially shared across agencies. Children and families may not always understand what happens to the information they submit digitally, who can access it or how long it will be stored.

For participation to be meaningful, service users must not only consent to contribute their views – they must understand the implications of doing so. This includes clarity around data sharing, the potential use of AI and their rights to view, correct or challenge digital records (Diaz, 2023). Consent in this context is not a one-off checkbox but an ongoing conversation grounded in trust.

There is also a broader question of control. Digital systems often prioritise the needs of the organisation for compliance, efficiency or auditability over the needs of service users. Participatory ethics require shifting this balance. Wherever possible, children and families should have real-time access to their data, the ability to annotate or respond to case notes and the choice of how they want to engage digitally. Anything less risks reinforcing paternalistic models of practice.

These concerns are magnified by the growing use of AI and predictive analytics in children's services. AI tools promise early intervention, more efficient case handling and pattern recognition across large datasets. However, these technologies often operate without transparency, using historical data that reflects entrenched social inequalities. Studies of the Allegheny Family Screening Tool (AFST), used in the US child welfare system, have raised significant concerns about racial disproportionality, algorithmic bias and the risk of reinforcing systemic inequalities under the guise of objectivity (Chouldechova et al, 2018; Saxena et al, 2020). These tools, which use historical data to predict future risk, have been found to disproportionately flag Black families and those experiencing poverty, promoting debate about fairness, consent and transparency.

In the UK, local authorities such as Durham and Hackney have trialled similar predictive analytics to prioritise caseloads and identify families at risk of future safeguarding concerns. However, few of these systems are subject to public scrutiny or include participatory oversight, let alone contributions from children, families or practitioners in their development. This raises significant ethical questions: Who decides the criteria used by the algorithm? What recourse do families have to challenge automated decisions? How are false positives or data errors addressed?

These systems are also opaque by design. Families are often unaware that predictive analytics are influencing how services respond to them. Even when they are informed, it is rarely clear what data is being used, how it is weighted, or how it might affect future decisions. Participation in this context means not only being informed but also being involved in the governance and ethical review of such systems.

Shier's (2001) model of participation calls for movement from openings to obligations – that is, from one-off consultation to embedded accountability. Yet, AI projects in social care have often bypassed public engagement with ethical reviews conducted internally or outsourced to third parties. This creates a disconnect between the rhetoric of 'data for good' and the lived experience of families, who may feel surveilled, misunderstood or unable to contest decisions made by opaque digital tools.

There is a growing call for algorithmic accountability in public services, including children's social care. This means establishing oversight boards that include service users, care leavers, community representatives and ethical experts to guide the development and review of automated decision-making systems. It also includes the right to explanation, ensuring that families can understand and challenge how decisions about them are made (Veale et al, 2018).

Without such measures, participation in the context of AI remains superficial. A digital feedback form does not compensate for a lack of say in the algorithm determining your support. Participation must therefore be extended beyond front-end platforms to the very infrastructure of decision-making, including the datasets, indicators and predictive models that increasingly shape outcomes.

## *Power, bias and the reproduction of inequality*

Finally, digital participation cannot be disentangled from power. As scholars such as Noble (2018) and Gillingham (2019) have shown, digital systems are never neutral – they encode the values, assumptions and blind spots of their designers. Algorithms trained on historic data can reinforce the same racial, class or gendered biases that participation is meant to challenge. Platforms designed without service user input may unintentionally exclude the very voices they claim to amplify.

This is particularly relevant in social care where systems are increasingly linked – for example, health, education and policing – and where digital records may follow a child for life. Participatory ethics demand not only that service users are included but also that they are recognised as experts in their own lives, with the right to question, shape and even resist the digital systems that govern them.

To avoid tokenism, digital participation must be underpinned by humility, accountability and reflexivity. Practitioners and organisations must ask: Whose voices are missing? Who controls the platform? Who benefits from the data? And, most importantly: What changes as a result of what service users say?

## Embedding participation into digital practice

The previous sections have outlined both the opportunities and the risks associated with digital participation in social work. While examples of promising practice exist, they remain the exception rather than the norm. To realise the transformative potential of digital platforms, participation must be embedded not as an add-on but as a core organising principle, reflected in the design of technology, the cultures of practice and the structures of governance. The following sections outline key principles and recommendations to support this shift.

### *Design with, not for: co-production from the outset*

Participatory digital practice begins with co-production. Service users, particularly children, young people and families with lived experience, must be involved in the design, testing and evaluation of digital tools. This means moving beyond consultation to shared decision-making about what tools are needed, how they function and how success will be measured.

Local authorities and service providers should establish participatory design panels or advisory groups, ensure that those involved reflect the diversity of service users (including disabled people, care leavers and those from racially minoritised backgrounds), and resource their involvement meaningfully (Diaz, 2023). Co-production builds tools that are not only more effective but more trusted and inclusive.

### *Embed rights-based frameworks into digital strategy*

As this chapter has emphasised, frameworks such as Lundy's (2007) model, Shier's (2001) pathways and Hart's (1992) ladder offer practical ways to evaluate and design for meaningful participation. These frameworks should inform not only front line tools but broader digital strategies at the organisational level.

Digital participation policies should be mapped against these frameworks, asking: Where are the opportunities for space, voice, audience and influence? Are there mechanisms for feedback and redress? How is participatory quality being monitored and improved over time? Embedding rights-based models into digital governance ensures that technology serves participatory ends rather than procedural or bureaucratic ones.

## Prioritise accessibility and equity

Accessibility must be a starting point, not an afterthought. This includes ensuring compatibility with screen readers, simple and intuitive interfaces, low-data functionality for those with limited broadband, and multilingual content. Platforms should be user-tested with diverse service users, particularly those with disabilities, lower literacy or limited digital experience.

Additionally, social work organisations should conduct digital inclusion audits to identify and address gaps in access and support. These audits should consider not only hardware and connectivity but also confidence, privacy and the availability of digital mediation (for example, practitioners helping service users navigate systems). Embedding participation requires eliminating the barriers that make digital spaces exclusive.

## Foster relational, not transactional, digital engagement

While digital tools can increase efficiency, participation is rarely fostered through speed alone. Digital engagement must be relational, focused on building trust, listening deeply and responding to what is shared. Wherever possible, digital tools should supplement rather than replace human interaction.

This might include enabling young people to prepare thoughts before a meeting by using an online form and then discussing their views in person or via video with a trusted adult. It might involve using secure messaging for follow-up conversations that build continuity between appointments. Technology should open space for dialogue, not close it down (Pink et al, 2022; Ferguson et al, 2022).

## Build capacity in the workforce

Participation depends on people, not just platforms. Social workers and other practitioners need the skills, confidence and organisational support to use digital tools in participatory ways. This includes training in digital safeguarding, inclusive communication, data ethics and participatory facilitation. Supervision and team meetings should include space to reflect on digital practice – what is working, what is not, and how participation can be strengthened. Digital champions or peer support models can help embed innovation while maintaining the values of relational and rights-based practice.

*Ensure transparency, feedback and accountability*

Finally, digital participation must be accountable. This means being transparent with service users about how their information is used, where their input goes and what decisions are shaped by it. Feedback loops should be built into platforms, whether through update notifications, co-authored plans or simple acknowledgements of receipt and response.

Organisations should also monitor participation metrics not only in terms of quantity (for example, how many users submitted feedback) but quality (for example, how feedback was used, how users felt about the process). Annual reviews or external audits of participatory quality can ensure that digital innovation does not drift into tokenism or exclusion.

## Conclusion

Digital technologies are reshaping the structures and rhythms of social work practice. From case recording systems and messaging apps to AI-driven decision support and online service portals, the digital turn in social care is both inevitable and accelerating. Yet, as this chapter has shown, the question is not simply whether we adopt new tools but how we do so, and for whose benefit.

Digital systems have the potential to democratise access, amplify voice and create new spaces for collaboration between practitioners and the children, young people and families they support. But this potential is not automatic. Without deliberate, rights-based design, digital participation risks becoming shallow, tokenistic or even exclusionary – particularly for those already marginalised by systemic disadvantage, poverty or discrimination.

Using frameworks from Hart (1992), Shier (2001) and Lundy (2007), we have examined the conditions under which digital participation becomes meaningful. Participation must involve more than presence or feedback. It must offer genuine influence. This requires safe and accessible platforms, co-designed with users; practitioners confident and supported to work relationally; and systems of accountability that ensure that voices are heard and acted upon.

Participation also requires resisting the drift toward performative or technocratic models of digital engagement, whereby speed and data take precedence over dialogue and care. Social work is a profession rooted in human connection, empathy and justice. These values must remain central as we move into increasingly digital modes of practice.

There is no single model of ideal digital participation. Context matters and tools will vary. But the core principles remain: inclusion, transparency, equity and responsiveness. When digital practice is shaped by these principles, it can open new routes to empowerment and shared decision-making. When it is not, it risks becoming another system of control.

Ultimately, digital participation is not about technology. It is about power, voice and relationship. The challenge for social work is to ensure that, as we embrace digital innovation, we do so in ways that uphold the rights and dignity of the people we serve and that deepen, rather than diminish, their ability to shape the systems that shape their lives.

**References**

Baginsky, M., Eyre, J. and Roe, A. (2020) *Child Protection Conference Practice during COVID-19: Reflections and Experiences (Rapid Consultation September–October 2020)*. Nuffield Family Justice Observatory.

Baginsky, M. and Manthorpe, J. (2021) 'The impact of COVID-19 on children's social care in England', *Child Abuse & Neglect*, 116(2): 104739.

Beaunoyer, E., Dupéré, S. and Guitton, M.J. (2020) 'COVID-19 and digital inequalities: reciprocal impacts and mitigation strategies', *Computers in Human Behavior*, 111: 106424.

Camden Council (2023) *Camden Council's Data Charter: Updates from Residents Panel 2023*. Available from: camden.gov.uk/data-charter

Chan, C. and Holosko, M.J. (2016) 'The utilization of technology in generalist social work practice and education'. *Journal of Technology in Human Services*, 34(1) 42–52.

Chouldechova, A., Benavides-Prado, D., Fialko, O. and Vaithianathan, R. (2018) *A Case Study of Algorithm-Assisted Decision Making in Child Maltreatment Hotline Screening Decisions*. Proceedings of the 2018 AAAI/ACM Conference on AI, Ethics, and Society, 134–40.

*Community Care* (2024) 'AI could be time-saving for social workers but needs regulation, say sector bodies.' Available from: https://www.communitycare.co.uk

Cook, L. and Zschomler, D. (2020) 'Child and family social work in the context of COVID-19: practice issues and innovations', *Social Work Education*, 39(8): 1050–62.

Diaz, C., Fitz-Symonds, S., Evans, L., Westlake, D., Devine, R., Mauri, D. et al (2023) *The Perceived Impact of Peer Parental Advocacy on Child Protection Practice: A Pilot Evaluation*. What Works for Children's Social Care.

Equality and Human Rights Commission (2023) *Artificial Intelligence Case Studies: Good Practice by Local Authorities*. Available from: https://www.equalityhumanrights.com

Eubanks, V. (2018) *Automating Inequality: How High-Tech Tools Profile, Police, and Punish the Poor*. St. Martin's Press.

Featherstone, B., White, S. and Morris, K. (2014) *Re-imagining Child Protection: Towards Humane Social Work with Families*. Policy Press.

Ferguson, H., Pink, S. and Kelly, L. (2022) 'The unheld child: social work, social distancing and the possibilities and limits to child protection during the COVID-19 pandemic', *British Journal of Social Work*, 52(4): 2403–21.https://doi.org/10.1093/bjsw/bcac055

Gillingham, P. (2019) 'The development of algorithmic tools for use in social work practice: challenges and opportunities', *British Journal of Social Work*, 49(3): 552–67.

Hart, R. (1992) *Children's Participation: From Tokenism to Citizenship.* UNICEF/International Child Development Centre.

Helsper, E.J. and Reisdorf, B.C. (2017) 'The emergence of a "digital underclass" in Great Britain and Sweden: changing reasons for digital exclusion', *New Media & Society*, 19(8): 1253–70.

Kids (2021) *Driving Digital Inclusion Programme.* Available from: https://www.kids.org.uk/digital-inclusion-programme/

Kong, S.T., Noone, C. and Shears, J. (2022) 'Social workers' sensual bodies during COVID-19: the suspended, displaced and reconstituted body in social work practice', *The British Journal of Social Work*, 52(5): 2834–53.

Koutsounia, A. (2024) 'AI could be time-saving for social workers but needs regulation, say sector bodies', *Community Care*. Available from: https://www.communitycare.co.uk/2024/10/04/ai-could-be-time-saving-for-social-workers-but-needs-regulation-say-sector-bodies/

Local Government Association (2021) *Digital discharge to assess.* Available from: https://lb2.local.gov.uk/case-studies/digital-discharge-assess#:~:text=The%20aims%20of%20the%20SCDIA%20Digital%20Discharge%20to,raft%20of%20associated%20patient%20benefits%20and%20service%20efficiencies

López-Pelaez, A. and Marcuello-Servós, C. (2018) 'e-Social work and digital society: re-conceptualizing approaches, practices and technologies', *European Journal of Social Work*, 21(6): 801–3. Available from: https://doi.org/10.1080/13691457.2018.1520475

Lundy, L. (2007) '"Voice" is not enough: conceptualising Article 12 of the United Nations Convention on the Rights of the Child', *British Educational Research Journal*, 33(6): 927–42. Available from: https://doi.org/10.1080/01411920701657033

Mishna, F., Bogo, M., Root, J., Sawyer, J.L. and Khoury-Kassabri, M. (2012) 'It just crept in: the digital age and implications for social work practice', *Clinical Social Work Journal*, 40(3): 277–86. Available from: https://doi.org/10.1007/s10615-012-0383-4

Noble, S.U. (2018) *Algorithms of Oppression: How Search Engines Reinforce Racism.* New York University Press.

Pink, S., Ferguson, H. and Kelly, L. (2022) 'Digital social work: conceptualising a hybrid anticipatory practice', *Qualitative Social Work*, 21(2): 413–30.

Ramsey, A.T. and Montgomery, K. (2014) 'Technology-based interventions in social work practice: a systematic review of mental health interventions', *Social Work in Health Care*, 53(9): 883–99. Available from: https://doi.org/10.1080/00981389.2014.925531

Saxena, N.A., Saleiro, P., Kasymov, A., Moura, R. and Raji, I.D. (2020) *Fairness and explainability in algorithmic risk assessments: A case study of the Allegheny Family Screening Tool*. In *FAT '20: Proceedings of the 2020 Conference on Fairness, Accountability, and Transparency*. ACM, pp 228–38.

Shier, H. (2001) 'Pathways to participation: openings, opportunities and obligations', *Children & Society*, 15(2): 107–17. Available from: https://doi.org/10.1002/chi.617

Steiner, O. (2021) 'Social work in the digital era: theoretical, ethical and practical considerations', *The British Journal of Social Work*, 51(8): 3358–74. Available from: https://doi.org/10.1093/bjsw/bcaa160

UK Parliament (2021) 'Remote learning: laptops and other devices', *House of Commons Debates*, 18 Jan, 687: c330–c332.

van Dijk, J. and Hacker, K. (2003) 'The digital divide as a complex and dynamic phenomenon', *The Information Society*, 19(4): 315–26. Available from: https://doi.org/10.1080/01972240309487

Veale, M., Van Kleek, M. and Binns, R. (2018) 'Fairness and accountability design needs for algorithmic support in high-stakes public sector decision-making'. In *Proceedings of the 2018 Chi Conference on Human Factors in Computing Systems*, pp 1–14.

# 12

# Concluding reflections

*Clive Diaz and Tim Fisher*

This chapter offers concluding reflections on the themes explored throughout this book. It argues that the future of child and family social work must be fundamentally participatory – centered on the rights, experiences and contributions of children, families and communities. The chapters in this book demonstrate that participation is not a peripheral concern but a legal, ethical and professional imperative.

The child welfare system in England and Wales, as in many jurisdictions, is characterised by a range of intersecting pressures. These include rising referral and care rates, workforce instability, growing socio-economic inequalities and increasingly complex family needs. These pressures are compounded by risk-averse organisational cultures, bureaucratic constraints and an often-adversarial dynamic between families and professionals (Featherstone et al, 2018; Gupta et al, 2016).

Despite these challenges, there is growing evidence that more participatory, rights-based and collaborative models of social work are not only possible but increasingly necessary. As this book has illustrated, interventions such as Family Group Conferences (FGCs), peer parental advocacy, and the Family Drug and Alcohol Court (FDAC) represent promising alternatives that prioritise engagement, trust and shared decision-making with families. These approaches provide a foundation for rethinking the assumptions that underlie child protection practice and for building more responsive and equitable systems of support.

## The ethical and emotional foundations of participation

Participation is grounded in international and domestic legal frameworks. Article 12 of the United Nations Convention on the Rights of the Child (UNCRC) (UN General Assembly, 1989) asserts that children have the right to express their views freely in all matters affecting them, and to have those views given due weight in accordance with their age and maturity. This principle is echoed in domestic legislation and guidance, including the Children Act 1989, 'Working together to safeguard children' (Department for Education, 2023) and Social Work England's professional standards.

Participatory practice and ensuring that families participate meaningfully in decision-making requires not only organisational support, such as reflective supervision and reasonable caseloads. Practitioners also need to have the emotional capacity and reflective competence to carry out the work. Child and family social work is inherently affective, involving regular exposure to trauma, loss, conflict and distress. As Winnicott (1963, p 174) observed: 'To work effectively with children, the first and most fundamental thing we have to know about is the strength of our feelings about the suffering of children … But we too are only human and we will find that our own tolerance levels will fluctuate.'

This emotional labour has profound implications for the enactment of participation. When practitioners are unsupported – working in understaffed teams, under pressure to meet compliance targets – the relational and reflective dimensions of the work are easily eroded. Defensive practice may emerge in response, diminishing opportunities for open, reciprocal engagement with families. Participation cannot be achieved simply through procedural reform: it also requires attention to the psychological and affective conditions that make meaningful dialogue and connection possible.

Theoretical models provide useful conceptual frameworks for understanding and evaluating participation. Hart's (1992) Ladder of Participation distinguishes between non-participatory (for example, manipulation, tokenism) and genuinely participatory practices (for example, child-initiated decision-making). Shier's (2001) 'Pathways to participation' introduces a graduated model for embedding participatory practice within organisations, thereby highlighting the need for supportive structures, resources and accountability mechanisms. Lundy's (2007) model proposes four essential dimensions for enabling participation: space, voice, audience and influence.

Together, these models challenge practitioners and organisations to move beyond rhetorical commitments and to engage meaningfully with children and families in shaping the decisions and services that affect their lives.

## Practice models that operationalise participation

Throughout this volume, several practice models have been presented that exemplify the principles of participatory social work.

Family Group Conferencing (FGC) as explored in Chapter 6 enables families to lead planning processes for the care and safety of their children. Evaluations of FGCs have found that they can improve family engagement, strengthen support network and increase the likelihood that children remain safely within their families (Pennell and Anderson, 2005; Morris and Burford, 2007; Papaioannou et al, 2023). However, concerns have been raised about the dilution of the model when implemented without adequate independence or fidelity to its original design (Cram, 2018).

Peer parental advocacy, as implemented in Camden and evaluated by Diaz et al (2023), offers a complementary model wherein parents with lived experience of the child protection system support others navigating similar processes. Evidence from pilot evaluations suggests that peer parental advocacy can build trust, improve communication between families and professionals, and promote more equitable and informed participation in meetings and planning (Tobis et al, 2020).

Finally, the FDAC explored in Chapter 5 offers a therapeutic, problem-solving approach to substance misuse that involves families in ongoing decision-making.

These models demonstrate that participatory approaches are not abstract ideals. When implemented with fidelity and properly resourced, they can lead to meaningful improvements in family experience and more meaningful shared decision-making. We believe that when parental advocacy, children's advocacy, FGCs and Family Drug and Alcohol Courts are effectively implemented, this will reduce the risk that families are harmed by the child protection process. Furthermore, these interventions can lead to a reduction in the rates of children in care, families feeling that their rights are being respected, improved and more trusting relationships between social workers and parents, and – ultimately – improved social work retention as social workers feel that their work is more helpful to families and less adversarial.

Our recent research on parental advocacy in England, Wales and Ireland (Diaz et al, 2023; Fitz-Symonds et al, 2024) together with our evaluations of mentoring programmes for care-experienced young people in two different sites in England, has highlighted the importance of relationships between professionals and the families they work with. It is essential that professionals are willing to be open to learning from and about families, and to share parts of themselves as well as acknowledging that they do not have all the answers. Good social work involves engaging with the internal worlds of the people we work with, taking their feelings seriously and showing a deep interest in their lives, including asking about their hopes and dreams.

## Systemic barriers and structural inequities

Despite the promise of these models, significant systemic barriers continue to inhibit the widespread adoption of participatory practice. These include the following:

- Bureaucratic overload: excessive form-filling and administrative requirements divert practitioners' time and energy away from direct work with families (Broadhurst et al, 2010; Diaz, 2020).
- Defensive cultures: fear of blame or litigation may lead to over-intervention or risk-averse decision-making, limiting practitioners' willingness to share power with families (Munro, 2011).

- Structural inequalities: families from racially minoritised groups, those living in poverty, and disabled parents are disproportionately subject to statutory interventions and under-represented in participatory forums (Bywaters et al, 2016).
- Language barriers: the use of professional jargon and risk-centric terminology can alienate families and reduce their sense of agency in decision-making processes (Kline, 1992).

Addressing these barriers requires systemic change. This includes not only reforms to policy and process but also investment in workforce development, supervision and organisational cultures that value and protect time for participatory engagement.

## Inclusion, belonging and co-production

Participation must also be understood in relation to broader questions of inclusion and belonging. A truly participatory social work system is one in which all children and families – regardless of background, identity or legal status – feel seen, heard and respected. This requires:

- culturally responsive practices that recognise the diverse forms of knowledge and care within families and communities;
- anti-racist and anti-oppressive frameworks that challenge systemic biases in referral, assessment and decision-making; and
- mechanisms for co-design and co-production, ensuring that services are shaped with, not just for, those who use them.

Belonging is a critical outcome of participation. When children and families feel that they belong within systems of support – that they are not simply cases to be managed but valued contributors to their own futures – then engagement, trust and outcomes are strengthened. As highlighted in Chapters 10 and 11, this is especially critical in youth-led and digital spaces where innovation must meet inclusion.

## Leadership and organisational conditions for change

Realising the promise of participatory social work requires committed leadership and the enabling of conditions at every level. Leaders must:

- promote participation as a core organisational value and performance measure;
- invest in participatory infrastructure, including advocacy, translation, facilitation and time;

- model participatory behaviours in their own interactions with staff and service users;
- develop systems of reflective supervision and critical inquiry that support practitioners to engage with complexity.

In addition, organisational cultures must reward curiosity, humility and openness – qualities that are often essential for participation but easily crowded out by compliance-driven agendas.

## Participation as the basis of just practice

Participation does not require perfection. It requires intention, openness and a willingness to share power. As social workers, policy makers, leaders and educators, the question is not whether we support participation – but how far we are willing to go to make it real.

This book has argued that participation must become a defining principle of child and family social work – not a procedural gesture, but a sustained commitment to equity, inclusion and power-sharing. The models and practices discussed – FGC, peer parental advocacy and participatory reviews – demonstrate that participatory approaches are not only feasible but essential. They contribute to better outcomes, greater trust and a more legitimate child welfare system.

Realising participation in practice, however, is not without challenge. Systemic barriers, structural inequalities and professional cultures shaped by risk and compliance can make it difficult for participation to thrive. Embedding participation requires deliberate effort: a shift in how services are designed, how professionals are trained and how organisations conceptualise success.

Yet, despite these challenges, there is cause for cautious optimism. Across the UK and internationally, practitioners, families and young people are co-producing new forms of practice. These efforts suggest that the profession is capable not only of critique but also of creativity. They reveal a vision of social work grounded in mutual respect, structural awareness and the belief that those closest to the issue are closest to the solution.

## Final reflections

As we close this volume, we want to move beyond theory and practice to speak to the deeper values that underlie this work. Reflecting on the future of child and family social work, it is clear that technical solutions alone will not suffice. What is needed is a reassertion of values: of justice, dignity, humility and hope. At its heart, this work is about love – not a sentimental or abstract love but a principled love. The kind of love that requires courage. The kind that calls us to fight for equity, to listen deeply and to create systems that affirm the humanity of those they serve.

Let that commitment guide us – as practitioners, educators, managers, researchers and policy makers – as we work towards a child welfare system where every child and family can not only be safe but thrive: a system in which participation is not a privilege but a right; not an ambition but a reality.

## References

Broadhurst, K., Hall, C., Wastell, D., White, S. and Pithouse, A. (2010) 'Risk, instrumentalism and the humane project – identifying the informal logics of risk management in children's statutory services', *British Journal of Social Work*, 40(4): 1046–64. Available from: https://doi.org/10.1093/bjsw/bcq011

Bywaters, P., Brady, G., Sparks, T. and Bos, E. (2016) 'Child welfare inequalities: new evidence, further questions', *Child & Family Social Work*, 21(3): 369–80.

Cram, F. (2018) 'Measuring the success of a family group conference', *Aotearoa New Zealand Social Work*, 30(1): 62–7.

Department for Education (2023) *Working together to safeguard children: statutory framework for multi-agency working to safeguard and promote the welfare of children.* Available from: https://www.gov.uk/government/publications/working-together-to-safeguard-children--2

Diaz, C. (2020) *Decision Making in Child and Family Social Work: Perspectives on Children's Participation.* Policy Press.

Diaz, C., Fitz-Symonds, S. Evans, L., Westlake, D., Devine, R., Mauri, D. et al (2023) *The Perceived Impact of Peer Parental Advocacy on Child Protection Practice: A Pilot Evaluation.* What Works for Children's Social Care.

Featherstone, B., Gupta, A., Morris, K. and White, S. (2018) *Protecting Children: A Social Model.* Policy Press.

Fitz-Symonds, S., Evans, L., Tobis, D., Westlake, D. and Diaz, C. (2024) 'Mechanisms for support: a realist evaluation of peer parental advocacy in England', *The British Journal of Social Work*, 54(1): 341–59. Available from: https://doi.org/10.1093/bjsw/bcad200

Gupta, A., Featherstone, B. and White, S. (2016) 'Reclaiming humanity: from capacities to capabilities in understanding parenting in adversity', *The British Journal of Social Work*, 50(6): 1797–813.

Hart, R.A. (1992) *Children's Participation: From Tokenism to Citizenship*, UNICEF International Child Development Centre.

Kline, M. (1992) 'Child welfare law, "best interests of the child" ideology, and First Nations', *Osgoode Hall Law Journal*, 30(2): 375–425.

Lundy, L. (2007) '"Voice" is not enough: conceptualising Article 12 of the United Nations Convention on the Rights of the Child', *British Educational Research Journal*, 33(6): 927–42. Available from: https://doi.org/10.1080/01411920701657033

Morris, K. and Burford, G. (2007) 'Working with children and families separated by incarceration: A summary of Family Group Conferencing research findings', in J. Taylor, A. Gibbs and E. McDonald (eds) *New Zealand and International Trends and Issues in Family Group Conferencing*, Ministry of Social Development (pp 143–57).

Munro, E. (2011) *The Munro Review of Child Protection: Final Report – A ChildCentred System*. Department for Education.

Papaioannou, K., Kuo, T.-L., Fugard, A., Sharrock, S., Roberts, E., Kersting, F. et al (2023) *Evaluation of Family Drug and Alcohol Courts*. National Centre for Social Research.

Pennell, J. and Anderson, G. (2005) *Widening the Circle: The Practice and Evaluation of Family Group Conferencing with Children, Youths, and Their Families*. NASW Press.

Shier, H. (2001) 'Pathways to participation: openings, opportunities and obligations', *Children and Society*, 15(2): 107–17.

Tobis, D., Bilson, A. and Katugampala, I. (2020) *International review of parent advocacy in child welfare*. Available from: https://bettercarenetwork.org/about-bcn/what-we-do/organizations-working-on-childrens-care/international-parent-advocacy-network-ipan

UN General Assembly (1989) Convention on the Rights of the Child, United Nations, Treaty Series, vol. 1577: United Nations.

Winnicott, D.W. (1963) *The Child, the Family, and the Outside World*. Penguin Books.

# Index

References to figures appear in *italic* type.

## A

Aboriginal children 124, 129
abuse and neglect 4, 24, 74, 77, 100, 123, 129
access to digital services 208, 213, 216, 217, 222
accountability 221, 222, 224
Administration for Children's Services 116, 120
adoption 15, 22
Adoption and Children Act 2002 52, 171
adult FGCs 107–8
adult social care assessments 212
adversarial systems 50, 57, 80, 131, 148, 161, 228
advocacy 5, 7, 54, 59, 111
  accessing services 180–1, 185
  collective advocacy 182, 185
  and digital participation 214–16
  independent advocacy 170–1, 179–80
  long term impacts 181–2
  professional perspectives on 174
  *see also* advocacy for CiC
advocacy for children in care 7, 184–6
  about 167–8
  effective advocacy 175
  ethical considerations 177–81
  future directions 181–3
  legal and policy frameworks 168–72
  in practice 172–7
  voices of young people 183–4
Allegheny Family Screening Tool 220
artificial intelligence 3, 25, 206, 212–13, 220
Au, Kar Man 87, 139, 149
  and FGCs 87, 94, 97, 107–8
austerity 16, 37, 183, 185
  impact on advocacy 177
Australia 111, 112
  child removal 124, 129
  children in care 14
  Family Inclusion (FISH) 126
  parent activism in 117, 118, 119, 122–5
AutonoMe 213
autonomy and digital tools 207

## B

Barking and Dagenham 213
Belgium, children in care 14
belonging, sense of 115, 145, 202, 231

Bennett, Jourdelle 13
best interests 93, 156, 161, 177, 179, 184
Birth Parent National Network (BPNN) 117, 125, 143
birth parents 14, 23, 73, 80, 124
Black families 114, 146, 220
  Black and African workers 39
Black Lives Matter 114
Boylan, J. 174, 178, 180
Braun, V. 150
Bunting, L. 17–18
bureaucratic overload 230

## C

California Families Rise 124, 131
Camden 61, 87, 117, 130, 230
  Camden case study 74–5, 148–54
  Data Charter 208
  data governance 211–12
Canada 111, 112
  children in care 14
  parent activism in 117, 122, 125
Cardiff and Glamorgan, FDACs in 81–4
career progression 40
child and family social work
  current context 3–6
  foundation and challenges 6–7
  support engagement 6
  tiered UK system 22
child deaths 15, 21, 53
child-friendly justice 56
Child-Friendly Leeds 212
child-led change 5, 56, 214
  advocacy in practice 173
child protection 10, 53, 59
  advisory panels 120
  care plans 22, 52, 56, 100, 168
  child removal 112–13
  children remaining with families 6, 74, 229
  child sexual exploitation 16
  colonial systems 112
  increasing referrals 17–18
  and parental advocacy 160–1
  and parental rights 156
  and virtual case conferences 210
Children, Young People and Families Act 142
Children Act UK (1989) 15, 52, 53, 89, 169–70, 171
  'wishes and feelings' 52, 57, 170, 185

235

Children and Families Act 2014  169–70
Children and Young Persons Act 2008  171
children in care  6, 9, 13–18
  children chairing reviews  62
  costs of  14
  leaving care  22, 23, 171
  number of  114
  outcomes of  14
  solutions to increasing rates  21–7, 230
  variation of rates of  13–18
  *see also* advocacy for children in care
Children in Care Councils (CiCCs)  7
  background  191–2
  findings  193–202
  methodology  193
  reflections  202–4
  using online services  191–7, 198–203
Children's Commissioner  54, 216
Child Welfare Organizing Project (CWOP)  116, 145, 146
child welfare systems, navigating  5, 61, 140, 145, 151, 177, 182
chronosystem  21, 26
Clarke, V.  150
co-design/co-production  148, 183, 208, 211, 222, 231
collaborative work  63, 80, 89, 92, 97, 142
collective action  145, 147, 149
colonialism and child protection  112, 114, 124, 129
commitment, three stages of  9
communication  148, 154
  and advocacy support  174
  challenges  57
  and child protection  141
  and digital technology  206
  at FGCs  89–90
  skills training  84
community  92, 95
  community activism  124–5
  community-based support  25
  community meetings  61
*Community Care*  33, 35, 47
confidentiality  156–7, 171, 177–8
Connelly, Peter  53
consent, informed  157, 220–1
Cooper, Andrew  42
cost-effectiveness
  of FDACs  80–1
  of FGCs  104
cost of living crisis  4, 16
court proceedings  22, 55, 73, 84
COVID-19  16, 33, 41, 185, 191, 193, 216
  children's voices during  210
  and digital tools  203, 206, 208
  and FGCs  100
  and inequalities  4
  research during  7

Crichton, Judge N.  74, 75, 84
criminal exploitation  16
critical theories  145–6, 154
Crow, G.  105
culture
  cultural inclusion  217
  culturally responsive practice  231
  cuts in services  16, 37, 185

**D**

Dalrymple, J.  167, 178, 179
data  26, 212
  control over data  220–1
  and decision-making  24–5
  ethics  218
  privacy and security  3, 7
death rates  4, 21
decision-making  50, 93, 155, 173, 229
  and artificial intelligence  3
  for children in care  167
  and families  89
  and parental advocacy  61, 139
  participation in  5, 6
  theories of participation  8
defensive culture  230
Department for Education  18, 170
deprivation  15, 18, 24, 149
  in Wales  16
Diaz, Clive  3, 139, 148, 191, 228, 230
digital participation  3, 6, 7, 206–7
  and advocacy support  185
  case examples of practice  211–14
  children's voices  214–16
  digital exclusion  216–22
  digital literacy  216–17
  embedding participation  222–5
  and organisational obligation  218
  and platforms  207–8
  and rights-based framework  222–3
  and service design  208, 222
  speed versus depth  219–20
  theoretical models of  208–11
  *see also* CiCCs
disabilities  52, 57, 171, 182, 223, 231
  and digital participation  216–17
disadvantage *see* structural inequalities
discrimination  35, 39, 224
diversity  11, 95, 149, 182
domestic abuse  16, 77, 100, 153, 195
Dove, Becca  149
drug testing, regular  83–4
drug treatment courts *see* Family Drug and Alcohol Court (FDAC)
Durham  220

**E**

early intervention  15, 21–3
Ecological Systems Theory  6, 13, 15, 18–21, *20*, 26

# Index

economic policy 23, 25, 26
educational attainment 14, 132
emotional distress 35, 36–7, 41
employment factors 24
energy prices 4
engagement 5, 8, 10, 142, 148, 193, 200
  digital engagement 214–16
England 6, 15, 100, 111, 223
  child protection in 17
  children in care 14
  Durham 220
  Leeds 212
  lockdown survey 193
  north-east England 193
  parent activism in 117, 119, 125, 127–9
  parental advocacy in 139
  Swindon 212–13
  Telford 117, 118
  see also London
environmental settings 20
Equality Act 2010 217
ethical considerations 74, 156–3, 219, 220, 228–9
  and advocacy for CiC 177–81
ethnic minorities 39, 146, 182, 220, 231
  and inequalities 4
Eubanks, V. 219
exclusion/inclusion
  AI tools and practice 212–13
  and belonging 231–2
  digital access 208
  digital exclusion 7, 216–22
exosystem 20, 26
experts in their own lives 34, 60, 102, 158, 184, 221

## F

families
  empowering families 23, 60–1
  family preservation 17, 23, 25, 26
  and predictive analysis 220–1
  private family time 97
  strengthening 7, 93, 94
  support for families 129
  see also Family Drug and Alcohol Court (FDAC); Family Group Conferencing (FGC)
Families First Prevention Services Act 2018 129, 143
Family Advisory Board 107, 148
Family Drug and Alcohol Court (FDAC) 7, 228, 230
  about 73–4
  cost-effectiveness of 80–1
  development of 76–8
  and empowerment 82
  evidence base 79–81
  and family reunification 79–80
  funding for 77–8
  keyworkers in 82–3
  positive results from 84
  principles and components of 75–6
Family Group Conferencing (FGC) 5, 7, 23, 25, 60–1, 142, 228, 229
  about 87–91
  challenges for research 99
  co-ordinators 95–7
  delivery of 95–9
  evidence from 99–105
  future of 105–9
  importance of 91–5
  painting 91
  and practitioners 104–5
  private family time 97
  reflections on 88, 92
  relationship repair 94
Family Inclusion Network 117, 125, 126
family inclusion theory 146
Family Justice Law Center 122, 128
Family Proceedings Court 74, 75, 79
Family Rights Group 100
father absence 24
Featherstone, Bird 21, 59, 142, 146–7
female social workers 34
feminist theory 147
financial instability 4, 21, 23–4
Finland 111
Fisher, Tim 148, 149, 228
  and FGCs 87, 88, 104, 106–7
Fitzsimons, P. 16
Fitz-Symonds, Sammi 3, 167, 191, 206
foster care 14, 16, 19, 22, 116, 123, 128
  foster carers 178, 180, 196, 199
Franklin, J. 25, 178
Frost, Liz 33
funding 18, 24, 158, 175–7, 183, 185
  for FDAC 77–8

## G

gender bias 221
Gillingham, P. 221
Give Us Back Our Children 125
grassroots activism 114, 117, 124–5, 142
Gupta, Anna 59, 146–7

## H

Hackney 220
harms 53, 79, 94, 146, 178
  of care system 14, 16, 114, 119, 131
  social determinants of 21
Hart, Roger 9, 167, 175, 222
  Ladder of Participation 8, 209, 219, 229
health inequalities 4
high-profile cases 15, 21, 40, 53
Hodges, H. 16

Holbrook, H. 17
homelessness 24

## I

inclusive practices 60–2
Independent Reviewing Officer (IRO) 52, 62
Independent Review of Children's Social Care 54, 59, 61, 63
indigenous resistance 112, 122, 123, 124, 125, 130
inequalities 145–7, 174, 230–1
 and artificial intelligence 3
 'automating inequality' 219
 digital exclusion 216–22
 systemic 220
intergenerational trauma of care 14
International Parent Advocacy Network (IPAN) 119, 125
international perspectives 7, 11
 and FGCs 104
 international research 159
 legal frameworks 51–2, 169, 172, 228
 and parent advocacy 143
 and parental advocacy 161
 *see also* Australia; New Zealand; United States
International Review of Parent Advocacy in Child Welfare 160
Italy 40

## J

Jacobsen, B. 24
judges 76, 84
 child-friendly judgements 56
 perception of 80
justice system 73

## K

Keddell, E. 17
Keeping Families Together Act 2023 123
Kentucky 119
keyworkers 82–3
kinship care 15, 23
knife crime 36
Knight, A. 178

## L

Ladder of Participation 8, 209, 219, 229
language barriers 180, 183, 212, 231
 and digital exclusion 217, 218
 digital tools 208
 large language models 213
 young people's terminology 199–200
leadership and change 231–2
learning disabilities, and digital access 213
leaving the care system 22, 23, 171
Leeds City Council 212

Legal Action for Women 127
Legally Stolen Children 122
legislation 52–3, 57, 89, 169–71
 child-friendly justice 56
 international 51–2, 143, 169, 172, 228
 legal advocacy 141
 legal and policy frameworks 6
 and practice implications 53–4
 Working Together 53
lived experience 147, 148, 149, 154, 230
 of CiC 174
local authorities 6, 148
 advocacy in practice 172–7
 characteristics of 16–17
 CiCCs during lockdown 197–201
 CiC statutory requirements 170–2
 and digital participation 211–14
 and FDACs 78–9
 parent activism in 117, 130
 parental advocacy in 139
 and retention of workers 33
 variation of rates of CIC 13
lockdowns 4
 impact on CiC 191–2, 198, 203
 *see also* CiCCs
London 74, 79, 105, 149
 Barking and Dagenham 213
 FGCs in 95
 Hackney 220
 social workers well-being 33
 Southwark 117, 130
 *see also* Camden
longitudinal studies 181–2, 185
Lundy, Laura 218, 219, 229
 Model of Participation 9, 207, 210–11

## M

MacAlister, Josh 52–3, 53–4
macrosystem 21, 26
Magic Notes 212–13
Māori people 89, 142
 and children in care 60, 88
 and FGCs 88, 112–13
marginalised communities 143, 145–6, 158, 160, 180
Marsh, P. 105
meaningful participation 6, 229
 in care plans 52, 56
 in child protection process 151
 for children in care 167, 172
 and CiCCs 191, 192
 and digital technology 209, 224
 and FDACs 73
 and FGCs 103
 inclusive practices 60–3
 and independent advocacy 180
 investment required for 202
 models for 8–9, 210

# Index

and parental advocacy 140, 145
rights-based framework 169 222
understandings of 57
media, working with 121, 128
Meindl, Melissa 73
mental health 14, 123, 153, 168, 183, 203
  support 77
  and using online services 194–5
mesosystem 19, 26
Microsoft Copilot 213
microsystem 19
Model of Participation 9, 207, 210–11
Morris, Kate 146–7
mothers
  and employment 24
  and FDACs 79
Movement for Family Power 117, 125, 127
Munro, Eileen 55
mutual aid ideas 144–5, 154

## N

National Centre for Social Research 80
natural instincts, restoring 94
navigating the child welfare system 5, 61, 140, 145, 151, 177, 179, 182, 230
neglect 16, 19, 21, 100
neoliberalism 37, 147
New South Wales 118, 122, 123
Newton, Elen 191
New York City
  parent activism in 113, 116, 121, 123, 127–8
  parental advocacy in 142–3, 145
New Zealand 15, 60, 88, 112, 142
  child protection in 17
  Māori people 60, 88, 89 112–13, 142
  parent activism in 122
Noble, S.U. 221
non-lawyer reviews (NLRs) 76, 83, 84
north-east England, lockdown survey 193
Northern Ireland 17, 100
  children in care 14, 15
Nørup, I. 24
Norway 15, 111

## O

Obasi, C. 39
Ofsted ratings 18, 37
Open College Network 117, 149
oppression 50, 58, 147, 211
  anti-oppression practice 10, 231
organisational change 217, 223, 230–2
  and obligation 218

## P

Parent, Family and Allies Network 125
parent activism
  and advocacy 7
  domains of 115–25
  future of 126–32
  litigation plaintiffs 122–3
  origins/development of 112–15
  parent leadership 130–2
  policy/legal changes 123–4, 127–30
  research in 118–20
  working with media 121–2
Parent Advocacy Network 117, 119, 125
parental advocacy 5, 59, 126, 131, 230
  Camden case study 148–51, 151–6
  critical theories 145–6
  definitions and significance 139–42
  ethical considerations 156–8
  future direction 159–60
  mutual aid/networking theories 144–5
  peer parental advocacy 7, 61, 111, 148–9, 232
  power theory 147–8
  rights-based approach 146–7
  strengths-based approach 143–4
  theoretical frameworks 142–3, 146
Parent Legislative Action Network (PLAN) 123, 128
parents
  empowerment of 82
  and oppression 58, 59
  parent-led change 5
  post-proceedings support 77
  and professional partnerships 58–60
  regular drug testing 83–4
  and substance misuse 73, 75
  writing their stories 121
  see also parent activism; parental advocacy
Parents Anonymous 145
participation 5, 7, 50–1, 171, 228
  children and young people 54–8
  children chairing reviews 62–3
  embedding participation 232
  and ethics 228–9
  experience of 11
  Family Group Conferencing (FGC) 60–1, 101
  inclusive practices 60–2
  key theories of 8–10
  and legal frameworks 51–4
  meaningful 210
  parent/professional partnerships 58–60
  peer parental advocacy 61
  and practice 229–30, 232
  Young People's Participation Project 55
  see also advocacy; digital participation; meaningful participation
Pathways to Participation 8, 207, 209–11
pay/conditions of work 40–1
peer parental advocacy 61, 111, 148–9, 232
peer support 5, 7
Pert, Hayley 3, 50

physical safety for social workers 35
Piel, M.H. 18
policy
　for advocacy services 183
　inconsistent policies 36
　policy advocacy 140
　policy reform 25, 111
Polkki, P. 57
poverty 4, 21, 25, 147, 220, 225, 231
　in Camden 149
　and child welfare 125, 129
　digital access 208
　families living in 146
　income factors 23–4
　poverty-aware approaches 26
Powell, Shane 3, 139, 141, 156, 157, 158, 206
power dynamics 9–10, 50, 224
　in advocacy relationships 157–8
　and Camden case study 151–2
　and children in care 168
　between children/professionals 178–9
　and digital technology 221, 221–2
　empowering families 58, 60–1, 89, 92–3, 101
　empowerment theory 143–4, 154
　FDACs empowerment 77, 82
　and parental advocacy 140
　and participation 232
　power theory 147–8
practice *see* social work practice
predictive analytics 220–1
preventive measures 22, 25
privacy and trust 218
problematic behaviour 22
problem-solving approach 73, 84, 230
procedural focus of social work 58–9, 63
professional advocacy 141, 154
Public Sector Equality Duty 217

# Q

Queensland 117, 118, 120

# R

racism
　anti-racism 231
　racial discrimination 39, 221
　racial disproportionality 220
　racist abuse 36
real-world applications 10, 11, 51
recognition, lack of 39, 40, 42
reflective supervision 38, 42–4, 156, 229
　reflective spaces 42–4
relationships 93, 98, 101, 103, 145, 230
　personal/close 19
　relational activism 149
　with support team 63, 80, 82, 103
remote working 4, 46

research 159–60
　advocacy in practice 172–7
　and FGCs 99
　longitudinal studies 181–2
resilience 19, 197
resource allocation 158
reunification 22, 23, 26, 79, 80, 84, 140, 142, 144
Review of Child Protection in England 58
reviews 62, 76, 83, 84
　children chairing reviews 62
rights 168
　of children 7, 51, 52, 169, 191
　and child welfare 156
　and digital strategy 222–3
　rights-based approach 9, 146–7, 206, 228
*Rise Magazine* 114, 116, 119, 121, 123, 127, 131, 160
risk-averse approach 15, 16, 21, 228
Rowley, Fae 111

# S

Saar-Heiman, Y. 59, 143, 144, 146
safe spaces, Y. 9, 195
safety for social workers 34–6
school
　educational attainment 14, 182
　lockdown closures 195, 196
　relationships at 19
Scotland 100, 111
　child protection in 17
　children in care 14, 15
Sebba, J. 14
service delivery 25, 33, 50, 51, 60, 152, 182
　and digital tools 206, 207
shame 34, 39, 58, 92, 106
Shier, Harry 9, 218, 222, 229
　Pathways to Participation 8, 207, 209–10
Shine Lawyers 123
slavery 112
social distanced meetings 203
social media 113, 121–2, 214–15
Social Model of Child Protection 147
social network theories 144–5, 155
social support theory 145, 146
social workers
　challenges of 3–5, 37
　and data management 24–5, 27
　and digital technology 211–13, 217–18, 223
　emotional distress 35–7, 41
　lack of recognition 39, 40, 42
　pay/conditions of work 40–1
　professional growth and FGCs 98–9
　remote working 4, 41, 46
　retention/vacancies 4, 6, 33

safety of 34–6
survey of 33–9, 39–47
training 57, 96, 115, 118, 199, 200
values of 11, 40, 46–7, 63, 211
workloads 6, 37–9, 42–3, 53, 174, 183
social work practice 5, 23–5
  advocacy for CiC 181, 182–3
  and digital participation 215–19, 222–4
  exploring participatory practice 6, 8–11
  inclusive practices 60–3
  and just participation 232
  and legal changes 53–4
  models of 229–30
  and parental advocacy 141–2, 159, 160–1
  reflective practice 2, 6, 10, 11, 158
  relationship-based practice 43, 85, 202
  and SEND children 57
  *see also* Family Drug and Alcohol Court (FDAC); Family Group Conferencing (FGC)
socio-economic conditions 15, 19, 21, 147, 157
Southwark 117, 130
special educational needs (SEND) 10, 53, 57, 170
*Stable Homes Built on Love* 54
Stabler, Lorna 55, 167
  and FGCs 21, 87, 98–9, 103, 106
stolen children 112, 122
strengths-based approach 84, 94, 143–4, 155
Strolin-Goltzman, J. 17
structural inequalities 4, 147, 174, 216, 224, 230–1
substance abuse 16, 24, 75, 123
  and reunification 79–80
supervision 38, 40, 44
support 101, 148
  collaboration with families 20
  for families 5, 19, 98
  personalised package of 75–6
  for PPAs 153
support network theories 144–5
surveillance 217, 218
Sweden 40
Swindon Council 212–13
system change theory 146
systemic issues 174, 230–1
  and advocacy 176–7

# T

teams in social work 44–5
team support 75–6
Telford 117, 118
theoretical frameworks 142–3, 154–5, 229
  critical theories 145–6
  digital participation 208–10

Ecological Systems Theory 18–21
empowerment theory 143–4
Family Group Conferencing (FGC) 100
family inclusion theory 146
mutual aid/networking theories 144–5
of participation 8–10
power theory 147–8
relational activism 149
rights-based approaches 146–7
social support theory 146
system change theory 146
Tobis, David 111, 140, 141
tokenism 9, 10, 179, 209, 219, 222
training 96
  advocacy training 180, 181, 182–3
  and digital tools 217, 223
  or online CiCCs 199–201
  of parent activists 116, 118, 127
  of social workers 57, 96, 115, 118, 199, 200
transparency 40, 89, 97, 178, 208, 218, 224
Trial for Change 75–6
trust 84, 93, 148, 212, 218
  building trust 152–4

# U

Ukraine War 4
United Kingdom 220
  care system 22
  children in care 13, 13–18
  court proceedings in 73
  FGCs in 95–9, 100, 105, 109
  Independent Review of Children's Social Care 59
  legislation/guidelines 169–70
  parent activism in 117, 119, 120
  studies from 11
  *see also* Northern Ireland; Scotland; Wales
United Nations
  Convention on the Rights of Persons with Disabilities 52
  Convention on the Rights of the Child 15, 51, 114, 169, 175, 179, 210, 228
United States 61, 111
  Allegheny Family Screening Tool 220
  Family Drug Treatment Court 74–5
  and FGCs 112–13
  parent activism in 116–19, 122–9
  parental advocacy in 126, 142–3
  *see also* New York City; *Rise Magazine*

# V

values 11, 89, 232
  of social work 46–7
verbal abuse 35–6

voices of lived experience 11, 51, 63, 102
  and advocacy support 183–4
  children's voices 53–7, 173, 202, 210
  and digital participation 206, 214–16
  of parents 83
  of social workers 38, 47
  of young people 183–4
vulnerability 56, 102, 181

## W

Wales 100, 111
  child protection in 17
  children in care 14, 15, 16
  FDACs in 74, 76, 81–4
  FGCs in 89
  legislation in 51–4
  study in 24
Washington 123, 125, 126, 127, 128, 129
Webb, C.J.R. 24
welfare system policies 24, 25, 26
well-being 101, 184, 203
Wells Street Family Proceedings Court 74, 75
Westlake, David 74
White, Sue 146–7
Wijedasa, D. 18
Winnicott, D.W. 229
Wisconsin 126
'wishes and feelings' 52, 57, 170, 185
women 14, 34, 79
  and child protection 24
  and oppression 114
Wood, Sophie 13, 17, 23–4
Working Together 170, 228
Working Together to Safeguard Children 53, 170, 228
workloads 6, 37–9, 42–3, 53, 183

## Y

young people 54–8
  and advocacy support 173–4, 183–4
  leaving care 171
  youth-led innovations 6
Young People's Participation Project 55

www.ingramcontent.com/pod-product-compliance
Lightning Source LLC
Chambersburg PA
CBHW051535020426
42333CB00016B/1942